The Constitution of Deliberative Democracy

The Constitution of Deliberative Democracy

· · · · · · · · · · · · · · ·

Carlos Santiago Nino

Yale University Press
New Haven & London

Set in Aster Roman type by Tseng
Information Systems, Inc., Durham,
North Carolina.

Printed in the United States of America.

10 9 8 7 6 5 4 3 2 1

*Library of Congress
Cataloging-in-Publishing Data*

Nino, Carlos Santiago.
The Constitution of deliberative
democracy / Carlos Santiago Nino.
    p.   cm.
Includes bibliographical references
and index.
ISBN 0-300-06748-8(c : alk. paper)

1. Democracy.   2. Civil rights.
3. Representative government and
representation.   4. Judicial review.
I. Title.
JC423.N54   1996
321.8—dc20   95-53688

A catalogue record for this book is
available from the British Library.

The paper in this book meets the
guidelines for permanence and durability
of the Committee on Production
Guidelines for Book Longevity of the
Council on Library Resources.

To my dear friend Owen Fiss

Contents

Acknowledgments

This book is the result of discussions I have had in several academic centers, including the University of Buenos Aires School of Law, the Center of Institutional Studies of Buenos Aires, the Yale Law School, and the University Pompeu Fabra of Barcelona. I owe a considerable intellectual debt to the colleagues and students whose objections and queries have been extremely useful in writing this book.

Chapter One

The Complexity of
Constitutional Democracy

Constitutionalism and democracy combine to form a system of government known as "constitutional democracy" (sometimes equated with "liberal democracy"). For many people, this is a happy marriage of two valuable ideals. They consider constitutional democracy a far higher form of government than either pure democracy or nondemocratic constitutional government.

Future historians will probably describe the closing decades of the twentieth century as the era in which the ideal of constitutional democracy spread swiftly around the world. During the late 1970s several countries of southern Europe abandoned aged dictatorships and adopted liberal democratic regimes. During the early 1980s most Latin American countries instituted constitutional-democratic governments, repudiating a long-standing tendency toward military rule and dictatorship. As that decade came to a close and the present one began, another wave of constitutionalism swept Eastern Europe and the Soviet Union, shattering the communist empire which had, at one time, seemed destined to last a millennium. Perhaps another wave of constitutional democracies will yet overtake those parts of Asia and Africa that are still subject to one-party rule.

The marriage of democracy and constitutionalism is not an easy one, however. Tensions arise when the expansion of democracy leads to a weakening of constitutionalism, or when the strengthening of the constitutional ideal entails restraint of the democratic process. Yet these tensions are not easy to detect with precision because of the uncertainty about what makes democracy valuable and which model of democracy maximizes that value, and because of the obscurity of the notion of constitutionalism.

Although almost no thinker today denies that democracy is the only legitimate system for governing a society, there is very little agreement about the source of that legitimacy. Is the value of democracy instrumental or intrinsic? Is it procedural or substantive? Does the value of democracy lie in the negative feature of avoiding tyranny and the monopolization of power, or is it associated with democracy's positive capacity for promoting personal self-realization? Does the value of democracy reside in its power to transform people's preferences or in its willingness to leave them untouched? Is democracy a political process isolated from the moral realm or a way of sorting out moral values and overcoming moral conflicts? Are the real subjects of democracy atomic individuals, or groups or corporations? Should democracy be restricted to the polity or be extended over other dimensions of civil society, such as the workplace? Which institutional arrangements are essential to democracy and which ones are merely contingent and instrumental? What about one-man-one-vote, periodical elections, freedom of expression, the division of powers, representation, political parties, judicial review?

As these and other questions are answered, extremely diverse models of democracy emerge. Each bears a different relationship to constitutionalism. For certain models, some requirements flow smoothly from the features that give value to democracy; for others, there is a factual and contingent, but real and important, tension between the institutional implications of the value of democracy and those which are involved in the ideal of constitutionalism. This tension can be resolved only through some accommodation and compromise between the ideals at stake. Sometimes the inconsistency, either complete or partial, between the ideals of democracy and constitutionalism is a logical one and can be overcome only by relinquishing some of those ideals totally or partially.

Above all, the relationship between democracy and constitutionalism depends mainly on the interpretation of constitutionalism. Notwithstanding the practical success of the constitutional ideal and the host of scholarly works devoted to celebrating it, the ideal itself remains vague and even somewhat mysterious. A few illustrations are in order. Consider England, the country commonly deemed to have pioneered the idea of constitutionalism. England does not have a written constitution; in fact, many scholars argue that since there are no procedures for subjecting ordinary legislation to constitutional review, the country has no constitution at all. Moreover, while it was the United States that introduced the idea of a written constitution, the kind of constitutional structure it adopted has, by and large, not been followed by other countries that are commonly considered paradigms of constitutionalism. Many such countries are monarchies; almost all have parliamentary or semiparliamentary systems of government, not presidential systems. The parliamentary system of government brings with it a weaker conception of the division of powers than the American one. Most of these countries that are considered paradigms of constitutionalism have a tradition of strong political parties, often combined with proportional representation, in contrast to the weaker parties and the majoritarian system of representation of the United States. Most do not have a federal structure, or if they do, it is of a very different character than that of the United States. Some of these countries do not provide for judicial review of legislation; again, if they do, it is quite different from that established in *Marbury v. Madison*. In fact, after reviewing these differences, the question arises: What do the many countries taken as paradigms of constitutionalism have in common which could serve to illustrate the core meaning of constitutionalism?

In very general terms, everybody agrees that constitutionalism means something like "limited government."[1] But the word has a range of meanings that vary in their conceptual thickness:

(i) Perhaps the thinnest conception of constitutionalism is associated with the basic idea of the *rule of law*, that is, of the preservation of some fundamental legal rules which limit at any point what a particular organ of government, be it democratic or not, can do.

(ii) A slightly thicker concept is more specific about the way in which governmental bodies are constrained by legal rules, requiring a constitution, though not necessarily a written one. Whatever its content, this constitution is entrenched, since its reform and abrogation are more difficult than ordinary laws', and it is held to be supreme with regard to ordinary laws.

(iii) A still thicker concept of constitutionalism includes formal restrictions that the constitution imposes on the laws subject to it, requiring laws, for example, to be general, precise, public, nonretroactive, stable, and applied impartially without making distinctions not recognized by the laws themselves.

(iv) We thicken the concept further by adding the idea of separation of powers, particularly with regard to an emphasis on the judiciary's independence from the bodies that enact the laws of the land.

(v) A decisive new dimension is added to the concept of constitutionalism when the constitution recognizes individual rights that cannot be encroached upon by any organ of the state.

(vi) By adding judicial review, constitutionalism grows even thicker, since an independent judiciary becomes the unique institution capable of protecting those rights and therefore is empowered to nullify legislation endangering them.

(vii) The thickness increases dramatically when democracy is added to the previous requirements, qualifying the origin of some of the offices of the state.

(viii) Finally, the thickness of the constitutional conception depends on the particular democratic model embraced and its specific institutional arrangements—for example, a collective, popularly elected legislative body versus an individual office, also popularly elected, comprising legislative and executive functions.

By assessing the presence or absence of these various features of constitutionalism, it is possible to compare and contrast varying conceptions and dynamics of constitutionalism. Even the thinnest sense of constitutionalism is of theoretical interest and of significant practical value. I refer to the requirement that a country have a constitution as the basis for its legal system. There is again considerable fuzziness surrounding the word *constitution*, but one can assume that it refers to a set of norms delineating the basic organization of political power and the relationship between the state and the individual, implying certain constraints on normal legislative activity. In this minimal sense, the constitution need not be written but may be customary, as in the British case. Above all, nothing is assumed about the content of such a constitution. It may have any content whatsoever. Hence it is not false to say that both the Soviet Union under Stalin and the apartheid government in South Africa had constitutions. Such an understanding of constitutionalism is extremely familiar to scholars working within the Latin American context. Constitutions have existed not only during periods such as the present when democracies prevail but also during military dictatorships. Military governments in Latin America have often tried to legitimize themselves by paying lip service to fundamental norms characteristic of this thin meaning of constitutionalism.

Some interesting questions may nonetheless arise under this thinnest sense of constitutionalism. The fact that rules exist which define, in some way or another, the organization of power and the relation of the state to its citizens, and the fact that these rules are not subject to normal legislative processes, may provide citizens with some baseline guarantees against sheer governmental caprice. Such are the advantages associated with the rule of law. An example of constitutionalism in this sense—and of its benefits—is the regime of Augusto Pinochet in Chile, which just a few years ago was replaced by a democracy. As is well known, the Pinochet regime sought to legitimize itself in 1980 by instituting a constitution that was ratified by plebiscite. Although Pinochet's constitution had many grotesquely undemocratic provisions, it is the general opinion in Chile that it helped restrain governmental abuses. In addition, many democratic advances were achieved by invoking constitutional provisions in litigation, as the courts were at times inclined to abide by them in order to save face before national and international opinion.

It is instructive to compare the Chilean experience with the Argentine one under the last military regime. Although the junta in Argentina enacted a basic "Statute of the Process of National Reconstruction" that placed some constraints on the exercise of power and declared the previously existing constitution to be in force regarding anything not governed by the statute, the junta showed extreme reluctance to abide even by its own normative system. This was most evident, of course, with regard to the human rights abuses committed in the "dirty war against subversion." In this context, the military government blatantly violated the laws in force when it prescribed draconian penalties and summary trials for terrorist acts. On the other hand, the very fact that the junta paid at least some lip service to legal norms meant to restrain its power was of vital importance. In a few cases the Supreme Court issued writs of habeas corpus on behalf of people who had been arbitrarily detained or had disappeared, some of which were honored with by the military authorities.

The notion of constitutionalism that is at the other extreme of thickness is, of course, of the utmost theoretical and practical relevance. The thickest meaning not only requires the existence of norms that organize power and are somewhat entrenched against ordinary legislative processes, but also, and preeminently, requires specific strictures on the procedure and content of laws regulating public life. These strictures are what define the concept of liberal democracy. They seem to be born of the combination of two ideals often held to be in permanent tension. First, there is the ideal of a participatory political process in which everyone affected by political decisions has an equal say in the formation of those decisions; I shall refer to this ideal as the democratic dimension. Second, there is the ideal of a limited government in which even the majority cannot encroach upon entrenched individual interests. This dimension reflects a libertarian ethos. Constitutionalism in this thick sense appears as a synthesis of the seemingly conflicting ideas of Rousseau and Locke.

When the evolution of constitutionalism throughout the world is surveyed, it is easy to perceive varying degrees of emphasis on the two components of liberal democracy—the thickest sense of constitutionalism. In the United States' historical experience, the element of limited government has been heavily stressed, despite some oscillation over time. This was partially effected through the division of powers. As Bruce Ackerman points out, the multifaceted division of powers prevents any political organ from claiming to represent the whole people.[2] In addition to this system of "checks and balances" and the federal structure of government, popular participation in elections, at least at the national level, is generally modest. Most important, the strong system of judicial review exercised by nonelected officials is conducive to broad interpretations of the Constitution's vague clauses concerning individual rights.

It is commonplace to stress that the European experience has differed greatly, placing a greater emphasis on the participatory or democratic strand of thick constitutionalism. In Europe, parliamentary governments unify popular representation in order to claim a greater degree of democratic legitimacy; this is compounded by a tradition of large electoral turnouts, sometimes enforced by legislation establishing obligatory voting. In addition, many European states are unitary. When they are federal, like the German Republic, the division of power is different from the American case, infringing less on parliament's pretensions to speak for the people. Judicial review is by and large foreign to the European tradition. Thus, the present expansion of constitutional control through special tribunals—namely, constitutional courts—preserves, more than the American system, the influence of the political process, as those courts have a more direct connection to the political process.

Observers from Europe and the United States have noted that the two components of liberal democracy—popular participation and limited government—do not operate exclusively. In both regions, currents of thought and of political action exist that accord varying importance to one or another component. Witness the recent resurgence of the republican intellectual movement in the United States, with its vision of democracy as participatory dialogue, as opposed to the pluralist or elitist view. In the European context, on the other hand, the expansion and deepening of European Community integration has tended to weaken both aspects of liberal democracy.

When we turn from Europe and the United States to Latin America, we find a curious mixture of popular participation and limited government. Most Latin American countries enacted constitutional systems similar to the North American model, but they also adopted paraconstitutional norms and procedures and other legal practices that reflect a strong Continental influence. Thus, on the one hand Latin American countries have employed presidentialist systems of government, usually with strong traditions of judicial review and significant federal components. In other respects, however, the Latin American countries have generally followed the European tradition. For example, the European influence can easily be perceived in the Latin American conception of the state and public administration, the role of political parties in the electoral system, the general structure of the legal system, the substantive and procedural laws on civil and criminal issues, and the structure of the judiciary. Latin America's uncomfortable adoption of the two strands of liberal-democratic constitutionalism is reflected in the fact that the two ideals—political participation and limited government—have been only partially internalized into the political culture of the population. Empirical research supports the hypothesis that people's adhesion to democracy is much stronger in terms of the participatory dimension than with the liberal dimension of tolerance and respect for rights.[3]

Constitutionalism seems clearly to require recognition of the mutual importance of the democratic and the liberal or rights-oriented dimensions of constitutionalism. Given the myriad institutional permutations of these values, it is important to create a normative framework for understanding them. That framework will in turn prove helpful to politicians and political theorists seeking to stabilize constitutionalism in different countries of the world.

Democracy as a Normative Concept

Constitutional lawyers and political actors often become involved in the process of consolidating democratic regimes. These individuals typically find conceptions of democracy relevant only from the perspective of subjective legitimacy and hence from the perspective of the stability and the functionality of the political system. Subjective legitimacy consists of the generalized belief of the population in the moral justifiability of the government and its directives. Democracy is therefore seen ultimately as an instrument to the end-goal of stability. In effect, those engaged in democratic transition who propose or enact institutional reforms are attempting to consolidate and to stabilize the democratic structures while averting threats of reversal to authoritarian alternatives. They seek to preserve and foster in the social conscience a sense that the system in force is legitimate, particularly in the face of probable shortcomings in satisfying social demands. One important aim of this book is to try to show that an essential dimension is omitted in this approach to the issue of institutional design. For me, the question is not of *subjective* but of *objective* legitimacy. My concern is not the beliefs of the community about what makes a political regime morally justified but what really makes it morally justified.

Political actors and scientists, concerned with the best political design for stabilizing democracies, are not impervious to the issue of their justifiability. They usually are firm partisans of democracy and take for granted that it is the best political system. They do not, however, consider that what makes it the best political system is relevant to ascertaining the means for its preservation. Instead, they typically adopt a "hyperrealist" perspective characterized by a very results-oriented process, concluding that whatever is responsible for making democracy the morally best system of government can be identified by certain factual features—regular ways in which the citizenship may affect a change of government, the division of powers, or respect for basic rights. Additionally, the morally best system of government is ostensibly exemplified by systems in force in some paradigmatic countries, such as the United States, Great Britain, Germany, and Spain. By simply identifying and replicating the phenomenon or results desired, these actors seek in a value-neutral manner the proper means for achieving or preserving that system.

This train of thought is mistaken. Democracy, as Giovanni Sartori says, is a normative concept and cannot be identified in depth without articulating fully the evaluative conception that justifies its distinctive institutions. In his words, "what democracy is cannot be separated from what democracy should be."[4] The inevitability of this normative inquiry is demonstrated by the inherent conflicts and tensions within the distinctive institutions of democracy, making it impossible simply to identify and adopt appropriate democratic institutions. Is democracy the phenomenon of representation, or is it instead an auxiliary institution imposed by the difficulties of direct democracy in a large society? Is it the separation of the executive and the legislative powers, or is it an optional arrangement that is not adopted in parliamentary democracies without loss of value? Is it the recognition of a bill of rights as limits to majoritarian decisions enforced by independent institutions such as a Supreme Court, or is democracy compatible with the complete sovereignty of parliament? Are political parties distinctive democratic institutions, or are they unnecessary in a more perfect working democracy? Is the proportional electoral system the most adequate way of democratic representation, or is it only one of diverse alternatives that must be chosen for technical reasons?

When we realize the full range of these questions, we come to the conclusion that there are no distinctive institutions of democracy outside of a value-laden theory that simply justifies a set of options. We cannot identify institutions commonly understood as democratic and work out a method for stabilizing them without systematically bringing to the fore the moral theory that justifies them. Simply put, reality does not tell us which institutions are essential and which are contingent in relation to a normative concept like that of democracy. We are unable to determine what contingencies we can manipulate to preserve the essentials of the concept. The "hyperrealist" who thinks otherwise is muddled.

The need for a normative conception of democracy is similar to the point that Ronald Dworkin makes in arguing that characterizing a practice necessarily involves an interpretive attitude toward it.[5] In a sense, democracy is a social practice, consisting of regular conduct and predictable attitudes. These practices make up institutions that in turn are oriented toward a certain goal or value. We cannot participate thoughtfully in the practice, nor can we understand it as intelligent observers, if we do not adopt an interpretive attitude, putting the conduct and attitude in the light of certain goals or values. The practice can be made compatible with different goals or values—though not with just any one that happens to come to our imagination—and so we must choose the one we think best justified. Once we do this, the interpretation of the practice in relation to that value may simply result in confirming the practice itself.

We will see some of democracy's characteristics as contingent and revocable, while others are central and therefore in need of expansion. By the same token, this process of rendering democracy as a normative concept should not lead us to move to the other extreme of utopianism. Not only would such an outlook result in striving for the impossible, it would characterize the factual components of present social practices as equal in democratic value. Thus, we start from the intuitive conviction that the political practices of, say, the United States or Sweden are more valuable than those of China or Libya since we cannot characterize the goal of democracy in such a way that these examples end up with equal democratic value. We must try to show that, imperfect as they are, the social practices of current democracies are closer to the ideal democratic state than systems that have no democratic traces. On the other hand, it is not utopianism in the negative sense to set forth an ideal that, though perhaps never fulfilled in reality, could still distinguish a gradation of real or possible situations according to how far or close they are to that ideal. A valid utopianism is distinguished from an invalid one by the fact that the former allows an evaluative assessment of real social phenomena.

In sum, we cannot begin to decide which institutional design is best for securing subjective legitimacy, and hence stability for democratic institutions, without articulating a fully developed theory that explains the essential elements that give democracy its value.

Constitutional Dialectics

Constitutionalism includes additional levels of depth in comparison to the analysis of democracy. As already indicated, we must begin by taking into account the problems arising from the normative nature of the concept of democracy. In addition, constitutionalism combines two elements, rights and democracy, and this combination creates its own problems. First of all, it is not easy to locate normative conceptions congruent with both of these two ideals. Democracy means, at minimum, majority rule, while individual rights require either unanimity or decision making by nondemocratic officials, such as judges and other "minority" institutions. How is it possible simultaneously to justify majority and minority rule and to trace proper boundaries between the two? Second, the task of combining the two ideals, democracy and rights, is not in itself sufficient fully to explain the notion of constitutionalism. Constitutionalism must also include the ideal of respecting a historical constitution and of the legal system that flows from it. For instance, many contemporary observers are concerned about certain measures taken by the government which seem violative of the constitutional text, including pardons of people not yet convicted of human rights violations and the enactment by decree of measures that properly should be enacted by congressional legislation. But these actions are not direct and obvious sins against the participatory and libertarian ideals of constitutionalism; those who object to them must be making a point about the historical constitution.

The historical dimension of constitutionalism is often concealed behind the recognition of rights because of two circumstances. The preservation of the historical constitution and of the legal system that flows from it is thought to be instrumental to the protection of rights. Moreover, the historical constitution often recognizes a set of rights in a manner which is considered to be morally acceptable, and so the observance of the historical constitution coincides with the respect of those rights. The recognition of rights in the historical constitution may, however, be less than ideal in several degrees, and sometimes the protection of someone's rights requires violating the requirements of the legal system. For instance, the preservation of the autonomy of somebody who objects to the military service may require desertion and the repudiation of his or her legal obligations.

The only practicable approach I perceive for undertaking a thorough analysis of constitutionalism is to focus tentatively on the elements of constitutionalism that seem prima facie to be the strongest bearers of the values associated with that notion. These elements consist of the historical constitution, democratic or participatory processes, and the protection of individual rights. Once these components of constitutionalism are examined and their value grounded, the next step should be to review the different conceptions justifying democracy so as to determine which ones withstand critical scrutiny. The institutional implications of the favored conception of democracy should be also acknowledged, allowing us to probe the relationship between that conception of democracy and the (other) dimensions of constitutionalism. (I added "other" parenthetically because of the decision to view democracy itself as a dimension of constitutionalism, which I consider justified in light of some linguistic usages and of the convenience of presenting the tensions between it and the other dimensions as *internal* to the constitutional ideal.) Once different justifications of democracy are discussed and one of them is adopted, the tension between democracy and the recognition of rights, and also the tension between democracy and the observance of a historical constitution, appear in a new light, thereby creating many implications for institutional design.

The aim of this book could thus be described as identifying the two dialectics of democracy that come from its being embedded within a complex constitution. First, there is the dialectic between the *ideal* aspect of the constitution, reflecting the constitutional dimensions of democracy and rights, and the *real* constitution, which reflects the historical dimension of constitutionalism. Despite the readiness with which different schools of thought accord priority to one or the other of these dimensions or consider each dimension to be mutually exclusive, I argue that both the ideal and the actual components of a constitution are sources of valid claims, and I attempt to show how these claims can be combined. Second, we will examine the dialectics between the constitution of rights and the constitution of democracy. In studying both existing constitutions and the ideal constitution, it becomes apparent that there is a possibility that substantive claims which are a priori valid may conflict with the results of legitimate procedures. In other words, rights recognized as belonging to the liberal dimension of constitutionalism may conflict with the results of democratic procedures that constitute the participatory dimension of constitutionalism. One of my purposes is to explain how rights and democracy can be combined in a coherent way.

This book, then, is in some ways a chart for sorting out conflicting claims based on the plurality of dimensions of constitutionalism. The theory I adopt places special emphasis on the dimension represented by democracy, once its value is grounded in what I will call deliberative democracy. By combining deliberative democracy with the dimensions of constitutionalism related to rights and the historical constitution, we can help constitution makers determine the most appropriate system of government and the division of power within it, the limits of participatory democracy vis à vis representation, the requirements of a valid electoral system, the role of political parties, the preconditions of decentralization, the system of government—presidential, parliamentary, or mixed—that maximizes the the value of democracy. We may even be able to define the legitimate scope of judicial review.

In determining the basis for each of the three dimensions of constitutionalism—democracy, rights, and the historical constitution—and the relationship among them, I shall take into special account the role each plays in the practical reasoning that leads to the justification of actions and decisions. The analytic framework of practical reasoning is particularly useful because it shows the significance of each dimension of constitutionalism at the most basic level of social experience—the formation of decisions. Moreover, the reference to practical reasoning keeps us connected with a notion of constitutionalism that is of practical relevance and not merely significant for the more speculative endeavors of a historian or anthropologist. The complex constitution that I want to analyze, locating the place that democracy has within it, is the one which is employed in the justificatory discourse of lawyers and judges, the structure of which also should be taken into account in external explanations, such as those of historians and anthropologists. Therefore, I shall try to explain how the democratic process, in combination with the respect for the historical constitution and recognition of rights, affects the premises of practical reasoning through which a judge, a government official, or even a common citizen attempts to justify a constitutional decision.

I shall begin this quest by discussing in Chapter 2 the relevance of the historical constitution in the practical reasoning of those people —specifically judges, but not only judges—who must justify their actions and decisions. This examination will shed light on the counterweight that the historical constitution exerts upon the democratic process. This effort becomes pressing once we confront the radical indeterminacy of the actual document and the fact that its enactment and observance must be justified, within the context of practical reasoning leading to a decision, on the basis of moral principles.

In Chapter 3 I propose a theory of rights. This theory may guide us in resolving the apparent paradoxes arising from the supposed indeterminacy of the historical constitution, yet it will also threaten the moral space reserved for the working of the democratic process. If rights, for example, can be individually inferred from presuppositions of our practical discourse and if these rights cover the whole of the moral space, there is very little space left for the operation of the democratic system. In short, this shrinking space for democracy is the problem the recognition of rights poses for the democratic process.

Doubts about democracy's relevance when rights are recognized and a historical constitution is respected are addressed in Chapter 4. Here I review a wide range of conceptions of democracy. In Chapter 5, still another conception of democracy—deliberative democracy—will be considered: I will try to show how this particular conception of democracy overcomes the counterweights posed by the historical constitution and recognition of rights. In Chapter 6 I will examine some implications for institutional design that emerge from the favored conception of democracy and its combination with the two other dimensions of constitutionalism. The emphasis on deliberative democracy will affect the choice of presidential or parliamentary systems of government, direct versus representative democracy, and various other basic decisions required by constitutional regimes. In Chapter 7 the particular implication of deliberative democracy for judicial review will be examined.

In the Conclusion I will comment on how the three elements of constitutionalism—the historical constitution, the constitution of rights, and the constitution of power—may be in a relation either of mutual tension or of reciprocal support. At its core, this book will advance a view of democracy that focuses on its epistemic value and explores the full range of its implications for constitutionalism.

• • • • • • • • •

Chapter Two

The Observance of the
Historical Constitution

Constitutionalism typically requires obedience to the historical constitution, the textual document created at a constitutional founding
and interpreted throughout a nation's history. This requirement per-
sists even when the historical constitution restrains the operation
of the democratic process and is not completely legitimized by it. A
discussion of this phenomenon, in tandem with our later discussion
of the foundations of individual rights, is necessary to determine the
moral space for the operation of democracy within a complex constitution, and to draw conclusions about specific institutional aspects
of that democratic system.

In examining the interrelationship between the different dimensions of constitutionalism in the context of practical reasoning, the
reasoning used to justify actions and decisions, two apparent paradoxes emerge. First, the historical constitution is, despite all signs
to the contrary, radically indeterminate as to its meaning. Second,
the historical constitution is seemingly superfluous in terms of justifying actions or decisions concerning issues supposedly regulated
by it. If the the historical constitution is either indeterminate or
superfluous, the observance of a historical constitution neither expresses a genuine requirement nor exerts any counterweight to that
of democracy. Thus, this chapter can be seen as an attempt to battle

this view of the historical constitution and to explain why the historical constitution is an essential component of the notion of constitutionalism.

The claimed indeterminacy and superfluousness of the historical constitution fly in the face of the almost sacred invocations of constitutions: the legendary battles across time and region in defense of different constitutions; the shared intuition that a constitution is, as Juan Bautista Alberdi, the intellectual father of Argentina's constitution, asserted, "the navigation chart of a country," without which it roams aimlessly; and widespread beliefs as to the sublime merits of some constitutions or the catastrophic defects of other. If the historical constitution were superfluous or indeterminate, it would not matter, in terms of the decision-making processes of judges, legislators, public officers, and ordinary citizens, if a constitution were to have one text or another, if it were sanctioned one way or another, or even if there were no constitution at all. In deciding, for instance, whether to grant legal recognition to a homosexual association, or whether to apply the death penalty to someone because of his or her political ideas, the justification of one or another option would not be based on a constitution but on other elements. The constitution would be regarded as one of the most monumental fictions of a Western culture that is not scarce in fictions, and this view would not be limited to only *some* constitutions. Its reach would be absolutely general: it would say that no historical constitution has any relevance for practical reasoning.

The Radical Indeterminacy of the Constitution

The first paradox, that of the radical indeterminacy of the historical constitution, appears when the constitution is conceived as a text or document, or as the speech-acts which lead to them, and requires that constitutional decisions emerge from "the four corners" of the text. However, the text itself cannot be employed in practical reasoning; the text is "too hard an object" to be forced into that immaterial operation! Rather, the text must be converted into propositions that can serve as premises of that justificatory reasoning. The process of transforming the text into propositions is a complex one.

In what follows I shall try to distinguish different steps involved in that process. I want to emphasize that several of those steps require use of normative considerations that cannot be extracted from the text itself or from other "hard facts." If we eliminate normative considerations involving moral principles from the process of converting texts into propositions, the process will lead to irreducible indeterminacies and to an indefinite number of propositions equally compatible with the text.

Converting texts into propositions that can serve as premises of justificatory reasoning involves several steps. First, one must ascribe meaning to the linguistic acts. Second, one must apply the general criteria ascertained above to the specific text in question. Third, one must overcome numerous remaining indeterminacies. Fourth, one must infer the logical consequences of interpreted material. Finally, one must apply the normative proposition to the specific facts of the particular dispute at issue.

Step 1: Ascription of Meaning to the Relevant Material

The task of ascribing meaning to linguistic acts, texts, and practices is a very complex and much debated evaluative step. In general, two major types of criteria compete for ascribing this meaning. The *subjective* one focuses on the interaction of the agent of the linguistic act, the author of the text, or the participants in the practice. The *objective* one, on the other hand, considers the common and regular use of the expressions employed in those texts, determined by certain conventions but independent of intentions. The difference between these two criteria is manifest in the split between the originalists, who take into account the beliefs and attitudes of the framers, and constructivists, who favor a progressive interpretation by taking into consideration the objective meaning of the terms employed in the constitution at the moment of their application. The role of legislative intent or of the intent of the framers in the process of legal interpretation is one of the most divisive in current legal discussion, creating in the United States, for example, profound academic, legal, and even political controversies.

At first glance, those who advocate recourse to intention for interpreting the constitutional text seem to possess very solid arguments. Clearly, the meaning of language depends on the intention of the person employing it, because language is a means of communication which is achieved as long as the intention of the person who emits is understood by the receptor. Why should legal or constitutional texts be different? If we are not disturbed by the transcendence of the issue and by the philosophical speculations that surround it, a constitutional or legal text is a linguistic act that seeks to communicate a message. Why should we turn it into something else by resorting to propositions that are alien to the process of communication? If the purposes of the law could be satisfied by other means rather than by the use of the language, these other means would be employed.

The reality is not as simple as this argument seems to indicate, however. Admittedly, when something is asserted, there is the intention of transmitting a belief. Similarly, when something is prescribed, there is the intention that the formulation of a normative proposition will serve as reason to accept this normative proposition. But why does the use of certain words permit us to conclude that the emissor intends to express a certain belief in a certain proposition, or intends that his formulation be absorbed into the practical reasoning of the receptor? This conclusion can only be maintained as a result of conventions that associate certain linguistic acts with determined intentions.[1] Convention determines that the use of certain words in a certain way will imply an intention, either of transmitting a belief or of asserting that the formulation of a proposition is a reason for accepting it. Sociolinguistic conventions allow us to permit associating particular words with a certain intention, but intention does not permit ascribing to words a different meaning than demanded by convention.

Although the intentions with which we use language generally defer to the linguistic conventions of our community, we sometimes make mistakes regarding linguistic conventions and improperly use words with which we want to express our intentions. The intentions of an emissor, for example, may be more profound than the meaning ascribed to the text by the linguistic conventions. This occurs in the cases of semantic or syntactic ambiguity. For instance, while the words "the bank was empty" can express different propositions, the intention of an emissor in a certain occasion will be one and not another of such propositions.[2] To choose among possibilities, we will have to select criteria for interpretation as well as to determine the level of abstraction with which the emissor is speaking.

These considerations demonstrate that the intention of a constitution maker is a construction stemming from a set of value judgments which are part of the ideal dimension of the complex constitution. This conclusion is not avoided by reference to the partisans of the objective method of interpretation, for the methods typically used in such a process are themselves indeterminate. Should we invoke the conventions common to the whole society, a particular community to which the law is being applied in a particular case, legal experts, judges? In light of these observations, one might assert that it is more honest to apply directly these value judgments for the selection of the meaning of the text to be interpreted without analyzing intent. As Alf Ross says, at the final stage the difference between a subjective and an objective interpretation is no more than granting more relevance to the circumstances of the context in which the norm was enacted than to those of the context in which it was applied.[3]

Step 2: Application of the Criterion to the Text

Once a decision is made about the general criterion ascribing meaning to the constitutional text along the subjective-objective dimension, then the criterion in question must be applied to specific materials. This is an empirical step, because, once it has been decided that the relevant materials must be interpreted according to the intention of their authors, or according to the common use of the language employed, or according to some intermediate alternative, the person who applies the norm to a concrete case must discover the true intention of the author or the pertinent linguistic conventions of the community. Clearly, this process can be very hard—particularly in the case of texts sanctioned a long time ago—and many times the empirical operations are again mixed with normative or logical considerations. In order to determine the intention of the author of the law, one must determine the level of abstraction of that intention, decide between various intentions expressed by diverse institutional organs or of collective organs, and choose among manifestations of intentions that sometimes produce incompatible results.

At this level of norm application, we perceive various semantic and syntactic indeterminacies produced by vagueness, an unavoidable and even useful characteristic of natural languages. A common example is vagueness by gradient, which appears when a word refers to objects or phenomena in the real world as a part of a continuum, without clearly indicating at what point of that continuum it is correct to use the word and when it is no longer correct. Another form of vagueness is when the word is not defined by a series of necessary and sufficient properties. Finally, there is vagueness caused by open texture. This type of vagueness affects all the expressions of the natural languages, for it is created by the fact that even when all the properties that permit the use of the word are there, the object may present extraordinary properties that make us doubt the propriety of such application. (H. L. A. Hart discusses this type of vagueness in describing the use of the word *vehicles* in an ordinance prohibiting their use in a park. He wonders about the ordinance's effects when confronted with the case of the child's tricycle.)

All constitutions present many examples of vagueness of one kind or another. For example, in the first section of the first article of the U. S. Constitution, the meaning of the expression "legislative powers" is extremely vague as to whether it comprises only enumerated powers or also covers implied ones.[4] The contours of those implied powers cannot be ascertained by the mere application of the text in the light of current criteria for ascribing meaning to it. Section 8 of the same article establishes the power of Congress "to lay and collect Taxes, Duties, Imposts and Excises, to pay the Debts and provide for the common Defence and General Welfare of the United States . . . ." A considerable controversy has arisen over the scope of the expression "provide for the . . . General Welfare of the United States." Does it only require that the federal spending has a "general" as opposed to a "local" purpose? Does it allow Congress to undertake spending that has regulatory purposes in areas over which it cannot legislate directly? The requirement of the Sixth Amendment that trials should be "speedy" is also vague, as well as the Eighth Amendment prohibition of "excessive" bail and "cruel and unusual" punishment.

Indeterminacies also arise from ambiguity. Often, it is easy to detect ambiguity because the diverse meanings have some connection, as in the case of the ambiguity called "process-product" in which the same expression refers to an activity and to the result of that activity. There are also ambiguities that arise from the metaphoric use of expressions. Shall the metaphoric or literal meaning control? Examples of ambiguity in constitutions abound. For instance, the word *commerce* of article 1, section 8, paragraph 3 of the U.S. Constitution may, as Chief Justice John Marshall said in *Gibbons v. Ogden*, have several meanings. One meaning is limited to the movement of commodities, not comprising navigation, while another refers to any exchange. Another ambiguity is provided by the expression "with foreign nations, among the several States" in the same clause. Does it refer to the commerce between private individuals where one lives in the United States and the other abroad, or both living in different States of the Union, or does it refer to commerce between political entities—either the United States and a foreign nation or different states of the Union?

The clearest cases of syntactic indeterminacy involve ambiguities that are not of words but of sentences which express more than one proposition, even when none of the words is ambiguous. This can occur when adjectives or adverbs are used after a series of nouns or verbs, and it is not clear whether they qualify only the last term in the series or the whole series; or with relative phrases that generate doubts whether they refer to all the terms of a preceding conjunction or disjunction; or with the use of the disjunction "or" that can have an including or excluding sense. One example of syntactic ambiguity can be taken from the Argentine Constitution. The first part of article 19 reads: "The private actions of men that in no way offend public order or morality, nor harm a third party, are reserved only to God and exempted from the authority of the magistrates." It is possible to make one of two claims. One is that the references to "private actions," to actions "that in no way offend public morality and order," and to actions that do not "harm a third party" all describe alternatives of the same property of the actions. The various alternatives are useful for making each other clear. Another reading holds that they are descriptions of different cumulative properties that must be present for an action to be exempted from the authority of the magistrates.

Step 3: Overcoming Semantic and Syntactic Indeterminacies

Semantic and syntactic indeterminacies cannot be overcome merely by resorting to the intention of the author of the text or to the current usages of language. This is true because the indeterminacies emerge when either a more subjective or objective criterion of ascription of general meaning to the text is being used, and this criterion does not itself offer a basis for the choice between competing constructions. For instance, the intention of the legislator, however constructed, might be compatible with both meanings of an ambiguous word used by him, or the linguistic customs might not signal a clear choice between two competing meanings suggested by the syntax of the sentence.

There have been attempts to solve these and other sorts of indeterminacies without resorting to normative considerations — that is, in a value-neutral way which would preserve the bindingness of the legal material over practical reasoning. For instance, in the Continental legal culture, a special type of theory about the positive law — so-called legal dogmatics — has emerged since the middle of the past century. It seeks to use mechanisms of legal construction which are supposed to overcome indeterminacies in a purely scientific and value-neutral way. I have tried to show in various other works that legal dogmatics as such constitutes a myth and in fact employs evaluative principles.[5] The concealment, though unconscious, is a function of applying analytic tools that are accepted as part of conceptual analysis but are then used normatively, in order to recommend modifications of the legal system which will overcome the indeterminacy in question. In short, the need to overturn indeterminacies in the process of transforming texts into propositions for practical reasons unavoidably requires recourse to value considerations.[6]

Step 4: Inferring Logical Consequences of the Interpreted Materials

In order to resolve individual cases, we need more than the normative propositions employed in assessing relevant legal materials. We must also infer their logical consequences and extract from texts logical consequences of norms identified in previous steps. As an operation of logic, we must appropriate rules of inference such as the rules of *modus ponens* or *modus tollens*.[7] In many cases this operation is so simple that it is done unconsciously. In other cases, the inference of the logical consequences of a norm or, above all, of a set of norms requires intricate logical operations that are sometimes made easier by resorting to the use of appropriate formal symbolism. It is in this step that the logical problems of interpretation appear. These logical indeterminacies involve both gaps and contradictions that signal the large role played by forces other than simple logic.

Constitutions may leave open a number of different gaps. One frequently mentioned in the U.S. Constitution concerns the right to privacy. As is well known, it is argued by some courts and scholars that this right is implicit in the liberty guarantee of the Fifth and Fourteenth Amendments. In the Argentine Constitution, one gap often mentioned is that regarding the right to life, a right not enumerated in the clauses of rights and guarantees.[8] Obviously, the right to life is presupposed by almost all the others and therefore might be said to be implicitly recognized by the Constitution. But one might reply that no matter how reasonable this interpretation may be, the normative system to which we are alluding is no longer the Constitution but a system expanded by the principles that are presupposed in the constitutional clauses.[9] Another clear gap in the Argentine Constitution is the absence in article 72 of the possibility of partial promulgation of a law that has been partially vetoed by the President.

In addition to the problems posed by logical gaps, legal texts often point to completely contradictory logical conclusions. There is a logical contradiction between two norms when the normative solution that one presents is incompatible with the one the other proposes. It is difficult to find explicit contradictions in a particular constitution given the limited number of clauses, the deliberation involved in its formation, and the vagueness of its text. There are, however, a few cases, particularly if we understand *lex specialis* (the principle that the specific prevails over the general) as a logical rule. One of the most striking cases is suggested by article 14 of the Argentine Constitution, which grants freedom of religion. It is very hard to reconcile this norm with article 2, proposing government support of Catholicism; with article 76, requiring the president to be Catholic; and above all with article 67, paragraph 15, prescribing the conversion of the Indians to Catholicism. Juan Bautista Alberdi, the author of the main draft of the Constitution, asserted that these clauses "far from being incompatible needed each other and are mutually complemented." However, freedom of religion is quite restricted if one's own money is used to pay taxes to support another religion, if one is excluded from the highest office of the country for reasons of religion, or if one is an Indian subject to laws promoting conversion.

As with other types of indeterminacies, the task of overcoming logical ones unavoidably involves evaluative judgment, even though it has been commonly argued and even assumed that it is possible and necessary to overcome legal indeterminacies by means of axiologically neutral operations. This pretension is vain, since without resorting to evaluative principles it is not possible to choose between two or more contradictory norms, or to fill up a gap. The different criteria of interpretation often alleged to resolve these problems themselves suffer from indeterminacies and, given their own inconsistencies and gaps, cannot be applied without making evaluative choices. Authors like Carlos Cossio or, even more important, Hans Kelsen assert that the law has no gaps. Kelsen's argument is based on the supposition that every legal system necessarily includes a principle of closure according to which everything which is not prohibited is permitted.[10] Alchourrón and Bulygin,[11] however, have demonstrated that Kelsen engages in a fallacy motivated by the ambiguity of the expression *permitted*.[12] They also distinguished logical gaps from axiological ones, where even when the legal system assigns a solution to the case, it does not consider as relevant a property that this type of case has and that should be relevant for assigning it a different solution.

Certain rules are often used for solving contradictions; the best-known are *lex superior* (the superior law prevails over the inferior one), *lex posterior* (the later law prevails over the previous one), and *lex specialis* (the special law prevails over the general one). Many times these rules are regarded consciously or unconsciously as logical rules, and therefore certain contradictions are not perceived as such. But all of these rules, particularly *lex specialis*, lack universal applicability and, more important, may contradict each other in certain cases. A special law may be, for example, previous to a general law.

Step 5: Subsumption of the Individual Case into the Norm's Domain

This is the step that entails applying a norm to a specific case. It requires a new derivation of logical consequences applicable strictly to the individual case once the relevant norm has been reconstructed and its indeterminacies resolved. On the other hand, this step requires the empirical operations that are necessary for determining the factual properties of the case, a process where normative considerations once again intervene.

Once all these five steps in the process of converting texts into propositions that can serve as premises in justificatory reasoning have been distinguished, one sees clearly the radical indeterminacy of the constitution understood as a document. If we subtract the evaluative considerations required in several of these steps, the constitutional text cannot determine by itself the course of justificatory reasoning since it is compatible with an indefinite set of propositions which contradict each other. The normative considerations themselves cannot be extracted from the text which itself requires them in order to be transformed into justificatory propositions. There are no neutral procedures that can help to produce that transformation. The process of interpretation resorts to moral judgments, which must be accepted as a result of intrinsic merits and not because they have been established.[13]

The indeterminacy of the constitution is not present in the same degree, however, if we conceive of it in a purely descriptive way, not as a prescriptive text or document but as a practice or convention generated not just by the enactment of the text but also by the actions, attitudes, and expectations of judges, legislatures, governmental officials, and the citizenry in general. In this way, the constitution is understood as a response to that text evolving over time. Naturally, constitutional practice itself has resorted to evaluative considerations to convert the text into propositions the acceptance of which has generated actions, attitudes, and expectations. But once the practice has a certain development and includes conventions for giving general meaning to the text, the text appears to later participants and observers as a more, though not completely, determinate entity, thus enabling one to infer justificatory propositions from the mere text.

This method of overcoming in part the paradox of radical indeterminacy may lead us to think that the historical constitution should be understood not as a mere document but as the practice generated by it. Even after having taken this important step, as we shall see, it is not easy to explain why a practice should be binding upon us even if that practice or norm can be defined.

The Superfluousness of the Historical Constitution for Practical Reasoning

The claim I want to explore here is that the historical constitution, whether it be seen as a description of current social practice or as a prescription for future practice, is not relevant, on logical grounds, for determining the validity of the other rules of the legal system. I will try to do this in an informal way by considering a central problem discussed by constitutionalists: the validity of international treaties that conflict with national constitutions.

Treaty provisions often appear to conflict with provisions of a country's constitution. For example, in Argentina, there is a debate concerning the authority of the Inter-American Court of Human Rights, established by the Inter-American Convention on Human Rights. According to the convention, the court's authority is supposed to prevail over that of national judges in countries, such as Argentina, that fully ratified the convention. This assertion of authority is, however, in conflict with article 100 of the Argentine Constitution, which establishes that judicial power is inherent in the Supreme Court and the lower courts, strongly implying that there can be no court of higher rank than the Supreme Court.

Three different positions can be distinguished regarding such apparent conflicts between national and international legal systems, each of which posits a different relation between the two types of law. "National monism" affirms that the validity of international law depends upon its consistency with the national legal order. "International monism" takes the opposite position: national legal systems derive their validity from international law—for example, from the principle of the effectiveness of international law—with which they must therefore be in accordance. Last, "dualism" maintains that each system has independent validity.

In the Argentine case, those who assert the priority of national law over international treaties look to article 27 of the Constitution. It states that treaties must be in accordance with constitutional principles of public law. Those who argue in favor of the prevalence of international treaties base their claim on articles 27 and 46 of the 1969 Vienna Convention, which prohibit nations from invoking their own internal law to justify their international behavior, unless the conflict between the treaty and the internal law indicates an absence of consent to the treaty or the treaty itself stipulates that the internal rule has transcendence.

Formulated this way, these arguments are vacuous because they are completely circular. Those who assert the priority of the national constitution over international treaties, basing their arguments on article 27 of the constitution, already presuppose the constitution's priority over the Vienna Convention. Similarly, those who argue in support of international treaties, basing their arguments on articles 27 and 46 of the Vienna Convention, have already assumed treaty law's priority over the constitution by considering the convention relevant for resolving the issue. Yet rules that purport to establish their own validity and assert their priority over other rules are absolutely empty, since they are self-referential.[14]

Thus, whenever we decide to apply a constitutional rule over a treaty, or when we decide, on the contrary, to apply a treaty over a constitution, we do so on the basis of considerations external to the constitution or treaty in question. We cannot rely on a constitution or treaty to establish its own validity. In other words, a constitution can assign validity to other rules only if it itself is valid, but it cannot be the basis of its own validity. Its validity is necessarily based upon basic principles or other supraconstitutional grounds. Indeed, this argument applies to any other rule as well.[15]

Since the constitution cannot ascribe validity to other rules if it is not valid itself, and since it cannot ascribe validity to itself, the constitution cannot on its own grant validity to other rules. It is thus necessary to resort to considerations external to constitutional practice to justify the obligatory character of legal rules. These considerations must be of a moral character when interests of different people are at stake. Only moral reasons have no basis in the enactments of authorities. In contrast, enactments unavoidably need to be justified by resorting to further reasons. As I have argued elsewhere, the rules of intersubjective practical discourse are such that we engage in a pragmatic inconsistency only when we assert moral judgments and do not act according to them.[16] In contrast, the reference to the content of a social practice—as is the legal system and its legal system when understood as descriptive terms—is perfectly compatible with an action which is the opposite of that required by its content.

This implies that legal discourse is a special type of moral discourse, an idea that Robert Alexy calls *Sonderfall*.[17] The thesis can be expressed in the same manner by saying that a social practice— such as a constitution seen as a social practice—cannot itself justify actions or decisions, but can only constitute a conditioning fact that determines the applicability of certain moral principles that justify actions or decisions.[18] When judges invoke the constitution to justify the application of a legal rule, they do not refer to the constitution as a social practice—that is, as a fact seen from an external point of view—they refer to it from an internal point of view as a normative, or moral, proposition. This practice of continually formulating normative propositions about the duty of applying certain rules in justifying actions or decisions gives rise to what, from an external point of view, constitutes a practice of recognition.

Up to now we have demonstrated that a constitution as text or as a social practice is not sufficient in itself to provide obligatory force or validity to the remaining rules of the legal system. Consequently, it cannot by itself justify decisions based on those rules. On the other hand, we have not proven a stronger claim—that the constitution is superfluous. In fact, the previous demonstration implies that even when a constitution understood as a social practice cannot itself generate justificatory propositions, it is relevant to such derivations.[19] The further step leading from the nonself-sufficiency of a constitution, understood as a text or as a social convention, to its superfluousness is based on an analysis of moral principles needed to legitimate a constitution.[20] Such principles may already contain everything that the constitution could contain. Therefore, the historical constitution may add nothing to its underlying moral principles.

The argument for this conclusion is pretty straightforward. It derives from the fact that the legitimacy of a constitution determined by moral principles will hinge on the fact that it has certain content —specifically, that it recognizes certain fundamental rights. If a constitution recognizes those rights or other content required by moral principle, it will be considered legitimate and be capable of conferring validity on the rules it recognizes. Once the constitution meets this requirement, it can serve as a justificatory reason. If it does not recognize the moral principles to which we must necessarily resort to justify it, we must reach a negative verdict about the justifiability of the constitution.[21] This means that only if the historical constitution contains the rights and other content required by its underlying moral principles, and excludes rules antagonistic to such rights, can it be relevant for practical justificatory reasoning. Since, however, such rights can be inferred from the moral principles themselves, a description of constitutional practice is superfluous to any justification.[22]

In short, a constitution is not legitimate and cannot be employed to justify actions or decisions if it lacks a certain necessary content. If it does include such content, it is superfluous because the justifications can be inferred directly from the moral principles that prescribe its contents. These crucial principles comprise what can be referred to as the ideal constitution, which consists of protection of rights and the establishment of democracy. Therefore, it appears that the constitution understood as a text or even as a social practice of recognition is superfluous, tout court, for generating justificatory propositions.

In Chapter 5, I will argue that an epistemic conception of moral discourse and democracy can demonstrate the relevance of government and legal rules, while keeping in mind that such reasoning has to be grounded in autonomous principles. This conception affirms the thesis that government, in order to be relevant, must be democratic, and at the same time it offers a way out from our uncertainty about the validity of, and our capacity to correctly perceive, intersubjective moral principles. Unfortunately, this way out, which is applicable to show the relevance of those positive laws which have democratic origins, cannot justify the relevance of most historical constitutions, intuitively of great importance to practical reasoning, because they did not in fact originate out of legitimate, fully democratic procedures, able to ground an epistemic presumption on the moral validity of their prescriptions.

We must therefore confront a troubling claim. Notwithstanding the rhetoric on the importance of one or another particular constitution, the text of a constitution and the factual circumstances surrounding its enactment and observance are superfluous for the central role we expect it to perform—having a logical impact on the practical reasoning of public officials and citizens, guiding them to decisions that are correct rather than arbitrary or discretionary. We will not, however, resign ourselves to this discouraging position, but instead take up the challenge to demonstrate the relevance of the historical constitution.

How to Take the Historical Constitution Seriously

One could dispute the conclusion that the historical constitution is irrelevant for practical reasoning by arguing that a constitution is fundamentally the most basic *convention* determining the collective life of a society. As such, it performs an indispensable social function, serving as a framework that both supports and constrains the democratic process. By returning to the idea of the constitution as a social practice or convention, we can overcome the paradox not only of the radical indeterminacy of the text but also that of the superfluousness of the constitution for practical reasoning. This is due to the fact that conventions may affect practical reasoning notwithstanding the principle that denies that ought-judgments can be derived from mere facts.

This is the thesis maintained by Neil MacCormick when, reflecting the influence of Hume, he asserts that constitutionalism is a prerequisite of operative democracy:[23]

The contemporary world reveals a sad plurality of failed experiments, as well as some considerable successes, all well short of perfection. It does seem that democracy works only where there is some form of well-established constitutional order drawing on a constitutional tradition of some serious standing, where the constitutional order utilises the separation of powers (to that extent removing adjudication from the democratic area to the extent of possible recourse to jury-trials) and where the security at least of constitutionally derivative rights is firmly upheld. In this sense, constitutionalism is a prerequisite for democracy.

MacCormick's thesis, supported by Hume's insights, provides a powerful argument for the relevance of the historical constitution for practical reasoning. A constitution is relevant because it embodies a country's fundamental convention: an agreement in time between diverse social groups about how the state's coercive power will be distributed, and about the limits of that power with regard to the individual. As a fundamental convention for society, the historical constitution—even if it limits democracy by establishing procedures or restrictions which do not maximize possibilities for democratic discussion and decision—provides in some imperfect way the basis for democracy itself. If we value democracy, we must also value its prerequisites.

However, MacCormick's argument is not completely clear about how a conventional constitution, which leaves the protection of a minimum set of rights to organs that are not fully subject to the democratic process, grants the stability and viability of an imperfect democracy. It is not easy to perceive the importance of the conventional or traditional character of the constitution in this argument, and to isolate it from the weight of the separation of powers and individual rights. Nor can we clearly infer any relation between the conventional character of the constitution and its content. At any rate, the argument that a democracy protected by a constitution which regulates and limits its functioning and which has traditional bonds is more stable and operative is sufficiently attractive, at least intuitively, to make it worthwhile to explore the consequences of conceiving the constitution as a convention or social practice. (But we will not discuss the obvious fact that a democracy is more stable when the constitutional norms that consecrate it have customary support. The principal thrust of MacCormick's thesis is less obvious: that a democracy is more stable and operative when the constitutional norms that limit it have conventional links.)

Conventions help resolve collective action problems. These problems involve situations in which the intentions of the parties may be frustrated because the parties cannot justify their behavior on the basis of expectations about the behavior of the other parties interacting with them. David Lewis illustrates this with a simple case: a telephone conversation is interrupted, and both parties understand the error of trying to reestablish their conversation by calling the other simultaneously.[24] In order to resolve this coordination problem, a convention has developed by which the party who called originally calls again. This may not be the best or fairest solution, but it is more convenient for everyone to respect this convention than to risk its disappearance, in light of the difficulty in reestablishing communications that would result if each person pursued his own idea of the appropriate response.

In describing a convention from the external point of view, we cannot ignore the internal point of view of those who participate in it. As I have argued elsewhere,[25] this is a general characteristic of human praxis. When examining an individual action, we cannot describe it as intentional if we do not consider the internal point of view of its agent, who acted according to practical reasoning founded on the normative and descriptive premises which constitute the propositional content of his or her desires and beliefs. From the external point of view, those desires and beliefs conceived as facts caused the action considered intentional. It is impossible to identify those desires and beliefs, however, or even causally to relate them to the action, without considering, as did the agent, the propositions that constitute its content and the logical relation between the propositions, and between them and the action. The action is caused by desires and beliefs which adhere to normative and factual propositions connected by certain logical relations. Similarly, with regard to social practices, we cannot identify the actions and attitudes that are a part of a practice if we do not consider the propositions to which agents adhere when they develop those actions and attitudes. For example, the gestures that constitute the practice of greeting could not be identified without assuming that those who practice them believe that those gestures are an appropriate way of greeting another. In turn, they adhere to the social obligation of extending salutations by employing one of the permitted gestures.

From the internal point of view of the actors in a legal system, the truly important point is not whether a norm belongs to the legal system in the descriptive sense, but whether that norm should be applied in order to justify an action or decision. According to how this question is generally answered from the internal point of view, the issue of the norm's membership in the legal system will be resolved from the external point of view.[26]

Dworkin's criticism of Hart's positivist conception of the rule of recognition can be interpreted as a rejection of the idea that a social practice can be useful in justifying actions or decisions, such as those of judges. This criticism, however, rests on a shaky foundation. By considering Hart's distinction between internal and external points of view, it can be seen that the rule of recognition appears as a social practice only from the external point of view. This point of view is not that of a judge resolving a case, but that of an observer—for example, a sociologist or an anthropologist—trying to describe a society's current legal order in an impartial manner. Though Dworkin's criticism may thus be unfounded, it still is useful in that it underscores a point that Hart does not in fact deny but does not emphasize enough: that those who adopt an internal point of view toward a practice such as a rule of recognition cannot be content with formulating descriptions of the practice that, as such, are compatible with any action or decision. They must instead formulate normative propositions which justify their decision to, for example, apply or not apply a norm.

Elsewhere I have said that Hart is not clear enough about the nature of the normative propositions that must be formulated from the internal point of view regarding legal norms (including the rule of recognition).[27] He seems to say that they are not necessarily of a moral nature, but may have a varied character. In contrast, I argue that all judicial justificatory propositions must in the end be derived from moral propositions that legitimize certain authorities. This is due to my assumption that, in practical discourse, ultimate reasons are autonomous in the Kantian sense. They are acknowledged because of their intrinsic merit, not because they originate from some legislative authority, divine or conventional.[28]

Imagine a social practice in which all participants engage in similar actions and attitudes, but they do so unconscious of their consistency; they rely only on ideal principles in shaping their conduct. These principles may be the same or they may be different. Would such a situation constitute a social practice or a convention? I think not. Not all convergences are conventions. For example, there may be a consensus against discrimination against women and people of color, but it is not the consensus itself that describes a practice or convention to this effect. Instead, what distinguishes a practice or convention is the self-consciousness of its participants, the fact that they know that they are participating in a social practice and, moreover, that the fact of participating in that social practice is part of the reason for acting as they do. Thus David Lewis defines a convention not only by a regularity of conduct but also by the fact that its participants expect that all other participants act in accordance with that regularity; they prefer to act similarly as long as others do so.

This is clear in the case of conventions that resolve problems of coordination and which lack a relevant moral solution—for example, the convention of driving on the right-hand side of the road, or of deviating to the right when faced with a pedestrian coming from the opposite direction. Such conduct is performed only because one expects that the other will do the same. But a similar thing occurs in relation to conventions that prescribe conduct that is not morally optional. (This implies that I am using the word *convention* in a more general sense than is employed in the literature of rational choice.) For example, there is only one social practice or convention for apologizing to someone whom we have offended or hurt, if we are conscious of what is regularly done and of what others expect us to do. Consciousness is a defining feature of a social practice or convention.

The role of the historical constitution as a convention or social practice becomes clearer if we understand the actors in the legal systems—the legislators, constitution makers, or judges, for example—as engaged in a collective enterprise of some duration. I use the analogy of constructing a cathedral to explain this point. A cathedral is constructed over a very long period. Consider the Cologne cathedral, completed by successive generations between the thirteenth and nineteenth centuries, or the Strasbourg cathedral, completed by sections between the twelfth and seventeenth centuries, or the "Sagrada Familia" of Barcelona, begun by Martorell and Villar in 1881, continued by Gaudi two years later, and still under construction. Assume that one of us is the architect in charge of continuing the construction of one of these cathedrals, knowing that we probably will not see it completed but that it will be done by others, perhaps in the distant future.

One will necessarily begin with aesthetic preconceptions—for example, that only the gothic style gives a cathedral the transcendence necessary for a place of spiritual inspiration. Then, on the basis of this determination, one can judge the merits of the incomplete work from which construction continues. If, for example, the cathedral was initially built according to another style—say, romanesque—one may have various reactions. One possibility might be to decide that what has already been constructed is worthless from an aesthetic point of view and that one should tear it down and start again. To reach such a conclusion, the architect must imagine that it is in fact possible to begin construction anew. Surely, it would be irresponsible to adopt a proposal, knowing it is impossible to start ex nihilo, unless he thinks that it is better that there be no cathedral at all than a bad one.

Another possibility is that those who manage the work's continuation conclude that, despite existing defects, it is still preferable to continue with the project rather than to abandon it and start anew. In this case, the architect must resolve a series of complicated technical and aesthetic problems. Let us suppose that continuing the work in a more attractive style implies structural changes that might endanger the stability of the cathedral. Or let us suppose that in fact the architect believes that there is none but the gothic style when it comes to cathedrals, and the romanesque style of the already constructed part is seriously deficient. He has to decide whether his contribution to the cathedral's design—which, to make things worse, may be concurrent with the independent contributions of other artists—should be in the gothic style, the romanesque, or some intermediate style that would harmonize better with what has already been constructed. Or perhaps it should be in some other style capable of neutralizing the aesthetic or functional deficiencies of the romanesque style. Of course, the architect has in mind an ideal image of the cathedral in the gothic style but cannot translate that image straight into reality because he knows well that he is not constructing the whole cathedral but only a part of it, maybe even a small part. He knows that if he designs that part according to his ideal cathedral, the result of combining it with what has already been constructed may be technically deficient or aesthetically horrendous, and the completed design may end up even worse than if the cathedral had been completed in the romanesque style in which it was started.

Moreover, suppose that our architect knows that he will not have the privilege of completing the cathedral but that completion will be left to others, some of whom may work concurrently with him. Knowing this, the architect will reasonably take into account not only what is already built but the way in which it probably will be continued by others. His choice of style must incorporate not only the past but also future contributions to the construction of the cathedral. (If, for example, the architect foresees that other architects will continue in the romanesque style, this may affect his decision to make a gothic contribution.) The necessity of taking into account future contributions obviously complicates the architect's decisions in particular ways, because future contributions may be partly influenced by present decisions.

The cathedral analogy demonstrates that there is a specific rationality for acting in collective enterprises. No matter what the generalized criteria are for defining the desirable in a collective work, those criteria are qualified when applied to efforts that contribute to a work but do not have control over the final outcome.[29] Someone who independently contributes to a collective work cannot adopt the simple strategy of molding reality to an ideal model. The problem arising is unlike that of obstacles to the realization of ideals, necessitating adjustments, or tactics designed to overcome them. Rather, it stems from the fact that we use principles that value actions due to preconceived final results, but we cannot produce those results through our own actions. We need the cooperation of other people whom we cannot control.

Because we can only make one contribution to a collective work whose final product we do not control, the rational choice may not be the most preferred alternative. Instead, the rational choice may be others with lesser merits. Given a cathedral with a romanesque foundation, it may be technically and aesthetically preferable to continue in the same or an intermediate style, instead of the gothic style which would be chosen if the cathedral's total construction were under one's control. This type of rationality, constrained by choices made by others in a collective work, may be called "second best," because it often entails a progressive retreat from the ideal model in the hope of bettering the collective action or work as a whole.

Constitution makers, legislators, judges, and administrators must be seen as participants in a collective work—the law—itself part of the complex of practices, institutions, habits, cultural attitudes, and basic beliefs that define a society. Only exceptional men and women, acting under exceptional conditions—like Napoléon or Lenin—can have almost complete control over the construction of an entire legal order and its network of practices, habits, expectations, and cultural attitudes. Normally, even great men and women can only hope to make an important contribution to the collective work of the law, which is the intentional or nonintentional product of the actions of millions of people over a long period of time. Each of those contributions is conditioned by the evolution of the law and other social practices of the past as well the future.

Given that constitution builders, legislators, and judges generally contribute to a collective work whose other past, present, and future contributions they cannot control and can only partially influence, their actions must follow appropriate guidelines of rationality. It would be irrational for a judge to resolve a case as if he were creating the whole legal order with his decision, or even the legal order relative to the question at hand. The judge must keep in mind expectations generated by decisions of past legislators and judges so that his conclusions will harmonize with his colleagues' simultaneous decisions. This result will be greatly aided by the principle that "like cases should be decided alike." Additionally, the judge will want his decision to serve as a useful precedent for the future. Otherwise, it might be ignored until it inspires opposition by future legislators and judges.

Here we see clearly the meaning of a historical constitution in the context of the collective work of the current law and its component group of social practices. Society's constitution, whether or not it is expressed in a written text, is a historical fact that represents the successful attempt to found the process with which we identify a society's legal order. Generally, there are many attempts of this nature, and only a few are successful. Those which are successful have a special character that compels the attention of all and enables their efforts to be coordinated around it. It is generally very difficult to recommence this process, although at times readjustments can be made that, because of their magnitude, are considered constitutional reforms.

The realization that practical reasoning is not addressed to justify individual actions and decisions but only contributions to a collective action extended over time, through a constitutional convention, allows us to overcome not only the paradox of the moral superfluousness of the historical constitution but also its radical indeterminacy. The historical constitution, which is relevant for practical reasoning, is not a mere text or document but is constituted by the regularity of conducts, attitudes, and expectations of successive legislatures, governmental officials, and generations of citizens generated by the enactment of that text. Therefore, the task of transforming the text into justificatory propositions is aided by the choices taken in this collective work, and the indeterminacies are much more restricted than if each of us had to confront the naked text in isolation.

This theory I am proposing must be distinguished from similar attempts to analyze social practices in terms of a collective enterprise. The approach is not Burkean: it does not attribute any inherent value to a society's traditions. Nor is it like the Dworkinian conception of integrity, which authorizes judges and other government functionaries to make decisions on the basis of the best principles used to justify the decisions and measures of other judges and legislators. My theory must also be distinguished from the communitarian conception defended by philosophers like Alasdair MacIntyre who, using the example of successive narration, assert that only in the context of shared social practices may a valid conception of the good be developed.

Unlike the above-mentioned conceptions, my approach is based on the fact that actions of legislators and judges develop in the context of a collective work they do not control. The judge or legislator is free to decide that the prevailing system of law, beginning with the constitution, has so little worth that it is worth risking a refounding, or even a situation of anarchy or dissolution of the legal order. The judge's decision must however be conceived as an integral part of the legal order, founded upon certain constitutional facts. Therefore, legislative, judicial, or administrative measures must contribute to preserving and even improving the legal order. Unlike Dworkin's view, this does not mean that measures must be justified on the basis of those same principles that justify the other contributions to the supposedly valuable legal order, given the impossibility of another foundational act.

It has often been maintained that there are prima facie values inherent in any legal order, whatever its content.[30] This assertion is of dubious validity. The values of peace and order, for example, are derived from the value of justice only when they are located in social situations where certain acts of violence are not justified. More inherent to the idea of a legal order is the value of predictability. But predictability is an instrument of some other value (as Max Weber showed when he related it to the market economy) and will depend on the latter's priority over other competing values. It is possible to say, however, that a current historical constitution and the legal order it generated resolve a problem of coordination in that the constitution is a completed historical fact compared to other historical attempts. As such, if the current constitution has any value at all, it is in the potential of its being reformed and perfected, a possibility not offered by other unrealized and unrealizable utopias. The fact that the legislator or judge could not have dictated his law or sentence without a legal order to grant him authority does not in itself imply a moral restriction on his decisions, since the legal order may be so bad in comparison with the ideal constitution that it is necessary to take advantage of that authority in order to destroy it. Without the preservation of the legal order, however, their future decisions will probably be completely ineffective.

This conception goes beyond Karl Popper's recommendation to consider traditions as conditioning factors in gradual social engineering.[31] It is not just a matter of taking advantage of some practices in order to change others. If the only way of taking morally justified decisions is to do so in the context of existing social practices founded by a constitution, it is necessary to preserve that constitution and the practices generated by it, even perhaps when they depart from the democratic orthodoxy. This necessity is only limited by the situation where the practices are so bad that they cannot be improved. Only in this worst case is it a morally justified decision, in light of the ideal constitution, to disregard the historical constitution and face the risk of not being able successfully to establish another.

Preserving the historical constitution and the practices generated by it is not relevant only from the external point of view. Instead, it necessitates attending to the internal justifications of those who have participated, are participating, and will participate in the establishment and development of the historical constitution and its practices. For example, a constitution can successfully establish itself at the base of a legal order as long as citizens over time accord the constitutional text and the historical facts that surround its creation a certain intrinsic authority. Nevertheless, as we have seen earlier, neither a text nor a combination of historical circumstances has the epistemological value to determine such principles. If justificatory reasoning is based on principles that we consider valid due to their intrinsic merit, or due to the procedures consistent with the ideal constitution's respect for rights and the democratic organization of power, the historical dimension of the constitution becomes superfluous. Whether there is or is not a coincidence in basic reasons, be they substantive or epistemological, is a matter of fact. If no convergence exists, the currency of the constitution and its practices will be diluted.

This problem places the theorist in a difficult position, almost like an atheist compelled to preach religion. One must seek to maintain conformity with rules of behavior that one believes are rationally justified but that would not be followed on the basis of their rational justification. Since judges and legislators can only issue morally justified decisions that will be effective if they do so within the framework of a successful historical constitution, perhaps its preservation and future improvement require that their reasoning accepts it as a basic moral fact.

I believe the solution lies in the adoption of a kind of two-tiered reasoning:

(i) At the first and most basic level, the reasons legitimating a particular social practice constituted by the historical constitution must be articulated. Here the requirements of promoting a democratic process of decision making and recognizing fundamental rights are applicable. They lead us to evaluate the legitimacy of the historical constitution in terms of whether it is the expression of a democratic consensus resulting from ample and free deliberation and whether it also provides a basis for forming consensus and deliberating with regard to norms of an inferior category. In addition, we can evaluate the degree to which the constitution recognizes those fundamental rights that are prerequisites for the proper operation of the democratic process.

At this first level of practical reasoning, it is important to take into account any realistic alternative to the preservation of the historical constitution. Even when it is far from satisfying the strictures of a legitimate democratic process and of the recognition of fundamental rights, it is possible that any other realistic alternative will be even further away. The most likely alternatives to the historical constitution may be an authoritarian government or anarchy, in which case the desiderata associated with the legitimacy of the historical constitution in light of the ideals of democracy and rights are even less satisfied.

At this first level, one must determine if the conditions of "precommitment" described by Stephen Holmes exist to justify constitutional limitations on democratic procedures.[32] According to Holmes, such limitations do not always disempower the majority but may instead allow it to resolve problems that it could not resolve in any other way by removing certain issues from the decision making sphere. Holmes described this as a form of legitimate paternalism, comparable to Ulysses' request to be tied to the ship's mast in order to keep on course while simultaneously listening to the sirens' song. Yet such constitutional limitations do not involve self-paternalism; they can better be viewed as current majorities protecting future possible majorities, perhaps against the harmful decisions of intermediate majorities.

However, the value of precommitment can only be an ex post facto justification: We cannot justify a priori constitutional limitations of democratic procedures on the ground that democracy is strengthened when we take issues away from its sphere of decision. Rather, the constitutional restrictions may prevent people from deciding future conflicts in the best possible way, that is, by majoritarian decision. This would be an illegitimate attempt by today's circumstantial majority to dominate future majorities. If this is so, it must not be evaluated at the level of practical reasoning. The guiding principle for such an evaluation is that "majority government" does not mean government of any group of citizens, whatever their number. It means government by what is essentially a conceptual construction: a larger number of raised hands in favor of certain solutions for certain issues, regardless of whose hands are raised and how the votes combine when joined with another issue under different circumstances. What must be preserved is the possibility of any given combination of hands against one particular combination. Many constitutional limitations can have this scope, but this cannot be determined in the abstract.

(ii) If the above first-level reasoning supports the legitimacy, even though still imperfect, of the historical constitution, it is possible to go on to a second level of reasoning. This is the application phase, where the historical constitution is applied to justify actions or decisions. The reasoning of this second level must be constrained to respect the results of the first-level reasoning. This means that justificatory reasons incompatible with the preservation of the historical constitution are excluded as long as the first-level reasoning demonstrates that the constitution is more legitimate, with regard to the ideal constitution, than any realistic alternative. Similarly, a rule that is impeccable according to moral principles may be disqualified or excluded if necessary for the preservation of the historical constitution.

This second stage does not imply that the principles and procedures of the ideal constitution have no relevance to legal reasoning, or that the latter is autonomous from morality. First of all, these principles and procedures are the last court of appeal at the first level of legal justificatory reasoning. Given the priority of the first level over the second, this hierarchy determines the results of the reasoning as a whole. Second, the principles and procedures of the ideal constitution are relevant even at the second level of justificatory reasoning as long as they are not incompatible with the conclusions reached at the first level.[33] The principles of rights and democratic procedures that are morally valid as part of the ideal constitution can be called upon to resolve the inevitable indeterminacies that remain in a constitution—even one conceived of as a practice or convention. These indeterminacies allow a constitutional practice to improve and evolve toward more acceptable forms of legitimacy, since it is often possible to find solutions that are normatively preferable.

Dworkin's conception of constitutional interpretation, in contrast, does not allow for this possibility. He tries to minimize chances for variation in legal interpretation by arguing that past decisions not only determine the solutions explicitly adopted but influence cases not explicitly resolved, since those cases must be decided according to principles used to justify past decisions. Thus, Dworkin maintains that there is no difference between cases that are solved according to the law and those that are not. I believe, however, that it is important to see the tension between the preservation and the evolution of the practice. While it is true that the use of past decisions in order to solve hard cases can fortify existing practice in terms of a specific problem, it is preferable to solve such a problem according to principles of rights and democratic procedures which are morally valid. This process makes the practice more consistent with the forms of legitimacy embodied in the ideal constitution, strengthens the historical constitution as a whole, and eliminates tensions with legal demands that might endanger its subjective legitimacy.

These two stages of constitutional practice present a kind of "tiered" configuration when converting the text into justificatory propositions.[34] The initial choices involve general interpretive criteria, such as overcoming semantic, syntactic, and logical indeterminacies. Nevertheless, our options are not completely precluded by those former determinations. Even when we rely on those determinations, we are extending them to new situations.[35]

As I have suggested, this approach corresponds to a kind of "second-best" rationality, since individual cases would better be solved if we were able to justify our actions and decisions on the basis of the ideal constitution. Yet we cannot do this outside of a constitutional practice. Thus, we must justify our actions and decisions in a form compatible with the historical constitution in order to preserve that practice if it is the best possible alternative to the ideal constitution.[36] At the same time, we should always seek to move closer to the ideal one.

This method of overcoming the apparent paradoxes of the radical indeterminacy and the moral irrelevance of the historical constitution generates a new approach to the interpretation, enforcement, and even modification of historical constitutions. In addition to the two dimensions of the ideal constitution—respect for individual rights and the democratic system of decision making—there is a third dimension. That dimension involves the preservation of the current constitutional practice as long as it is basically compatible with constitutional ideals and potentially can achieve greater satisfaction of those ideals in the future. This view of the historical constitution's impact on practical reasoning requires an articulation of the two dimensions of the ideal constitution in whose light the historical one must be evaluated: the ideal constitution of rights and the ideal constitution of democracy. These two dimensions may conflict if they are not suitably combined.

Chapter Three

The Ideal Constitution of Rights

In Chapter 2, I demonstrated what might be deemed to be "the fundamental theorem of legal theory." This theorem holds that actions and decisions, such as those taken in constitutional matters, cannot be justified on the basis of positive laws, as in the historical constitution, but only on the basis of autonomous reasons, which are in the end moral principles. Presumably those moral principles establish a set of fundamental rights. I also established the role of the historical constitution in practical reasoning: Constitutional conventions or practices are not premises of justificatory reasoning but objects of justification in the first stage of that reasoning. These practices in turn serve as the basis for justifying particular actions and decisions in the second stage. This demonstration of the relevance of the historical constitution in practical reasoning, however, was not achieved at the expense of principles establishing rights. Those principles are still considered the ultimate basis of justification in practical reasoning, in the light of which the historical constitution is or is not legitimized.

It is now appropriate to evaluate the bases and implications of principles establishing rights in practical reasoning. Only when we undertake this inquiry can we determine the counterweight that the recognition of rights exerts on the legitimate scope of the democratic process. That scope may be larger or more restricted according to the grounds and implications of the recognition of moral rights. Moreover, recognition of rights may affect how the historical constitution acts as a counterweight to the democratic process. Allegiance to a historical constitution may restrict the operation of the democratic process when necessary to preserve a constitution, that is, the instrument that makes possible the operation of democracy. This depends, however, on the justifiability of the historical constitution itself, which is in turn a function of the extent to which the historical constitution respects moral principles establishing rights.

The object of this chapter is to describe a theory of rights that gives content to this counterweight to the democratic process. My purpose is to articulate that part of the ideal dimension of the complex constitution that deals with individual rights, and hence with the just distribution of social and natural goods as it should be recognized by the state. Of course, historical constitutions may depart considerably from what I would like to defend as the content of an ideal constitution of rights. As I argued in the preceding chapter, the extent of that departure must be considered in evaluating the actual constitutional practice to determine whether one is justified in abiding by it. Moreover, even if one is committed to abiding by it in particular cases, we have to decide whether the historical constitution should be brought closer to the ideal, even if that weakens continuity over time. If so, we need to confront the tension created when we interpret the practice to make it come closer to the requirements of the ideal constitution while at the same time weakening continuity.

The core of this section will be devoted to restating, in a somewhat different manner, what I presented in *The Ethics of Human Rights* as the foundation and general content of a liberal conception of social and political morality.[1] I will also address the implications of the liberal conception for a few particular rights, those essential to the justification of democracy.

The Notion of Individual Rights

The constitutional rights we are going to analyze are, in the first place, *legal rights*, since they either are or ought to be recognized by the legal system. It is well known that legal rights respond to a varied typology that has been described by W. N. Hohfeld, Hans Kelsen, and others:[2]

(i) *rights-liberties*, which involve only the absence of a prohibition and cannot by themselves provide any sort of protection;

(ii) *rights-authorizations*, which are generated by permissive norms, although their status as belonging to an independent category or as reducible to some of the others depends on how those permissive norms are conceived;[3]

(iii) *rights-privileges*, which correlate to active or passive duties of other people, belonging either to certain specific classes or to a universal class;

(iv) *rights-claims*, which include the possibility of presenting a claim to some organ in order to enforce the correlative duties;

(v) *rights-powers*, which involve the ability to enact norms in order to alter the legal relationship of other people;

(vi) finally, *rights-immunities*, which are correlative to the lack of power of others to alter the legal status of the holder of the right.

Constitutional rights are often a conglomerate of these different categories of rights, mainly vis à vis the different organs of the state.

Behind these categories of rights, there are different kinds of duties. They include the absence of the duty to do something or to omit to do something on the part of the holder of the right; the duty of others to perform some action toward that holder or to abstain from interfering with his action; the duty of the organs of the state to provide certain benefits to the holder of the right or to abstain from interfering with his conduct and enable him to use the state's coercive power against those not complying with their correlative duties; and the duty to recognize the norms enacted through exercise of legal power to do so and not to recognize the norms enacted outside that power. To be a beneficiary of a constitutional right is to be a beneficiary of a set of duties.

We saw in Chapter 2, however, that legal norms are not sufficient to justify actions or decisions like those typically grounded in the invocation of constitutional rights. When we resort to a constitutional right to justify a certain decision (including criticism of a decision already adopted), we are ultimately resorting to principles of social morality which endorse the constitutional-legal norm establishing the right in question. Constitutional rights are in the last instance moral rights, since they derive from principles that have the properties of autonomy, finality, supervenience, publicity, universalizability, and generality.[4] These are the distinctive features of moral principles.[5]

Although all legal rights invoked in justificatory contexts are moral rights, not all moral rights are of a legal character. Whether they are legal depends on two circumstances: the concept of law that is employed and the existence of certain prescriptions. With regard to the first point, there are many descriptive and normative concepts of law. There are certain descriptive concepts which refer to the norms which in fact some organs have enacted (the most common concept refers to the judicial recognition of the relevant norms). As we have seen, there are normative concepts which refer to the norms that certain organs ought to enact or apply, including the norms legislators ought to enact, or judges ought to apply, or judges ought to apply if they were enacted by the legislature. A moral right may or may not be of a legal character, depending on the normative or descriptive concept of law employed and the existence or absence of the corresponding enactment.

In what follows, I shall refer to constitutional rights under a certain normative concept of law with which we identify the ideal dimension of the complex constitution. This concept of law takes into account the moral duty of judges and state officials in general to recognize legal norms establishing the right in question. Accordingly, the concept of rights I invoke is also a normative one: Rights that should be recognized as part of the constitutional ideal cannot be determined without articulating a conception of political and moral philosophy.

The Liberal Conception of Rights

There have been many attempts to ground moral principles establishing rights. Some have based them in intuitions of a supra-empirical reality, in contingent social conventions, in the enlightened self-interest of social agents, or in subjective preferences of some people. All such efforts, however, fail to sustain the strong claims implied in the assertion of those rights. The intuitions may be counterpoised by other intuitions of contrary content. Often, social conventions may not be favorable to the recognition of rights. Moreover, there are many situations in which the self-interest of some people may lie in crushing the rights of fellow human beings.

The only way to overcome these dead-ends and give a solid foundation to rights is to rely on the presuppositions of the practice of moral discussion in which we engage when we evaluate actions, decisions, institutions, and practices that may affect the basic rights of people. Those presuppositions of moral discussion define the validity of the principles used in the evaluative framework. To participate in the practice and to deny those presuppositions necessarily assumed when participating in it or their implications is to incur a *practical inconsistency*.

Admittedly, this form of meta-ethical constructivism—which relies on the assumptions of the practice of moral discourse and not on the results of any manifestation of that practice—is itself a form of conventionalism.[6] This is true because it takes as its "archimedean point" of moral justification the presuppositions of a social practice. But two caveats are in place here. First, what validates a moral judgment is its conformity with the underlying requirements of moral discussion, not the fact that those requirements are conventionally accepted. Second, the conventions that constitute the practice of moral discussion are much broader, more general, and more stable than the specific substantive moral standards, such as the proscription against torture. While it is true that throughout history and geography some radical changes are produced in the presuppositions of moral discussion, they are extremely rare and exceptional. The most noticeable change lies in the rejection of criteria of validation that are based on the prescriptions of human, traditional, or divine authorities. These criteria have been replaced by ones deeply embedded in our present practice of moral discourse, which resort to the counterfactual prescription of whoever assumes a position of impartiality, rationality, and knowledge of the relevant facts.

A central presupposition of the post-Enlightenment practice of moral discussion is that every authority or convention is subject to criticism, except perhaps the very practice of criticizing. The role of criticism is associated with liberalism because this feature of the moral discourse of modernity reflects the value of moral autonomy. In effect, moral discussion is designed to overcome conflicts and to achieve cooperation through consensus. That consensus presupposes the shared, free acceptance of principles to justify actions and attitudes. In other words, one who participates in the practice of moral discussion necessarily assumes, either as an end in itself or as a means for some other end, the value of acting on the basis of the free adoption of moral principles—that is, an adoption not grounded in authority or conditioned by threats or inclinations but based on reasons (which are defined in terms of impartiality, rationality, and knowledge of the relevant facts). In the end, participation in the practice of moral discussion presupposes the value of acting on the basis of reasons.[7]

The Principle of Personal Autonomy

The general presupposition about the value of autonomy refers to the free acceptance of both *intersubjective* moral principles and *self-regarding* ideals of personal excellence. Intersubjective moral principles evaluate the actions of individuals according to their effects on the interests or welfare of other individuals (such as the prohibition on killing other people). Ideals of personal excellence evaluate actions for their effects on the quality of the life or the moral character of the agent (such as the ideals of a good parent, a good patriot, or a good Christian, of a rewarding sexual life, and so on).

When the value of autonomy refers to the first kind of moral principles—those of intersubjective character—it has the power of limiting itself. It is necessary to restrain the autonomy of some in order to preserve the autonomy of others. This restraint occurs when the standards of behavior that some individuals freely accept adversely affect the autonomy of other individuals to act according to moral standards that they freely would accept. Of course, this requires us to avail ourselves of some principle which allows us to balance between the autonomy that is lost and that which is preserved when interfering with the choices of individuals.

Note, however, that the same possibility of self-limitation of the value of autonomy is not involved when it refers to the free adoption of ideals of human excellence or of personal virtue. This is true because the adoption of those ideals, by definition, cannot affect in itself the interests of other people. While the adoption of many personal ideals may have consequences which harm the autonomy of people, this is due not to the adoption itself but to the tacit acceptance of some intersubjective standard which allows for action that harms the autonomy of others. It is, thus, the adoption of such a standard and not that of the personal ideal which transgresses on the value of autonomy. Accordingly, from the general presupposition of the value of *moral* autonomy, we can derive the more specific liberal principle of *personal* autonomy proscribing interference with the free choice of ideals of personal excellence. The attempt to impose personal ideals is self-frustrating and, hence, irrational. Democratic discussion and decision, which render a coercive imposition legitimate, have no epistemic value when they refer to personal ideals because the requirement of impartiality, on which that epistemic value is based, is not relevant to their validity.[8]

The recognition of this principle of personal autonomy, a distinctive feature of a liberal conception of society, excludes perfectionism, that is, the position according to which it is a legitimate mission of the state to impose ideals of personal virtue. Some authors have maintained that liberalism based on the principle of personal autonomy implies a version of perfectionism, since personal autonomy is part of an ideal of human excellence.[9] This claim deserves several replies. First, though it is true that personal autonomy gives value to the life and character of individuals, it is also the object of an intersubjective principle—that of not interfering with the choice of life plans on the part of other people—and this principle is derived from the presupposition of moral autonomy in practical discourse. Second, even when it is maintained that the intersubjective principle of personal autonomy cannot be interpreted in all its depth without resorting to the value of personal autonomy as part of an ideal of human excellence, it is nevertheless distinctive of that value to proscribe any interference with the choice of any other aspect of ideals of human excellence. Third, it is precisely that feature of the value of personal autonomy which makes the adoption of it contrary to perfectionism, since it would be absurd to define perfectionism so that there cannot logically be a nonperfectionist position.

The principle of personal autonomy determines the content of basic individual rights, since from it we can infer the goods that those rights protect. These goods are the necessary conditions for the choice and realization of personal ideals and plans of life based on those ideals. Prerequisites for the choice and realization of life plans include psycho-biological life, bodily and psychological integrity, freedom of movement, freedom of expression, access to material resources, freedom of association, freedom to work, access to leisure, and freedom of religious practices.

The value of personal autonomy is, if taken in isolation, an aggregative value. This means that when there is more autonomy in a social group, there is more value in that group regardless of how that autonomy is distributed. This, however, seems to contravene intuitions deeply ingrained in liberalism. If, for instance, an elite achieves enormous degrees of autonomy by subjecting to slavery the rest of the population, making the total amount of autonomy greater than would exist if autonomy were more evenly distributed, this would not be a satisfactory state of affairs from the liberal point of view. Kant captured that intuition in the second formulation of the categorical imperative which prohibits treating people only as means and not also as ends in themselves. In a slaveholding society, the masters would be using the slaves as mere means for their own ends, since the former produce or countenance the reduction of the latter's autonomy so that they may enjoy greater autonomy.

The Principle of Inviolability of the Person

Several contemporary philosophers have asserted that the main fault of a conception of social morality exclusively based on aggregative values lies in its disregard for the independence and separability of persons.[10] They argue that the aggregative conception treats the interests of different individuals as if they were the interests of one and the same person. While it is rational to give priority to the more important interests of a particular individual, it is not rational to do similarly when the interests involve different people. The requirement of impartiality which defines moral validity does not seem to be constructed upon the assumption of a comprehensive viewpoint, which incorporates the interests of all those concerned. It is plausible to conclude, therefore, that moral discourse presupposes this idea of separability and independence of persons. As Thomas Nagel says, impartiality is based on the adoption in successive and separate ways of the points of view of each of the people affected.[11] The very idea of autonomy implies the separability and independence of people, since it presupposes being able to distinguish the life-plan decisions adopted by the agent concerned from those adopted by other people.

These considerations lead to the defense of a second principle as part of a liberal conception of society—the principle of the inviolability of the person.[12] This principle limits that of personal autonomy. In its first formulation, the principle of inviolability of the person proscribes the diminishment of one person's autonomy for the sole purpose of increasing the autonomy enjoyed by others. It excludes positions of a *holistic* character. Holistic positions do not take into account considerations of distribution since they admit, as a matter of principle, interpersonal compensations of benefits and harms or burdens. Among the holistic conceptions, the collectivist view is of particular importance. Collectivists recognize the existence of a collective entity which constitutes an independent moral person with irreducible interests. This is clear, as Elie Kedourie says, in the case of some post-Kantian authors such as Fichte, who maintain that the autonomy of individuals materializes only through their belonging to the whole of the state that confers reality upon them.[13] The state, in this view, is not a mere collection of individuals addressed to satisfy individual interests but is over and above the individuals.

Collectivism is subject to objections of both an ontological and an ethical nature. The most plausible conception of collective persons is that which conceives of persons as logical constructs, since the propositions about collective entities are equivalent to a complex set of propositions about individuals and their factual and normative relationships.[14] But even when we assign an independent logical status to collective persons, it is hardly plausible to consider them irreducible units from the moral point of view. The principle of personal autonomy implies adopting a subjectivist conception of self-regarding interests, and there is no subjectivity without a psyche. From what we know through present science, there is no autonomous psyche without an independent nervous system. The same conclusion can be reached by considering that moral discourse presupposes adoption of the points of view of all the people affected. It would be very strange to suppose that a state or a university has a distinctive point of view.[15] This does not mean that it is senseless to speak of the interests of a country, but the propositions about those interests should be translatable to propositions about interests of individuals.

The Principle of Dignity of the Person

The combination of the principles of autonomy and inviolability of the person is insufficient for constituting a liberal conception of society and for deriving the set of individual rights normally associated with that conception. The two principles guarantee that the autonomy of an individual may not be sacrificed in order to increase the autonomy of other individuals. But this guarantee also would apply to the very agents concerned, prohibiting them from engaging in any kind of arrangement that might damage their own autonomy. Thus, the principle of personal autonomy would imply, paradoxically, a permanent supervision of individuals in order to disqualify any personal decisions that restrict their own autonomy, even if the net result is to enlarge the autonomy of other people.

The rejection of the above antiliberal implication of the former two principles necessitates a further principle that directly limits the principle of the inviolability of the person. This new principle must authorize restrictions in the autonomy of individuals, when those restrictions are consented to by the very individuals concerned. A more precise formulation of this principle, which I call "the principle of dignity of the person,"[16] permits one to take into account deliberate decisions or acts of individuals as a valid sufficient basis for obligations, liabilities, and loss of rights. Thus, it is possible to envision a dynamic process where rights can be transferred and lost so that some individuals may diminish their autonomy in favor of actions of others.

The limitation that the principle of dignity of the person places upon the principle of inviolability of the person may cancel the limitation that the latter places on the principle of autonomy of the person. Therefore, when the principle of dignity of the person applies (since the person affected consents to a normative relation resulting in a loss of autonomy), the prohibition on restraining the autonomy of an individual in order to increase that of others is overridden. This manifests itself in the fact that legal institutions which establish obligations and liabilities depending on the consent of the people affected—such as contract, marriage, and criminal laws—should be justified on the basis of promoting autonomy in society at large.[17] Individuals who, for instance, commit a crime may be punished in order to prevent further crimes and, consequently, to promote a greater aggregative amount of autonomy. Such individuals are not entitled to complain that they are being used as mere means because they have agreed to assume liability for punishment when they voluntarily commit a crime while knowing that liability is a necessary, normative consequence of the act.

This third principle of a liberal conception of society excludes "normative determinism." At its most basic level, determinism maintains that every event, including human actions, is caused by biological, psychological, or socio-economic factors. Normative determinism is a position which infers from this descriptive hypothesis that voluntary human actions should not be taken as sufficient normative conditions of obligations, liabilities, and rights. This is itself a normative proposition which, as such, could not simply be derived from the descriptive hypothesis of determinism without engaging in an illegitimate derivation of "ought-judgments" from "is-judgments."

Such a derivation could only be done on the basis of some major premise of a normative character. As I have tried to show elsewhere, however, it is not easy to see what that premise might be and how it might be grounded.[18] This is all the more true when the conclusion that would derive from it would lead, once generalized, to an unintelligible conception of society. Negating the principle of dignity of the person would lead not only to the rejecting of the institution of criminal responsibility—since it is based on the consent of those subject to punishment[19]—but also to the rejection of institutions such as civil contracts, marriage, and political representation.

In adopting the principle of dignity of the person against the claims of normative determinism, we must confront the challenge of dealing with exceptions in situations where consent is commonly considered to be invalid due to a failure of the will. In certain cases the will of the agent is overcome by external factors, such as coercion or mental disturbance. In my view, excuses from punishment or compensation as a result of a failure of will that nullify contracts are compatible with the principle of dignity of the person.[20] The consistency exists insofar as we take into account not the fact that the will of the agent is caused but rather that it is caused by factors which operate in an unequal way on the agents in question. If mental immaturity, coercion, necessity, or mistakes affect in a relatively equal way all the members of the relevant social group, it would be absurd to permit those circumstances to invalidate contracts or marriages, or to deny compensations for torts or punishments for crimes committed within that group.

These three principles—autonomy, inviolability, and dignity—constitute a broad basis for deriving an ample set of individual rights that conform to the substantive ideal dimension of the complex constitution. The principle of personal autonomy determines the goods that are the content of those rights; inviolability of the person describes the function of those rights by establishing barriers of protection of individual interests against claims based on interests of other people or of some collective whole; and the dignity of the person allows for a dynamic handling of rights by permitting consent of individuals to serve as grounds for the liabilities and obligations that limit them. These three principles define a liberal conception of society, a conception which rejects the implications of perfectionism, holism, and normative determinism.

Who Enjoys Rights? Who Must Respect Them?

Any limitation on the class of holders of moral rights on the basis of certain factual properties, such as belonging to the human species or possessing rationality, presents an almost insurmountable difficulty. We must ask why those factual properties should necessarily be relevant to certain higher normative principles. If we do not resolve this problem, we risk a dogmatism analogous to that of the racist who considers morally relevant physical differences without an ulterior moral justification.[21]

Though this problem requires more extensive discussion, I can say here that the solution consists in acknowledging that the principles establishing fundamental rights are unconditional and extend toward everybody and everything. Certain factual conditions control not who are the holders of the rights in question but who actually is able to enjoy the benefits provided by them. For instance, certain psycho-biological conditions are preconditions to enjoying the good of personal autonomy. A determinate development of the nervous system is a condition to feeling pleasure and pain. The attribution of a separate existence, which underlies the principle of inviolability of the person, also requires also some psycho-biological conditions. The capacity to make decisions and to perform certain voluntary actions, which allows for the application of the principle of dignity of the person, also presupposes a certain psychological and biological development. Hence, when fundamental moral rights—like constitutional ones—are deemed *human* rights, this alludes to the very important, but logically contingent, fact that we believe that those rights mainly benefit members of the human species. This conception of the addressees of individual rights has important implications for issues like abortion and discrimination.[22] However, there are classes of superior nonhuman animals which may partially enjoy some aspects of those rights, such as rights that imply that infliction of pain has negative value.

An important question with regard to constitutionally guaranteed human rights asks whether they should benefit people outside the borders of a certain country. For instance, the United States Supreme Court, in *United States v. Rene Martinez Verdugo-Urquidez,*[23] ruled that the guarantee of the Fourth Amendment against search and seizures undertaken without a judicial warrant did not apply outside the territory of the United States.[24] The argument of the majority of the Court was that the expression "the people" used in the

Fourth Amendment refers to the national community, and the Court held that only members of that community are protected by that guarantee. Justices William J. Brennan, Jr., and Thurgood Marshall dissented, adopting a universalistic vision of constitutional rights. They pointed out the contradiction inherent in maintaining that while the government is constitutionally authorized to act abroad in order to combat crime, it is not constrained in its action by the same constitution to protect the individual rights. In my view, the dissent is the correct approach according to the principles of constitutional liberalism, since the recognition of rights must necessarily be universal, notwithstanding the fact that the efficacy of such recognition is limited to the national territory.

Our framework also can be used to examine who must preserve constitutional rights and who can be made responsible for their violation. In principle, the class of those who are morally bound to respect human rights is also a universal class, since any a priori discrimination in the duty to protect and promote those rights is not justified. As previously suggested, however, such duties are subject to conditions related to the possibility of complying with them and with the distribution of the corresponding burdens. With these limitations, the duties protecting constitutional rights are in many cases fulfilled in a direct way—such as in duties of noninterference. In other cases, they are fulfilled through institutional mechanisms, such as contributions of different forms, particularly taxation, that maintain the state structures which protect and promote those rights. These state structures include the police, the administration of justice, and a system of social security. The state is often considered the main offender against human rights. This emphasis is understandable insofar as it is assumed that there are legal mechanisms able to confront human rights abuses committed by nonstate actors, but absent when committed by the state. But it is necessary to underscore the need to establish such mechanisms.

Two Challenges to Liberalism:
Communitarianism and Egalitarianism

The liberal conception of society is generally criticized for not being able to absorb ideals of fraternal community, equality, and democracy. While liberalism is said to be based on the values of autonomy, inviolability, and dignity of the person, it allegedly ignores other essential aspects of the human condition. Critics argue, first, that liberalism fails to recognize the role that membership in a community plays in the life and character of individuals in defining their identity, conditioning their moral reasoning, and choosing plans of life. Second, liberalism arguably gives an undue weight to autonomy understood in merely negative terms, protecting formal liberty and disregarding the claims of equality and social justice.

The Communitarian Challenge to Liberalism

Philosophers like Alasdair MacIntyre, Charles Taylor, and Michael Sandel have tried to show how the traditions and conventions that define a community, many of which may eventually be reflected in a constitution, are necessarily approximations of propositions that justify actions or decisions. These traditions and conventions are used, for example, in justifying decisions based on individual rights or the democratic process. This conception of the addressees of individual rights has relevant implications for issues like abortion and discrimination.[25]

Taylor tries, for example, to show in an almost syllogistic way how appeal to individual rights presupposes membership in a specific community defined by specific traditions.[26] He alleges that the ascription of rights depends on the recognition of the capacity for certain activities, such as expressing opinions, developing a spiritual life, and feeling pleasure or pain. He then argues that the ascription of rights implies not only the recognition of certain human capacities but also the recognition that such capacities are valuable. If something is valuable, there is a duty to expand and preserve it as well as to create the conditions on which its materialization and expansion depend. But, he states, most of the capacities underlying the protection of individual rights are conditioned by membership within a given society, since their practice requires elements such as language, a conceptual scheme, and institutions that are inherently social.[27] The conclusion is, of course, that the ascription of rights presupposes the duty of preserving those communal bonds that make possible the development of the precious capacities protected by rights.[28]

Elsewhere I have maintained that communitarianism seems attractive only in light of its valuation of each society's peculiar form of solidarity, and of the social contribution to individual development.[29] Communitarianism appears questionable when we perceive that the logical development of this position can lead to collectivist and perfectionist implications, derived from its implicit adoption of a conservative and relativist conventionalism.

It is not these less plausible characteristics of communitarianism that demonstrate its theoretical weakness, however, but rather a more fundamental inconsistency. On the one hand, it embraces conventions and social practices, but on the other, it questions the current practice of moral discourse which, as MacIntyre recognizes, is characterized by those features of liberalism that communitarianism condemns.[30] These features include the idea that morality is principally composed of rules that would be accepted by any rational individual under ideal circumstances; the requirement that such rules be neutral with respect to the interests of different individuals; the requirement that moral rules be neutral in relation to conceptions of the good that individuals support; and finally, the requirement that moral rules be applied equally to all human beings independent of their social context. Hence, current practices of moral discourse seem to exclude the possibility of justifying actions or decisions on the basis of reasons whose validity is socially relative—dependent on their acknowledgment as social conventions—and whose content varies from society to society. Communitarians are thus inconsistent in both emphasizing the importance of conventions to moral reasoning and opposing those that constitute the foundations of the social practice of moral discourse. The post-Enlightenment moral discourse of our civilization, as epitomized by Kant, requires that ultimate justificatory reasons be autonomous (their validity should not depend on their context but on their acceptability under ideal conditions) and also universal (applicable to all situations that do not differ in relevant circumstances).

This rejection of the philosophical basis of communitarianism does not deny that membership in a community and bonds of fraternity and friendship are extremely important goods in the development of personal autonomy. As such, the political organization, beginning with its constitution, ought to provide the material basis for those goods. This requires granting everybody ample freedom, not only negative but also positive, to engage voluntarily in the most varied associations and organizations of communal life, be they partial and circumstantial or total and lifelong. Of course, the essential precondition for this freedom is the possibility of voluntarily joining and leaving these communities, a freedom of special importance in the case of children. It also requires individuals to be exposed to other forms of life outside the community in which somebody has been born and raised. Finally, the state will have to intervene in order to overcome problems of collective action that affect the possibility of free communitarian engagements.

The Egalitarian Challenge to Liberalism

The egalitarian criticism of liberalism implies that philosophy is antagonistic to a commitment to support the neediest citizens, since that support often involves interfering with choices of individuals. Although liberalism should not be reduced solely to the defense of the free economic market, the market and private property must occupy a central place in liberal institutions addressed to promote personal autonomy. This centrality must be assured despite the obvious fact that the protection of the market and private property may often consolidate and even expand initial inequalities.

There has been a strong egalitarian trend within liberalism, ever since Kant and Mill, that makes one wonder whether the supposed tension between liberty and equality is real. The suspicion that it is only illusory emerges when we consider that the two values have different structures. Liberty is not a relative value: I am free regardless of how free others are, despite any causal interdependencies between my own freedom and that of others. Freedom is an absolute value, the extension of which does not depend on how it is distributed among different individuals, nor does it a priori include a criterion of distribution. On the other hand, equality is a value which necessarily refers to the distribution of some other value. Equality is not a value if it is not predicated on another situation or property which is in itself valuable. It is not, for instance, valuable to be equal in our height or in our conditions of slavery.

This suggests the possibility of combining the two values: what is required is an equal distribution of liberty. But then one might ask, why should this combination be accepted in place of another criterion for distributing autonomy? One could choose, for instance, to maximize autonomy by equalizing people in relation to some other value, such as the satisfaction of their needs. The answer to this question may be provided by examining the violations of rights that liberalism recognizes.

Liberalism endorses rights such as the right to life, to bodily integrity, and to property, and guarantees freedom from aggression and from torture. Recognition of these rights raises a further question: Why are those very same rights not violated when people are left to die or suffer bodily harms for want of food or medical attention or when they lack the necessary resources to pursue their chosen plans of life? The usual reply rests upon a distinction between the two types of cases. In the first, individual rights are being violated by the person, normally a public official who executes the attack or aggressive act. The second case involves not a violation of rights but their nonsatisfaction due to natural events or at most to involuntary actions of human beings. In this view, all that public officials do is to allow that nonsatisfaction to occur. Even in the worst of situations, this is considered much less serious than provoking the nonsatisfaction in the first place.

But this reply seems to depend on an unjustified moral distinction between *actions* and *omissions*. Why not say that the public officials who did not ensure that the ill get adequate medical attention, or even the citizens who did not contribute sufficient taxes, have killed or caused bodily harm by omission? There are many situations in which the differences between actions and omissions either do not appear or are not significant. By way of response, some point to the fact that the act committed shows a greater degradation of the agent than the corresponding omission; others state that positive actions are always deliberate, whereas omissions are frequently involuntary; some argue that the former generally provoke greater scandal and worse exemplary effects than the latter.

Elsewhere, I have argued that the examples typically used in the discussion of this problem do reveal a difference between action and omission—specifically, that the omission does not *cause* the disvaluable result which is indeed caused by the action in the parallel example. The government official in charge of public health who does not assign enough funds to hospitals creates a necessary condition of the death of the patients. But he does not cause that death as he would if he shot those patients with a machine-gun. The official's intervention, or lack of it, is comparable to that of the person who made or sold the machine-gun.

Despite these distinctions, it is reasonable to ask why omissions in these and other similar examples do not cause the results which violate human rights and to inquire into the moral relevance that they are not causes but only conditions of those results. Consider the mother who does not feed her baby and thereby causes his death. The reason seems to be that the ascription of causal effects to conduct, mainly to the omitted conduct, depends on normative standards which establish a duty of acting in a positive way. Such standards distinguish the case of the mother from the case of a neighbor who might also have fed the child but did not have the duty to do so and, hence, did not cause his death. According to this logic, it is not that we have the duty of acting or of not acting when such action or inaction causes a result that violates a certain right. Instead, we cause a result that violates some right when we have a duty of acting or not acting in order to impede that result.

Since it is generally concluded that a right such as the right to life is not violated by not providing people with food or medicines, it presumably follows that there is no duty to provide such resources. From where does the definition of that duty emerge? As part of the positive morality of our societies, we judge intuitively that it is different to abstain from providing food to hungry people than to shoot them with a machine-gun. Therefore, the assumption that there is no duty to provide food to the needy corresponds to a standard of that very positive morality. That standard has an impact on the principle of inviolability of the person, since it implies that nobody should be sacrificed for the sake of increasing the autonomy of others in the case where resources are not provided for satisfying the needs of somebody. In this way, we avoid restraining the autonomy of others, since the failure to provide the resources in question is not a cause of the fact that the autonomy of the person in need is diminished.

But how is it possible to justify this standard of positive morality which limits the duties to perform positive actions to extremely rare cases? As we have seen, liberalism assumes that any social practice or convention is subject to criticism. Therefore, the fact that this standard is part of social morality is not a sufficient reason to accept it. One might say that this standard protects the very value of autonomy, since it would require restrictions in individual choice and actualization of plans in order to satisfy the needs of others. This answer is a *petitio principii*, since it presupposes, on the basis of the very same standard under discussion, that the autonomy of the individuals whose needs are not satisfied are not adversely affected by omission. In the end, it seems that the standard which limits positive rights cannot be justified in any way at all. The "conservative liberalism" which avails itself of this view in order to justify an extremely lean conception of rights is more conservative than liberal. It starts from a noncritical acceptance of standards of positive morality, thus contravening the liberal requirement of subjecting every social convention to critical examination.

At the same time, it is not easy to articulate a liberal position which abandons the more restrictive standard of positive morality, with its limited view of the duty of positive behavior toward other people. If that standard is removed, any action or omission that may be a necessary condition of results that violate rights may itself be a violation of rights. This would mean that anything we do or omit to do may infringe on the principle of inviolability of the person, since the act or omission may involve the reduction of the autonomy of somebody, almost surely by increasing that of others. If this inviolability principle were infringed upon in practically every case, it could not serve to limit the principle of autonomy of the person. And if that were so, only the autonomy principle would serve as the basis of a liberal conception of society, since the principle of dignity of the person would also vanish because its function is to limit the principle of inviolability of the person. If the principle of autonomy of the person were taken in isolation, it would constitute an aggregative principle that did not respect the separability and independence of the persons, leading to a holistic approach such as utilitarianism.

To avoid this result, I propose a second version of the principle of inviolability of the person. This version proscribes only those restrictions which diminish a person's autonomy to a level inferior to that enjoyed by others.[31] Thus, one may restrain the autonomy of some if this results in increasing the autonomy of people who are less autonomous than those whose autonomy is being diminished. This principle resembles the prescription involved in Rawls's difference principle of increasing always the welfare of those who are the least well-off. The principle does not impose a strict equality among individuals: differences in autonomy may be justified if the greater autonomy of some serves to increase the autonomy of lesser autonomous people or has no effect in the latter's autonomy. This is an idea of equality not as leveling but as nonexploitation: greater autonomy is illegitimate when achieved at the expense of a lesser autonomy of other people.

Two great conceptions of equality have dominated the history of philosophical reflection and are in considerable tension. The first conception of equality focuses on the idea of *leveling*. According to this conception, a situation of inequality between persons exists when persons are located in different positions with regard to some relevant dimension. Ideally, all moral persons are equalized in the amount of goods, resources, and satisfactions which are considered significant, such as in the value of personal autonomy. Obviously, this result is impossible to achieve in practice, and there are then divergences over which situations come closer to that ideal.[32] There is the additional problem that if I am satisfied with my possession of the relevant good in a degree x, the fact that I now realize that there is somebody who has that good in the degree $x + 1$ may lead to a complaint based on envy.

These doubts require our focus on the alternative conception of equality—equality as *nonexploitation*. This conception is perceptible in Locke when he maintains that men are not made to be instruments of others, and is clearly articulated by Kant through his famous second formulation of the categorical imperative prohibiting persons from being treated only as means. The idea culminates in Marx's idea that workers are exploited in the capitalist system of production through the appropriation of their surplus labor.[33] Additionally, the principle of the inviolability of the person is related to the idea of equality as nonexploitation.[34]

The articulation of the idea of nonexploitation through the second formulation of the principle of inviolability of the person creates a convergence with the idea of leveling. In effect, the inviolability of persons is affected now by harmful acts or omissions only when the autonomy which is reduced comes out to be less than the autonomy which is expanded. This seems to assume a certain value in the leveling of people in terms of autonomy. But this convergence does not imply total devotion to the equality principle. There are many cases of differences in autonomy which are unobjectionable according to the second formulation of the principle of inviolability of the person. The greater autonomy of one may be expanded, for instance, without having any causal effect on the scope of the more restricted autonomy of others. Differences in autonomy are also unobjectionable when the reduction of the inferior autonomy has been consented to by the person concerned, making relevant the principle of dignity of persons.

The idea of equality as leveling has an independent validity when it applies to the conditions concerning participation in the process of democratic discussion and decision. The justification of democracy which I shall present in Chapter 5 requires an equal participation of those affected by decisions in order to maximize the epistemic quality of the process. This requires an equal voice and equal vote, along with all the preconditions for that equality to be substantive and not merely formal. Since the determination of the differences that favor the least favored people must be done through the democratic process, there would not be any guarantee that those decisions were made impartially if the process itself were affected by favoring greater participation from those who are in the worse position.[35]

This reformulation of the principle of inviolability of the person prevents us from falling into either a conservative or a utilitarian position. It provides ample positive rights, but not every action or omission infringes on the principle of inviolability of the person. The reformulation recognizes as violations only those restrictions which diminish the autonomy of people less autonomous than those benefited by the action. This is true notwithstanding the effect on the total sum of autonomy available in the relevant social group. Despite the fact that this presentation permits combining the values of liberty and equality—ascribing value to the equal distribution of autonomy—the tensions between these two values do not disappear completely. The point may be reached in which an excess of positive duties to promote the autonomy of the least autonomous people removes all possibility of individuals autonomously to develop plans of life.

This form of egalitarian liberalism is the only approach that is not contingent on social conventions and makes room for the three principles of autonomy, inviolability, and dignity of the person. It is a liberalism that is far from being antagonistic to so-called social rights, such as the right to health, a dignified shelter, and a just salary. Instead, it shows that "social rights" are the natural extension of classic individual rights. This view is contrary to the claims of some that individual or negative rights have greater priority than social or "positive" ones. Similarly, it demonstrates the error of those who argue that the recognition of these social rights—through so-called social constitutionalism—requires rejection of classical liberalism by restraining individual rights.

Rights and Their Implications for Democracy

I have attempted in this chapter to articulate, in a very cursory manner, the basic content of the ideal constitution of rights. The rights identified are based on the principles of autonomy, inviolability, and dignity of the person and are derived from the assumptions of the social practice of moral discourse. Ultimately, the justification of democracy, the foundation of judicial review, and even the relationships between the different dimensions of the complex constitution are supported explicitly or implicitly by this account of rights.

We now may make a preliminary examination into the interplay between the recognition of rights and the operation of the democratic process in adopting collective decisions. This dynamic seems to be more problematic than the relationship between rights and the historical constitution. The rights we have explored are derived not from the democratic process but through reflections on the presuppositions of our practice of moral discussion. Once we discovered those rights, their function seems to be precisely to limit the operation of the democratic process by disqualifying collective decisions that ignore them. If the democratic process denies the inviolability of the person, for instance by instituting a form of slavery, or ignores the autonomy of the person by promoting perfectionist policies, recognition of the rights emerging from our core principles would *ipso facto* invalidate these decisions. This is the basic intuition behind the idea that when constitutionalism is added to democracy, there are democratic decisions which are precluded by the liberal recognition of rights. This counterweight provided by the recognition of rights upon democracy has implications for institutional design, including questions related to judicial review of democratic decisions, division of power, representation, and minority rights.

Traditionally, the counterweight that rights exert on democracy has not been so extreme as to prevent democracy from having its own important sphere of operation. If the scope of rights is restricted, as is proposed by classic liberalism, many important social issues will be decided not by the recognition of rights but by the democratic process. These issues may involve questions with regard to which a valid moral system may have solutions but ones which are not the concern of rights. Furthermore, the moral system may be silent with regard to these issues, either because any solution is morally indifferent or because the moral system is indeterminate as to the right solution. In fact, one role for positive law is to fill the gaps in the moral system. If the positive law is morally justified because it originates in a democratic process, which we assume is morally legitimate, positive law converts into morally right solutions decisions which were hitherto morally indifferent or morally indeterminate.

But what if this analysis is wrong and the scope of rights is not so restricted? This is in fact a consequence of adopting the liberal egalitarian outlook, interpreting the principle of inviolability of the person so that it is infringed when the autonomy of somebody is restricted in order to promote a greater autonomy of others. This implies that rights are not only negative but also positive, that is to say that the autonomy of a person is harmed not only by actions that prevent people from having certain goods necessary for that autonomy but also by failing to provide people with those goods which are the content of welfare rights. When we introduce positive rights into our moral space, that space is enormously extended. A good deal of the actions and omissions of people have intersubjective significance since they affect other people. This is even truer, of course, of the actions or omissions of public authorities. A policy that assigns resources to national defense instead of housing, or to housing instead of education, or that relies more on the market than on public distribution of goods may affect individual rights. Each policy option may expand the autonomy of certain groups of people at the expense of those who enjoy less autonomy. Therefore, interpersonal morality acquires an enormous scope, and rights occupy most of it.

Once we accept the constructivist proposal of grounding moral principles establishing rights in the presuppositions of the social practice of moral discourse, any person, particularly someone trained in exploring the structures of individual thought and social practices (such as a moral philosopher), can have access to those principles and have authority to assert implications concerning rights.[36] Therefore, we must confront the problem that a robust theory of rights, ostensibly supported by reasons to which anybody may have access, pushes the democratic procedure out of the moral realm. Even more troubling is the fact that this theory of rights may legitimize a historical constitution which guarantees the rights but does not establish a democratic system for taking collective decisions.

Confronted with this challenge, many thinkers have believed it essential to a liberal conception of society—and to the constitutional ideal which incorporates the recognition of rights—that democracy be justified in such a way that its value depends on the fact that its operations do not invade the moral space occupied by rights. This approach would create a sharp separation between politics and morality, implying that it is not the mission of democratic politics to transform the interests and preferences of people and groups in a moral way, or in a way which leads to the protection and promotion of rights. Others have maintained, on the contrary, that politics is inherently moral and that the operation of democracy is relevant to defining the rights that we have. This distinction will soon become important in the review of conceptions of democracy in the following chapter.

Chapter Four

Alternative Conceptions of Democracy

What justifies democracy? Is it the process or something inherent in the process? If democracy were justified by the value of its results, the appeal of democracy would be weak. It would be contingent on the fact that better results are not achieved through some other procedure and subject to the claim that democratic procedure sometimes produces morally unacceptable results. If democracy is justified, instead, in the light of values inherent in its distinctive procedure, its worth should be weighed against the results achieved through it. Unlike practices that we value because of some intrinsic procedures (such as games or sports), the results of the democratic procedure are not morally irrelevant but of immense moral importance. How this tension between procedure and substance is overcome should be taken into account in the evaluation of theories of democracy.

Justifications of democracy adopt two radically different approaches for overcoming these problems. They differ primarily in the way each approach incorporates concerns of morality into explanations of and justifications for democracy.[1]

First, many theories try to carve a sphere for the operation of politics, specifically of democratic politics, within which moral issues are not contested. Giovanni Sartori writes, for instance, that the realm of politics is not the realm of ethics. To introduce morality into politics, he states, is to play with fire.[2] The democratic process, in such a view, takes as given the interests and preferences of people (even when they are egotistic and morally blameworthy) and assumes that people act on the basis of those preferences. Democracy generates dynamics of collective action that produces morally acceptable results but does not try to modify the preferences and interests of people in a morally virtuous direction.

Such views of democracy generally start from a pessimistic view of human nature and of the possibility of changing self-interested inclinations of persons. They also assert that democracy makes the best of those self-interested inclinations. This pessimistic approach includes a conception of factions as self-interested and as a threat to the rights of individuals, but is tempered by a belief that democracy may neutralize without dissolving the power of these factions through a series of mechanisms that create results which are respectful of individual rights.

Those who take this view frequently assume a skeptical or relativist meta-ethical posture, doubting the existence of objective reasons for disqualifying people's preferences as immoral. They often argue that the very pretension of having found those objective reasons leads to authoritarian political enterprises and interventions into people's private lives. Instead, the virtue of the democratic process, they argue, is that nobody can disqualify the preferences of another participant as immoral and the system seeks to accommodate everybody's preferences without judging their moral content. Ultimately, according to this approach, the result of this morally neutral process is morally valuable.

The second family of theories justifying democracy adopts the exact opposite approach regarding the capacity of democracy to transform the preferences and inclinations of people, thereby inserting the democratic process into the moral realm. According to those who subscribe to this theory, democracy's virtue lies precisely in the inclusion of mechanisms that transform people's original self-interested preferences into more altruistic and impartial ones. Democracy not only produces morally acceptable results but produces them through the moralization of people's preferences, perhaps through the moralization of people themselves. This implies a much more optimistic view of human nature and of how it may be molded through social mechanisms according to some values.

Of course, those who support this second family of justifications of democracy are not relativistic or skeptical in meta-ethics. They believe there is a possibility of giving objective reasons for the morality of certain outcomes, and that the democratic process itself helps determine the morally right result. Furthermore, they struggle to overcome the charge that this objectivism may lead to a moral authoritarianism and to models of democracy which are quite impervious to the recognition of liberal rights.

These two families of justifications of democracy differ with respect to liberal rights. The first family appears sympathetic to the recognition of liberal rights through its insistence that democracy does not interfere with the moral realm constituted by those rights. In fact, its supporters have coined the expression "liberal democracy," sometimes equated with "constitutional democracy" or "representative democracy," to refer to this distinctive form of government. According to the defenders of the first family of views, this is the only kind of democracy that acknowledges the weight that the two other dimensions of constitutionalism—recognition of rights and historical constitutionalism—exert upon democracy.

The second family is, on the other hand, almost always understood by its opponents, and sometimes by its very defenders, as antiliberal or at least nonliberal. The views in this second family are frequently deemed "populist democracy," "social democracy," or "participatory democracy." Sometimes the defenders of these views acknowledge that they reduce or even eliminate the counterweight of the two other dimensions of constitutionalism to democracy— recognition of rights and the historical constitution.

The main thrust of this book is to show that this whole handling of the issue is wrong. Those who view democracy as operating outside the moral realm and leaving untouched individual preferences and interests are mistaken, since they cannot overcome the problem of the moral superfluousness of government and the tension between procedure and substance. I wish to justify democracy in terms of its power to transform people's interests in a morally acceptable way. At the same time, I will show that this view of democracy deserves to be considered part of the liberal tradition because it properly acknowledges the counterweights of the two other dimensions of constitutionalism previously analyzed—history and rights.

These different views of democracy are not merely speculative but have important consequences for pervasive issues of institutional design. Democracy is not simply a descriptive concept whose institutions can be factually identified. It is also a partly normative concept, shaped by moral theory, and the specific institutions it calls for will depend upon the theory used to justify it. Such institutions, for periodic elections and free speech, may be universal for all forms of democracy, but others are vitally dependent on the justificatory conception adopted. The conception I defend in the next chapter has very different institutional implications than those required by competing notions of democracy outlined in this chapter.

Group One: Conceptions of Democracy That Take People's Interests as a Given

Various theories of democracy take as given people's interests and preferences. These theories include utilitarianism, elitism, pluralism, and consensualism. These four approaches, plus the variant of utilitarianism contained in classic economic analysis, do not view democracy as transformative of interests and preferences, but simply accept these interests and preferences and leave them as found.

The Utilitarian Approach

Utilitarianism evaluates actions and institutions according to their consequences for a certain intrinsic good. There are several varieties of utilitarianism according to the nature of that intrinsic good. The traditional version is hedonistic, since it defines the good in relation to the attainment of pleasure and the avoidance of pain. In light of the recognition that pleasure cannot exhaust the whole good, the most favored version of utilitarianism today defines the good in relation to the satisfaction of preferences and the subjective interests of people, whatever their content. There are also versions of utilitarianism that identify the good with some ideal state of affairs, regardless of the object of people's preferences. While far removed from the original form of utilitarianism, which was based on some sort of subjectivism about the good for people, there are idealistic versions which, though not strictly subjectivist, may still qualify as respecting the utilitarian intuition. These include forms that identify the good with personal autonomy, and even perhaps those which include within the intrinsic good respect for certain rights.[3]

Utilitarianism distinguishes itself by not discriminating a priori between possible recipients of the intrinsic good but by including among them every being that is physically capable of enjoying the good in question. This implies that utilitarianism does not recognize racial, religious, gender, or national barriers to the holders of the good, and may even go beyond the human species.[4] Conversely, certain human beings—for example, those in an irreversible coma—may be excluded as holders of the good on the basis of not being capable of enjoying it. Therefore, utilitarianism is profoundly individualistic in the sense that every individual is a possible candidate for being a moral person. No supra-individual entity, such as the state, qualifies since it does not possess the physical capacities necessary to enjoy the good.

On the other hand, there is another essential aspect of the linkage between the good and its holders which makes utilitarianism anti-individualistic. The propagation of the good among individuals defended by utilitarianism is aggregative, in the sense that the good increases by summing up the participation in it of different individuals regardless of the distribution of that good among those individuals. In this way, utilitarianism allows interpersonal comparisons of the good of different individuals. While the distributive quality of a primary good may be seen as part of a more complex good, the most important component is the aggregation of the participation of different individuals in this more complex good.

There are also both necessary and variable features of utilitarianism concerning the objects or phenomena evaluated by the principle of utility. The necessary feature is that utilitarianism refers to actual instances of human praxis, not to ideal ones.[5] The variable feature of utilitarianism involves whether the objects evaluated are individual actions (envisioned by act-utilitarianism), rules and practices (rule-utilitarianism), whole social and institutional structures, or dispositions or inclinations of character.

In the different versions of utilitarianism, the way in which moral theory justifies democracy is paradigmatic of this first family of views. If democracy is justifiable, it is because it takes the interests or preferences of individuals as given. The state has no role in meddling with the interests of individuals, which must be respected and taken into account on an equal footing, even when those interests are egotistic. This gives highest priority to the principle of personal autonomy, discussed in the preceding chapter, and to the right of privacy flowing from it.

If democracy is morally justified under a utilitarian account, it is because the democratic system increases the good constituted by the total amount of pleasure over pain that people enjoy, or the total amount of preference satisfaction over the frustration of preferences, or the total amount of personal autonomy possessed by people or the enjoyment of rights.

The problem of justifying democracy by its beneficial consequences for the intrinsic good is that it is too *contingent* a way of ascribing value to democracy. One must corroborate in each case whether it is true that the actual consequences of maintaining the democratic system are more conducive to the intrinsic good than those resulting from alternative systems of government. If act-utilitarianism were adopted, for example, there could be a multitude of cases in which a nondemocratic government in general or a single decision in particular would contribute the common good more than a government of democratic origin or a decision adopted democratically. But even if rule-utilitarianism or institutional-utilitarianism is assumed, there are many occasions when a suspension of democratic institutions may increase public happiness. For many, the mere fact that these issues are subject to hard empirical evidence and debate is offensive to democratic sensibilities.

One obvious utilitarian justification of majority rule focuses on a straightforward way of achieving a social value (general happiness, welfare, utility, and so on) even out of self-interested individuals. Majority rule maximizes social utility, since a majority of individuals satisfy their preferences in this way. Maximum social utility, according to this view, cannot be secured by any other system that allows preferences of the few to prevail over those of the many.

The shortcomings of this simple proposal are well known. Majority rule by itself does not satisfy the utilitarian principle, since in order to maximize preferences, their intensity must be evaluated. Simple majoritarian rule may have anti-utilitarian results insofar as the interests of the majority may be much less intense than those of the minority. Thus, the degree of aggregate preference satisfaction is less than with an alternative solution. To overcome this problem, the utilitarians must search out more unorthodox devices, such as plural votes, or mechanisms for vetoes by minorities with intense interests.

A much more important shortcoming involves the deep misunderstanding of the logic of impersonal preferences when this argument endorses the idea of an aggregate satisfaction of preferences. This idea has some viability when it deals with personal or "internal" preferences, such as the preference for sports, opera, or chocolates. I may, for instance, maximize the preference satisfaction of my children with opposite tastes regarding sweets if, instead of buying one big chocolate bar that one loves but the other hates, or a bag of candies that provokes the converse response, I buy a little bar of chocolate and a small bag of candies. But how to proceed with impersonal or "external" preferences, such as the preference for the prohibition or permission of abortion? I cannot compromise opposite preferences of this kind by enacting what Ronald Dworkin calls "checkerboard" legislation (for instance, a law permitting abortion only on some days of the week).[6] Impersonal preferences are "imperialistic" in that they are not satisfied by making room for opposite preferences.[7] Instead, they exclude the opposite. Going further, one may say that this confusion between personal preferences (including personal plans of life) and impersonal preferences (the content of which may include standards of interpersonal morality) is one of the main weaknesses of this whole family of views regarding the justification of democracy.

Another method of showing a close connection between the democratic process and the intrinsic good is to locate such good in moral autonomy and to assert democracy's inherent bias in favor of autonomy, since democracy allows people to govern themselves according to laws freely chosen. But this view overlooks the distinction tension between procedure and substance. Even if we admit that the democratic procedure enhances people's moral autonomy, the content of the laws enacted may be extremely prejudicial to that autonomy. It may well be that a law enacted in an authoritarian manner, without respecting the choices of the people, will promote more autonomy in the long run than the law the majority would approve. Again, this issue refers to particularly contingent empirical circumstances. A much deeper flaw of this attempt to justify democracy relates to a general problem of utilitarianism. In the democratic process, it is not true that everyone realizes her moral autonomy in the sense of being governed by the laws she gives to herself. Only the members of the majority—supposing a direct democracy—are subject to the laws they choose for themselves. This is obviously not the case with the members of the dissenting minority, who are subject to laws that others have chosen.

Of these general criticisms, I believe the most important is that utilitarianism does not take into account the separateness and independence of persons, for it allows interpersonal compensation of benefits and burdens. This is tantamount, as Kant would say, to using people as mere means for the ends of other people. As we saw in Chapter 3, this use of people goes against the principle of the inviolability of the person.

As John Rawls says in a famous passage, utilitarianism establishes for society the same rule of choice that is valid for single persons.[8] This rule gives preference to the most important interests at the expense of the less important ones. When this is applied to interests of different persons, including the supposedly objectively valid interest in autonomy, there is no way of avoiding the charge that the person whose interest is sacrificed is being exploited at the expense of the person whose interest is protected. This holistic way of looking at society clashes with one of the basic liberal tenets. Utilitarianism is also subject to objections focusing on its conceptions of the good. Of course, the hedonistic conception of the good has been criticized many times for being too narrow. Not all preferences are for pleasure and not every satisfaction of preferences brings pleasure. A preference-oriented conception provokes, as we have seen, special problems for the justification of democracy due to its lack of distinction between personal and impersonal preferences. This is particularly important since it maintains the preservation of ethical subjectivism. Utilitarianism treats as subjective all the views of social morality, which are the content of preferences the satisfaction of which should be maximized. But it does not treat as subjective the preference for the utilitarian principle itself. This principle is, of course, given a privileged place in controlling the treatment of all other preferences. Therefore, the supposed neutrality and tolerance of utilitarianism over all conceptions of social morality is not valid.

While utilitarianism seems neutral with regard to all personal preferences not incompatible with it that could be processed through the democratic system, it is debatable whether this neutrality is well grounded under some versions of utilitarianism. If the basic good to be maximized is the satisfaction of people's preferences whatever their content, the common reply is that people do not see their good in this way. People do not value something because they prefer it, they prefer it because they value something on independent grounds. The utilitarian conception of the good implies an implausible disconnection between the internal and the external points of view toward preferences.[9] From the internal point of view, preferences are not seen as mere psychological facts but as value judgments of different sorts which are taken as valid. This is of course overcome if the good is identified with something that is independent of people's preferences, such as personal autonomy.

Many believe, however, that when utilitarianism adopts this sort of objective conception of the good, it loses one of its most important, valuable, and distinctive features.

Finally, utilitarianism can be criticized for relying on the actual consequences of the institutions in question—in this instance, democracy—for the promotion of the intrinsic good. This reliance raises at least three important difficulties. First, it is extremely difficult to detect all the consequences of a given action or institution. Second, the attribution of causal consequences to an institution like democracy is not a purely factual operation but involves normative and valuative judgments.[10] Third, a decision taken on the basis of perceived results is frequently self-defeating. Structures of collective action ensuring that decisions take into account actual effects for the attainment of some end in fact often frustrate that end.

In reviewing the utilitarian justification of democracy, we must assess whether it acknowledges the counterweight to democracy represented by the two other dimensions of constitutionalism. With regard to preservation of the constitutional convention, this seems to be accomplished only if we adopt the variety of rule-utilitarianism or institutional-utilitarianism which asserts that the principle of utility should be applied not directly to actions but to rules or institutional structures. There is the further problem of sorting out whether rule-utilitarianism refers to ideal rules or to actual ones. I believe that the distinctiveness of utilitarianism is preserved only under the latter option, since, as we just saw, the first seems to converge into the Kantian handling of the universalizability requirement on moral judgments. On these assumptions, rule-utilitarianism would justify the value of a democratic practice or convention. But the evaluation according to utilitarianism is more complicated when we try to distinguish the value of a democratic decision-making process and the value of preserving a constitutional convention that is not entirely democratic. This evaluation would help us appreciate the tension between these two dimensions of constitutionalism and estimating their relative weights. It is not easy to estimate realistically the utilitarian value of a democratic procedure or of particular democratic decisions independent from a practice of which they are a part.

The inability of the utilitarian justification of democracy to acknowledge properly the counterweight represented by the rights dimension of constitutionalism is much more clear. The aggregative feature of the intrinsic good that belongs to utilitarianism seems to leave no place for rights as barriers to the maximization of the satisfaction of people's preferences. If democracy materializes its supposed value because the majority satisfies its preferences, or expands its autonomy, or even promotes the rights of its members, any external counterweight constituted by rights which the majority cannot override seems to limit the maximization of the good.

As for the ability of utilitarianism to overcome the paradox of the superfluousness of government and its laws, this issue is also open to question. If those participating in the democratic process are themselves morally responsible, they should apply the utilitarian principle when they vote. In applying this principle, they should try to foresee the impact of their vote, along with remaining votes and other aspects of constitutional practice, on the intrinsic good. Once a democratic decision is taken, that good—either in isolation or in the whole—should be appreciated by whomever must decide whether to apply that democratic decision to the resolution of a particular case. If act-utilitarianism is adopted, there is no reason why the judgment of the last decision maker regarding the course of action that most maximizes the good should be subject to the majority's decision. Indeed, this judgment may be a product of mistaken individual judgments about what maximizes the satisfaction of the majority's preferences. If rule-utilitarianism is adopted, there could be reasons for observing a particular democratic decision even when it does not, in the judgment of the adjudicator, maximize the good. Nevertheless, this adjudicator must balance the negative value of that majoritarian decision against the supposed value of maintaining the democratic practice. One wonders why the adjudicator would not prefer a practice in which people can appeal directly to the principle of utility in making decisions, without having to acknowledge the "gravitational weight" of democratic decisions that may work against the principle of utility. Although one may respond that people reveal their real preferences through democracy, there are many other ways of revealing preferences—polls, for instance. These other avenues do not have the binding character of democratic decisions and are not distorted by the judgments of the people who participate in the process about what satisfies the majority's preferences.

The Economic Conception of Democracy

The economic conception of democracy is a variant of utilitarianism. Democratic politics works like the market, these theorists argue, in the sense that there are producers of some goods—politicians and their policies—which compete for the favor of consumers. The consumers are the voters who negotiate with the producers until an optimal equilibrium is reached.[11]

Under a more normative approach, the optimal equilibrium to which democracy-as-a-market is supposed to lead involves a state of affairs that is socially beneficial, no matter what the preferences or interests of the participants in the process. Therefore, the economic justification of democracy, like the economic analysis of any institution, relies on an "invisible hand." A socially valuable state of affairs is achieved by a structure of collective action which generates a dynamic that tends toward this valued state, although the actors may be indifferent or exclusively concentrating on their self-interest.

The economic analysis of the legal and political system in general and of democracy in particular has led some theorists to peculiar views about how democratic legislation operates and should operate. Richard Posner believes that legislation is "sold" by legislatures to politically effective interest groups following unprincipled deals in which those groups offer different kinds of benefits in return.[12] Free-rider problems arise, but the division of powers and rights that limit the democratic and legislative process are designed to overcome them.[13]

As with utilitarianism, one of the basic problems that the economic justification has to overcome is how to reflect preference intensities in the political process. James Buchanan and Gordon Tullock have proposed the rule of unanimous consent, under the hypothesis that it would create a dynamic of negotiation between a minority with intense preferences and a majority with opposite but weaker ones, so that a process of vote trading or "logrolling" over different issues would emerge.[14] These authors consider that unanimity, not majority rule, is the first choice from the perspective of an ideal constitutional convention. However, the transaction costs involved in reaching unanimity makes majority rule the clear second-best option. One should also note an important distinction between markets and elections in registering intensity of preferences. Unlike a market, electoral competition almost always has an "all-or-nothing" character, and "negotiations" between offerers and consumers of political goods are rather different than in the case of commercial goods. Also, the concern with efficiency is misplaced. What is its relation to justice?

One extreme response would be to subsume efficiency under justice. This occurs if we employ a principle of justice of a utilitarian nature.[15] However, as already discussed, the utilitarian principle is objectionable as a principle of justice, since it does not take into account the separability and independence of persons, which makes relevant the distribution of resources among them. This objection is applicable to the principle of efficiency when it is subsumed under the utilitarian principle of justice. In fact, the Paretian criterion of efficiency—where there is no state of affairs in which an individual is better off—takes into account some distributive considerations, but that which it values is highly questionable from the point of view of justice. Its only barrier against interpersonal compensations is phony. Whether somebody would be worse off in an alternative state is completely irrelevant from a moral point of view if we do not know whether his present position is just. Of course, there are many situations in which, to achieve just solutions, we must worsen the position of somebody. For example, if a person steals from another, the object must be returned to the owner. As Allen Buchanan says, a social situation in which the overwhelming majority has nothing and a few have everything may be Pareto-optimal, since a change toward a more just situation surely would worsen the condition of the privileged minority.[16]

The other extreme way of relating the principles of justice and efficiency is by subsuming justice under efficiency. This occurs when the value of justice is seen as a subjective preference and is considered in finding out whether an individual's preferences are frustrated in the application of the criteria of efficiency. But this maneuver implies a grotesque distortion in the principles of justice. Nobody who defends a principle of justice does so as a subjective preference that should be equated with opposite preferences of other individuals. The preference for principles of justice, unlike preferences for personal life-plans or their components, has, as I argued in the previous section, an "imperialistic" character. Preferences for justice displace those opposing them insofar as they are grounded on true judgments and cannot be satisfied if they are made compatible with opposite ones. Furthermore, the very attempt to maximize subjective preferences, including those for justice, already responds to a principle of justice, namely, that of utilitarianism.

Considering the nonviability of these two extreme forms of relating the principles of justice and efficiency, the most reasonable alternative is to conceive of these principles as mutually independent. If we proceed in this way, we must admit the priority of considerations of justice over those of efficiency because the structure of practical discourse determines the supremacy of moral reasons over prudential ones. We must recognize efficiency concerns are not ethically neutral but imply a distribution of resources which may be seriously in tension with the concerns of justice. On the other hand, one might take efficiency into account to assess the value of, for instance, the market insofar as it does not oppose considerations of justice and prescribes maximum results with minimal costs.[17] Besides, in the Paretian version, the principle of efficiency reflects the idea of mutual advantage that is taken into account in the appraisal of social situations.

In sum, the economic vision of democracy evades the paradox of the moral superfluousness of government only because it skips moral judgments and principles of justice altogether. Nor can it account for the counterweights of the two other dimensions of constitutionalism—rights and the historical constitution. The economic view of democracy cannot explain why rights and a constitutional convention should be recognized if they produce inefficient solutions. It should also be mentioned that the economic theory makes the democratic process prone to problems of collective action that arise in situations in which the participants are motivated by self-interest. These collective-action problems include the prisoner's dilemma, the assurance dilemma, the chicken game, and the battle of the sexes, all of which may be considered pure coordination problems.[18]

The Elitist Theory of Democracy

The vision commonly called "elitist" similarly assumes people's interests or preferences should be taken as given in the political process. Members of this school are resigned to the fact that people's preferences tend to be self-interested and do not think that a political system should be designed to transform them. Instead, elitists try to make the best of this somewhat sad feature of human nature.

The elitist vision of politics in general and even of democracy in particular was anticipated by Max Weber in his famous "Politik als Beruf," published in 1918.[19] Weber demonstrates the continuous process of professionalization and exclusion in the political process, leading to a small group who really make the decisions and a majority of people who are apathetic and at most have a role in selecting those in charge for a time. This feature of politics is aggravated because of the formation in many countries—mainly in the Western

Europe of his time—of a further group of people: the bureaucrats. These bureaucrats make possible the working of the economy but are mostly beyond politicians' control.

Joseph A. Schumpeter constructed an elitist theory of democracy with a more normative dimension.[20] He contrasts what he calls "the classic theory of democracy" with his own, elitist, theory. He characterizes the classic theory as the view, prevalent in the eighteenth century, which sees democracy as a method of generating political decisions to materialize the common good, allowing the people to decide questions through the election of the individual who should carry out its will. He criticizes this view as mythical, saying first that there is no such common good. Second, he argues that even if the common good could be defined in a satisfactory way, it would not imply definite consequences for particular problems; several options will always remain open. Third, as a consequence of the vacuity of the concept of the common good, the idea of a general will vanishes in the air. Even when we try to interpret this notion of general will by connecting it with the will of concrete individuals, insurmountable problems appear. For example, the will of individuals is not usually clear and defined, generally does not take into account relevant circumstances and consequences, and is often adversely affected by propaganda, pressures, and especially the phenomenon of mass psychology.

These conclusions regarding the classical view of democracy led Schumpeter to propose an alternative theory. According to this theory, the democratic method is an institutional system used to reach political decisions, within which some individuals acquire the power to decide through a competitive struggle for the people's support. This view of democracy does not overlook the impact individual will has on the political process; it also establishes an analogy between competition for leadership and economic competition, revealing a variety of ways in which this competition may express itself. Moreover, this theory of democracy reflects the relationship between democracy and individual liberty, since such a competition presupposes freedom of expression and freedom of the press so that people may choose their leaders. Finally, this theory avoids the problem of equating the will of the people with the will of a majority of persons, since Schumpeter's alternative does not believe in the former.

Schumpeter believes that his vision of democracy has certain practical implications. He argues that the presidential system, not the parliamentary system, better fulfills the vision of the electorate directly deciding who will lead them. Political parties should not be understood as groups pursuing the public welfare through certain principles they have adopted. Instead, parties are important in that they are machines for political competition. The stability of democracy depends on having good leadership (perhaps a professional one), a restricted scope for democratic decisions, and a stable and well-qualified bureaucracy to assist the political leadership. The electorate should not interfere with the decisions of the elected leaders and should not give instructions to them. Finally, there must be a high degree of tolerance for the opinions of others.[21]

The trouble with this view, as Hannah Arendt has pointed out, is that it consecrates an oligarchic form of government and allows the domination of the many by the few.[22] The nonegalitarian character of Schumpeter's view is compounded by the fact that it would require functionally an extended apathy, associated with the poorest and least-educated sectors of society.[23] Parties therefore have the effect of further dominating policy questions, and the responsibility of governments toward the electorate diminishes. As Samuel Huntington emphasizes, the equilibrium between the elites may collapse if the system is overloaded with demands coming directly from vast sectors of society.[24]

One may retort that there is nothing intrinsically evil in political inequalities as long as they are the result of fair procedures. But it is doubtful that any group of individuals, having enhanced power over others, has the capacity to represent faithfully and impartially the interests of others. It is obvious that elites with access to power will give priority to their own interests over those who participate merely by saying "yes" or "no" to the elites' requests to stay in office. While the competition to obtain public favor would lead some benefits to be granted to them, there is no mechanism, under this theory, to ensure equal benefit to the public and the leaders.

It is indeed true that democracy requires that elites compete for the favor of the electorate, impeding any one elite from gaining too much power and creating a tyranny. This is a remarkable achievement, since the competition between the elites may be a mechanism that provides protection of the rights of individuals. But this strikes me as only a negative value, one that can be achieved through different mechanisms and does not explain the special value of democracy. Moreover, we are still left with the paradox of the superfluousness of government and its laws and the ensuing tension between

procedure and substance. It is always possible that a different decision will better avoid monopolization of power than the one which
results from competition among the elites. In fact, refusal to abide
by the result of the competition may be a way of opening up competition to new players, widening the group of elites that participate in
the struggle for power. One wonders whether this view of democracy
is nothing more than a legitimization of the crude confrontation of
interests constituting the status quo.

The moral skepticism characteristic of Schumpeter's elitism also
makes one doubt whether it will support liberal constitutionalism.
The defense of the historical constitution or constitutional practice
is not based on its role in a justificatory reasoning which has moral
principles as basic premises. Rather, it is grounded on a conservative and relativistic appreciation of existing practices. The elitist
conception of rights is also quite weak, as is shown when Schumpeter is able to justify little more than freedom of expression. Any
reference to moral principles grounding a stronger set of rights will
surely limit the power of elites over the common populace.

Pluralist Democracy

The pluralist conception of democracy is a variant of the elitist view. Its specific contribution is to introduce groups or factions
as the main actors in political competition rather than individual
persons who together constitute elites. The idealists of the French
Revolution believed that factions can be excluded from the political forum. But pluralists consider factions an unavoidable outcome
of the self-interested nature of individuals and of their tendency to
associate in order to defend collectively that self-interest.

Inherent in pluralism is an ambiguity between the description
of actual systems and normative ideals that ascribe value to them.
Robert Dahl, a major figure in this movement and inventor of the
concept of polyarchy, shifted from a description that appeared to
be intertwined with the ascription of positive moral values to a description now clearly separated from the value of its referent. Dahl
begins with a critique of "populist democracy," the rule that privileges those policies which are socially adopted as those preferred by
the greater number of people.[25] He reminds us of technical, ethical,
and empirical objections to this view of democracy. The technical
objections recognize that individuals sometimes do not have preferences for one alternative over others, and that there can be ties

among the preferences of people, in which case no course of action is justified and no voting method is practicable. In describing ethical objections, Dahl mentions the difficulty in grounding the postulates of egalitarianism and popular sovereignty on an acceptable meta-ethical basis, the failure to consider intensity of preferences, and the absence of an explanation why these two values—egalitarianism and popular sovereignty—should be maximized. By way of empirical objection, he says that the theory does not tell us what individuals or groups should be included in the political system. He also points out that the theory does not account for cases in which the majority may undermine the democratic system itself.

In contrast to populist democracy, Dahl proposes the polyarchic model.[26] In his article "Polyarchy, Pluralism, and Scale," Dahl distinguishes populism from a regime of polyarchy by the presence of widespread suffrage, which is coextensive with the right to run for political office, fairly conducted free elections, freedom of expression, the existence of competing sources of information, a high degree of freedom to form relatively autonomous organizations, and the responsiveness of governments to elections.[27] Dahl also connects this model of polyarchy with what he calls "organizational pluralism," which has antecedents in Otto von Gierke, Leon Duguit, and Harold Laski. According to Dahl,

> Polyarchy is a kind of regime for governing nation-states in which power and authority over public matters are distributed among a plurality of organizations and associations that are relatively autonomous in relation to one another and in many cases in relation to the government of the state as well. These relatively autonomous units include not only organizations that are, legally and sometimes constitutionally, components of the government of the state but also organizations that legally are—to use a term that in this connection seems singularly inapt—"private." Legally, and to an important extent realistically, they are independent, or mainly independent, of the state.[28]

Dahl also makes clear that, though pluralism is necessary, inevitable, and desirable for polyarchy, it may also have undesirable consequences, such as maintaining unjust inequalities among the citizens. The main thrust of Dahl's more recent book *Democracy and Its Critics* is to explore the possibility of transcending pluralistic polyarchy, to achieve a more participatory democracy which overcomes minority rule and verges toward a more equal society.[29] Theodore J. Lowi asserts that pluralism has become the intellectual basis in the neocapitalist public philosophy, which he calls "interest-group liberalism."[30] According to Lowi, a vulgarization of pluralism in political theory has turned into the philosophy of interest-group liberalism through the acceptance of several assumptions: organized interests are homogenous and easy to define; every duly elected representative of any interest represents all those with that interest; organized interests emerge in every sector of our lives and adequately represent most of those sectors; and the role of government is to ensure access to the most effectively organized groups and to endorse agreements reached among competing leaders.

One may easily recognize the legitimacy of factions if one starts from the idea that politics has a realm separate from morality and that one should not expect people to change their self-interested inclinations or to act on impartial grounds. In this view, it is perfectly permissible for people to come together in associations to defend their interests in politics either directly or through the mediation of political parties. Parties are required to defend not certain principles but only the interests of certain factions. In that respect they are like the "corporations" or corporatist interests that have plagued the young democracies of Latin America. These corporations include the military, church, trade unions, and entrepreneur associations. They constitute centers of power and privilege within the state apparatus that are also used by politicians as a way of controlling sectors of civil societies.[31]

The pluralist acknowledges that while factions cannot be suppressed, they can be neutralized or placed in an equilibrium to avoid any from acquiring excessive power. This is the great insight of James Madison, who, in the famous *Federalist* number 10, defines factions as "a number of citizens, whether amounting to the majority or minority of the whole who are united and actuated by some common impulse or passion, or of interest, adverse to the right of other citizens, or to the permanent and aggregate interests of the community." Clearly, Madison had the same concern for the dangers that factions involved for the consolidation of a democratic system as was reflected in the *Le Chapelier* law of the French Revolution. There was an important difference, however. The idealists of the French Revolution sought to prohibit factions and held an optimistic view of human nature which assumes that people's self-interested inclinations can be transformed and that the tendency to defend these inclinations through factions can be suppressed. Madison did not share that assumption, but he nonetheless believed that mechanisms could be created to redirect the self-interested inclinations of the people and that the operation of factions could be channeled toward the public good. Indeed, for the pluralist, democracy can be seen as a device for achieving an equilibrium that neutralizes the power of factions, since it invites factions or political parties to compete for the favor of the electorate. The pluralist characterizes democracy as an institutional arrangement conceding the right to decide to those factions or groups of individuals that win the struggle for the people's vote.

According to pluralists, the great virtue of liberal or constitutional democracy is that it prevents any group or faction from monopolizing power. Moreover, if a proper division of powers is in effect, the equilibrium between different groups or factions can be achieved synchronically, since a party, group, or faction most probably can control only one of the centers of power in the "horizontal" divide (among the different branches) or in the "vertical" one (among the different territories). Pluralism favors a dispersion of popular sovereignty in different mechanisms of expression and in different centers of representation. For pluralists, the phenomenon of representation is an asset, since it allows dispersion of sovereignty and locates decisions in spheres that may be better protected from the direct pressures of constant factions or interest groups.[32]

Although the realist aspect of pluralism highlights the inevitability of elites and factions, one may rightfully question this inevitability as well as the effectiveness of factions to prevent monopolization. Throughout history, humanity has adapted itself to a variety of social structures and shown that it is capable of overcoming pure self-interest when conditions encourage the spread of a public spirit. The arrangement of social and political institutions according to the pluralist creed may freeze the status quo constituted by the corporatist structure. Moreover, factions and the so called corporations do not represent the whole population, and their power is not proportional to the number of their members. As a result, the individualist basis of democracy is compromised. There is no guarantee that the interests of each citizen will be given equal weight, even though they may choose among the competing power coalitions. Finally, any conception of democracy which grants a privileged position to associations of crude interests implies an antiliberal vision of the moral person, since it identifies persons with certain interests rather than with the capacity of choosing between diverse interests.[33]

Along with these equality-oriented concerns, Theodore Lowi emphasizes three dangers of pluralism: the atrophy of institutions of popular control, the creation of new structures of privilege, and the conservation of agency-group relationships. These dangers are connected with an even deeper problem—antagonism to law. In the pluralist conception, government is not separate from the struggle of interest groups but responds directly to the equilibrium reached in that struggle, and law simply reflects that equilibrium. It has no inherent worth. (As a result, the historical constitution is undermined.[34]) One sees this phenomenon distinctively in Latin America, where the struggle between the corporatist groups results in a serious deterioration of the rule of law.[35]

Lowi also points out that pluralism defends a distorted vision of how groups operate. Often, a group does not face an equally powerful group in order to ensure competition. Groups are not always based on voluntary membership and the equilibrium resulting from the competition of groups does not always serve the common good. Imperfections in group competition may create phenomena similar to the formation of cartels in the market.[36] Finally, one must take account of the coordination problems that arise in any model based on self-interest. Social phenomena like inflation, corruption, and civil strife often arise because of situations which involve structures such as the prisoner's dilemma, the assurance dilemma, and the chicken game. Groups or factions are moved by the goal of maximizing their members' interests, but ultimately they merely frustrate those interests. The theory of democracy that views it as a competition of factions does not include mechanisms through which these self-defeating phenomena are neutralized.

Consensual Theories

Consent is perhaps the oldest justification of democracy. As consecrated in the United States Declaration of Independence, this theory sees democracy as the only way a government can be compatible with personal autonomy. Each person remains truly his own sovereign, and the government can only interfere with the path he has traced for his life insofar as he, in one way or another, has accepted that interference. Also under this theory, the paradox of the superfluousness of government and its laws would be completely overcome, since those laws would be, by definition, the moral principles that one autonomously accepts. This vision of democracy would also accord perfectly with the principle of the dignity of the person, which may legitimize burdens, obligations, and liabilities on the basis of the consent of the people whose autonomy is so limited.

There are two quite different kinds of consensual theories: those relying on hypothetical consent and those based on actual or real consent. Hypothetical consent is formed by contractarian theories, which assume that if under some counterfactual conditions the institution at stake would be accepted by those subject to it, a value is thereby conferred on it. This value exists even if, in the actual world, those people who are not under the privileged conditions have not consented to that institution.

The main contemporary example of a justification of democracy based on hypothetical consent is Rawls's theory of justice.[37] Rawls justifies the institutions that are part of the basic structure of society according to two principles of justice which, according to him, would be unanimously accepted in an ideal situation that he calls "the original position." He imagines a gathering of free and equal moral persons who have the capacity for choosing life plans under "circumstances of justice." The circumstances include moderate scarcity of resources and a sense of vulnerability concerning attacks by others. These persons are rationally self-interested and seek to maximize their access to primary goods, but are subject to a "veil of ignorance" which prevents them from knowing the particular circumstances of themselves and their society. They must unanimously adopt principles that satisfy formal features of universalizability, publicity, and finality and which bind them when they return to normal conditions of life. Rawls argues that those persons would choose two principles: equal political liberty and equal social and economic resources. The latter holds true except when inequality would further the interest of the least well-off in society.

Rawls argues that when the principle of equal political liberty is applied to the political procedure defined by the constitution, it gives rise to the principle of equal participation. This principle transfers the notion of justice as fairness, which requires an initial position of equality, from the original position to the constitution as the higher-order system for making rules.[38] The constitutional process should, as far as is feasible, preserve the equal representation of the original position. As a practical matter, this requires a representative body with authority to determine basic social policies and to which the executive must explain its actions. Moreover, political parties should not be mere interest groups but should advance a conception of the public good. Equal representation of the original position also requires majority rule, since any other procedure of collective decision making guarantees a less extensive equality in the influence of the outcomes. Rawls further believes that constitutional constraints to majority rule, such as judicial review based on certain constitutional rights, may be justified if they are acceptable to all representative citizens in an ideal constitutional convention as a more secure way of realizing certain liberties, thereby outweighing any loss in the principle of equal participation. Interestingly, Rawls says that democracy does not reflect intensity of preferences. In fact, he argues that democracy must not do so, since this is a question of feeling, and the democratic procedure should be judged not by how much it reflects feelings but by how likely it is that its outcome will be just.

While I cannot evaluate here Rawls's theory of justice in full, I do agree with those who have criticized theories of hypothetical consent on the ground that they can only justify hypothetical, not actual, solutions and arrangements.[39] Whenever this is acknowledged, there is a tendency to look for an alternative meta-ethical basis for Rawls's principles of justice, which turn out to be either self-interest or intuitions determined through the technique of reflective equilibrium. However, I do not believe that these are the real meta-ethical foundations of Rawls's theory of justice. Self-interest is neutralized by the veil of ignorance, and intuitions have no independent appeal if one rejects the view that they reflect a certain moral reality.

As I shall explore more fully in Chapter 5, I think Rawls wants to capture with the heuristic device of the original position some structural features of practical reasoning. If so, Rawls's theory is not really based on consent and should not be included among these consensual theories of democracy. Nevertheless, it is worth noting that the justification he provides for democracy is quite incomplete. Why would the person in the original position not decide that the best way of securing rights established by the two principles is by leaving government in the hands of the wisest and morally best members of society? What is the scope of democracy once a strong set of rights such as those established in the original position is acknowledged? (This simply reintroduces the paradox of the superfluousness of government and its laws.) If we would find in the ideal constitutional convention that basic liberties are more secure when protected through nondemocratic constitutional means, why should we not conclude the same with regard to economic and social rights?

There are, of course, other theories of democracy based on hypothetical consent. Martín Farrell, for instance, maintains that individuals in a state of nature, with knowledge of the relevant circumstances, approximately equal in intelligence and physical power (though not in wealth), would hypothetically subscribe to a contract in which a democratic government, limited by individual rights, would be established.[40] His prediction as to what they would do, of course, depends on his description of people in the state of nature. Farrell describes a state of nature in which everybody is de facto free and equal and that assumption largely determines the contract agreed upon. In the state of nature, however, the majority may decide to enslave or even to kill a certain minority for their own enjoyment. So, why would everybody not agree to establish a political system within which each member of that minority has a vote worth half as much as the vote of members of the favored majority? This would seem to be quite a bargain for the minority compared to, for instance, being eaten by the majority. Moreover, if the individuals and their possessions were secure from threats from others, there would be no reason to enter a contract altogether.[41] Along with this particular shortcoming, this theory shares the same weakness as all those based on hypothetical consent. One must ask why the fact that we would accept democracy under conditions "close" to real has any bearing on whether we should accept it under real conditions.

These weaknesses make us turn toward theories of actual consent. Before analyzing them, I should emphasize that the possibility of justifying actions or institutions involving sacrifices or burdens for certain individuals on the basis of their actual consent is grounded on the principle of dignity of the person and the voluntarism associated with that principle. As previously discussed, this principle opposes normative determinism and establishes two conditions for the acceptance of obligations, responsibilities, and burdens. The first requires that people act with knowledge that the acts in question carry certain normative consequences. This does not require that individual to say, "I consent to such and such obligation." Such speech acts may be useful for evidentiary reasons but are not necessary. Many consensual obligations are undertaken in other ways. For instance, we incur the obligation to pay a taxi by getting into it, or the obligation to pay for a meal in a restaurant by asking for it. The act signifying consent must, in a minimum sense, be voluntary in that it cannot be a product of reflex reaction or external compulsion. At the same time, it does not require the absence of any outside force. Also, the act cannot be affected by circumstances that are distributed highly unequally among the individuals of the relevant group.[42]

The second condition for consent to have justificatory force is the existence of norms or practices that make the voluntary act in question the basis for obligations or responsibilities. Consent is always the child of norms or practices, since it requires foreseeing that the act constituting consent has normative consequences which imply obligations. They may be legal, social, or a part of positive morality. The possibility of these norms belonging to an ideal morality seems to be excluded, however, since such norms would have to rely on a preexisting consent. On the other hand, the positive norms that constitute consent ought to be justified on the basis of ideal moral principles, since otherwise the most horrible practices would be justified on the basis of consent. This justification should not consider the question of distribution, since consent is relied upon to overcome distribution, but should consider some aggregative social goal which the social practice is said to satisfy.

Actual consent theories, like the hypothetical ones, also acknowledge the counterweight that the other two dimensions of constitutionalism exert upon democracy. Social practices or conventions are essential for constituting consent. In fact, as the normative consequences of the voluntary act become more foreseeable, the consent becomes more genuine. Furthermore, rights are necessary preconditions of consent because, without their fulfillment, consent cannot be free. The main difficulty of the theories of actual consent is, however, to identify the *acts* which constitute that consent.

John Locke thought that the act was constituted by possessing land in a certain country, lodging there, or even traveling through its territory: "Every man that hath possession of any part of the dominions of any government doth thereby give his tacit consent, and is far forth obliged to obedience to the laws of that government during this enjoyment, as anyone under it, whether this possession be of land to him and his heirs forever, or a lodging for only a week: or whether it is barely travelling freely on the highway."[43] But for most people, the acts described by Locke are not entirely voluntary. Often, one's ability to sell all possessions and leave the country in order not to "lodge" or travel through its highways is materially impossible.

Moreover, they are not in anyway tied to democracy. Under Locke's theory, any form of government would be consented to by its subjects and would thus be morally acceptable.

If one wants to justify democracy on the basis of the actual consent of the people, an act typically confined to democratic regimes must be used as constitutive of consent. Of course, that act is voting. There is a problem, however, in determining the degree of abstraction used in describing that act. If the act is described as "voting for a particular rule or for a particular candidate," one can easily say that ensuing obligations are consented to only by the people who voted for a particular laws or candidate. The problem is that we also need to justify the moral obligation of those who voted against that law or candidate.

The relevant description, therefore, must be more abstract. In fact, some argue that it should be framed in terms of just "voting," as proposed by Peter Singer in his book *Democracy and Disobedience*.[44] He says that the requirements of genuine consent are too demanding to justify democracy and that we must be content with a notion he deems as "quasi-consent." Singer asserts that it is not plausible to maintain that the mere participation in the democratic process amounts to even tacit consent. Instead, for Singer, democracy is a situation which generates obligations *as if* there had been such consent. According to him, the generation of quasiconsensual obligations is a common phenomenon which occurs when people act so as to create expectations that a practice has been accepted. This happens, for instance, when a group of friends develops a practice of going out for drinks and paying in turns, and it is assumed that one will pay when one's turn arrives. In the same manner, participation in a democratic process creates the expectation that the result of the process will be accepted. Otherwise, it would be meaningless.

Unlike Singer, I am prepared to grant that in situations like the ones he describes, one finds genuine, though tacit, consent. The practice which the friends who drink together have developed includes the obligation to pay when one's turn arrives as a normative consequence of the free participation in the outings. Each friend who goes for drinks knows he is undertaking that obligation, and consent gives rise to the possibility of claiming that he complies. But I do not believe that voting is sufficient to constitute the consent that is required for this justification of democracy. For one thing, no act that expresses consent can be obligatory. If I were obliged to get into a bus, either by sheer force or by a norm stipulating that obligation, I would not be consenting to pay the fare by simply entering the bus. Similarly, one could argue that where voting is compulsory, as in Argentina or Australia, this consensual justification of democracy would not apply. This is a special problem for those of us who are inclined to justify, under certain conditions, mandatory voting.[45]

Second, there is the problem of nonperformance—the fact that the obligation does not arise if the act constituting consent is not performed. It would be a phony act of consent if I were equally obliged even when I did not perform that act. If I would be obliged to pay bus fare whether I entered voluntarily or not, it would be ridiculous to say that I consented to pay the fare as a result of getting voluntarily into the bus. If my consent to the laws arising from the democratic process is constituted by my voluntary participation in it, my omission to perform that act should imply that I am not under an obligation to abide by those laws! However, a legal system that exempts from its obligations those people who have not participated in the political process is obviously an impossible one. By simply not voting, one could be above the law.

The failure of this consensual justification is especially significant in view of the inability of this entire family of views to justify democracy regardless of its impact on the transformation of people's preferences. Of all the above theories, only the consensual one, if it were plausible, would overcome comfortably the paradox of the moral superfluousness of government and its laws, as well as properly acknowledging rights and the historical constitution as counterweights to democracy. When this theory is discarded, as the other members of this family of views have been, we are required to turn our attention to the other, radically different, family of justifications for democracy.

Group Two: Conceptions of Democracy That Transform People's Preferences

The theories of democracy previously discussed take as given— sometimes happily and sometimes grudgingly—people's interests and preferences. The theories that follow start from the opposite idea. They hold that in order to justify democracy, one must conceive of it as a mechanism that transforms the original interests of individuals. These conceptions do not separate politics from morality, since they acknowledge that politics involves moral inclinations, moral judgments, and moral responsibilities. The treatment of these views will be much briefer than that of the former ones, not only because they are fewer and less developed (and less dominant in theoretical circles), but also because I will devote the entire next chapter to defending one of these particular conceptions.

The spirit of Rousseau hangs over these theories. Despite his general justification of political institutions on the basis of the consent involved in the social contract, he grounds majority rule on the basis of the transformation of each individual's will into a general will aiming at the common good. The mechanism for this transformation has always intrigued political philosophers, who have proposed interpretations that relate to the conceptions we shall review by incorporating in their interpretations collectivist assumptions, perfectionist aspirations, or the merits of public deliberation.

It is important to note that if any of these transformative theories proved sound, we would be able to overcome problems of collective action, for those problems arise when people act in a self-interested way. The transformation of people's interests through a particular mechanism may change the order of preferences of the actors in the political process so as to overcome problems like the prisoner's dilemma. These transformative theories include popular sovereignty, perfectionism, and dialogism.

Popular Sovereignty

The first and most traditional justification of democracy is based on popular sovereignty. In democracy, according to this idea, the people as a whole are autonomous because it is the only system that guarantees self-government. Democracy is the government not only for and of the people but also by the people.

In light of the important and often misinterpreted influence of Rousseau on this view of democracy, it is useful to begin with one crucial passage of *The Social Contract* that deals with the sovereignty of the people. Rousseau argues:

> It must be clearly understood that the clauses [of the social contract] in question can be reduced, in the last analysis, to only one, to wit, the complete alienation by each associate member of each individual member to the community of *all his rights*. For, in the first place, since each has made surrender of himself without reservation, the resultant conditions are the same for all: and, because they are the same for all, it is in the interest of none to make them onerous to his fellows.

Furthermore, this alienation having been made unreservedly, the union of individuals is as perfect as it well can be, none of the associated members having any claim against the community. For should there be any rights left to individuals, and no common authority be empowered to pronounce as between them and the public, then each, being in some things his own judge, would soon claim to be so in all. . . .

In short, who so gives himself to all gives himself to none. . . . As soon as the act of association becomes a reality, it substitutes for the person of each of the contracting parties a moral and collective body made up of as many members as the constituting assembly has votes, which body receives from this very act of constitution its unity, its dispersed *self*, and its will. The public person thus formed by the union of individuals was known in the old days as a *City*, but now as the *Republic* or *Body Politic*. . . . In respect of the constituent associates, it enjoys the collective name of The People.[46]

Rousseau viewed politics as deeply intertwined with morality. He was profoundly concerned about how morally right solutions are reached in the political process. He also thought that this goal of politics is achieved if the social contract matches the transformation from the state of nature to civil government. Unlike the will of private individuals and of factions, the will of the sovereign people can never err. This means, among other things, that the sovereign will cannot affect the rights of the individuals or of the whole group. On the other hand, Rousseau's concerns about factions, later reflected during the French Revolution, were quite evident. For Rousseau, factions produced a general will only with respect to their own members, not with regard to the state as whole, even if we add up the different factions.

The most obscure and disputed feature of Rousseau's theory is how the subjects of politics are transformed through the fulfillment of the social contract. In fact, two answers are suggested by the text. The first points to changes that take place in the individual through the exercise of dormant faculties. The passage from the state of nature to civil society "substitutes justice for instinct in his behavior, and gives to his actions a moral basis which formerly was lacking. . . . By dint of being exercised, his faculties will develop, his ideas take on a wider scope, his sentiments become ennobled, and his own soul be so elevated."[47] The fulfillment of the social contract changes individuals by inspiring in them sentiments of justice rather than mere selfish instincts, by broadening their ideas, and by developing their faculties. But it is not quite clear in Rousseau how this process of transformation of people takes place, particularly when mechanisms commonly used to affect those changes, such as collective discussion, are discarded.[48] It is also unclear whether this transformation directly produces the right solutions, the expression of the general will, or whether an intermediate link is necessary.

The second answer to the question how the general will is constituted relies not on a transformation *in* the subjects of politics but on a transformation *of* the subjects. Rousseau thought that the Sovereign People was a different moral subject than the mere collection of individuals who compose it. This notion is employed currently in the law when legal corporations and associations are distinguished as legal subjects from their members. A similar conceptual move can be made in the normative realm of morality by accepting the existence of "moral collective bodies" or "public persons" which have rights, liabilities, and obligations different from those of their individual members. Of course, these entities must act through individual people, the officials of the corporations or associations in question. In the case of the people—or, more properly, The People—as a moral collective body, the "official" able to ascribe decisions to the People may be the collection of individuals or a majority acting under certain conditions. This transformation of the subject of politics caused by the emergence of an entity distinct and separate from the individual citizens may transform preferences in the direction of morality, since only some preferences are compatible with the structure and constituent elements of this new entity.

In this regard we can understand the assertion of Rousseau: "Now, the Sovereign People, having no existence outside the individuals who compose it, has, and can have, no interest at variance with theirs." This phrase can be understood as a sort of anticipation of the Kantian distinction between phenomenal and noumenal existence, because it implies that the fact that this collective person has no empirical dimension—having no pleasure or pain, desires or inclinations—means that it has no interests varying from those of its constituent members. This ensures its impartiality, an interpretation confirmed by what Rousseau says a few lines later. "The sovereign, by merely existing, is always what it should be." In other words, this moral collective entity has indeed an existence, but an existence which is not material but normative.[49]

In my opinion, the view of democracy as popular sovereignty can only be understood through this organic or collectivist conception of the people. It is obvious that the idea of government of the people by the people (immortalized in Lincoln's famous Gettysburg Address, with the addition of the clause "for the people") is a fiction if "people" is understood in other senses. If "people" denotes the whole collection of individuals composing the relevant population, democracy does not guarantee that the people govern itself. The phrase "of the people" refers to that whole collection, but "by the people" may refer only to the majority of that group. If "people" denotes the majority itself, it is again true that democracy does not guarantee the government of the people by the people, since now "by the people" refers to the majority, but "of the people" cannot refer only to it, because the majority governs the whole relevant population. Of course, the same is even more true if "people" denotes a subsector of the whole population, like the poor or the proletariat. In that situation, it would mean that a sector, such as a majority, of a sector, such as the poor or the proletariat, would govern the whole population.

The only way in which the word *people* can be used in the description of democracy as government of the people by the people is by assuming that it refers to a moral person. The fact that in one case the relevant decisions are taken by a sector (the majority) and in the other case the effects of those decisions are felt by the whole population does not affect the fact that in both cases the decisions and the obligations arising from them are ascribed to the same collective entity. An analogy can be found in a corporation where the decisions of the board of directors and their normative consequences affect all shareholders.

If sound, this view of democracy based on popular sovereignty would, like the consensual theories, overcome the paradox of the superfluousness of law. The will of the sovereign people would determine the common good and also the content of the moral principles. Law, when enacted by the people, would constitute morality. Thus, it could not be morally superfluous.

Of course, this view of democracy is entirely dependent on a collectivist moral philosophy, which in turn depends on a collectivistic ontology, of which I am most skeptical. These doubts are based on ontological criteria derived from Occam's decree requiring us to economize on the postulation of entities. They also are based on a conception of the moral person which requires a subjectivity and the fact that such a subjectivity is not usually ascribed to collectives. Moreover, this conception of democracy has frequently and quite rightly been accused of allowing for authoritarian practices. One may easily move from the position that the collective moral person (The People) is represented by the majority deciding under certain rules designed to protect minorities to the position that the moral person may be represented by a sole leader or an enlightened minority.[50] The justification of democracy based on popular sovereignty cannot acknowledge the counterweight to democracy implied in the recognition of individual rights. As Rousseau said, the decision of The People can never go against the rights of individuals. "In short," he said, "who so gives himself to all gives himself to none." Nor is there an acknowledgment of the other dimension of constitutionalism associated with the preservation of a continuous legal practice. There is no apparent connection between that legal continuity, the constitution of the general will, and the satisfaction of the common good. It may well be that the general will abrogates today what it has enacted earlier.

Perfectionist Theories

Perfectionism conceives of democracy as a method of promoting certain virtues of individuals. These goals include self-realization, particularly in connection with the capacity to be involved in public life, and the spirit of fraternity or social solidarity. According to this view, democracy achieves the transformation of people's interests by moralizing people themselves.

Despite his general utilitarianism, John Stuart Mill can be viewed as part of this school. He begins his defense of "representative government" in a utilitarian vein, articulating criteria of good government that depend on elements of social well-being, or the good state of society. It turns out, however, that some of those elements relate to attributes of human beings. Progress, for instance, requires mental activity, enterprise, and courage. He writes:

> We may consider, then, as one criterion of the goodness of the government, the degree in which it tends to increase the sum of good qualities in the governed, collectively and individually; since, besides that their well-being is the sole object of government, their good qualities supply the moving force which works the machinery. . . . We have now, therefore, obtained a foundation for a twofold division of the merit which any set of political institutions can possess. It consists partly

of the degree in which they promote the general mental advancement of the community, including under that phrase advancement in intellect, in virtue, and in practical activity and efficiency; and partly of the degree of perfection with which they organize the moral, intellectual, and active worth already existing, so as to operate with the greatest effect on public affairs.[51]

Once he establishes this criterion of good government, Mill demonstrates that representative government—the government in which "the sovereignty, or supreme controlling power in the last resort, is vested in the entire aggregate of the community"[52]—is the one which best satisfies it. This move requires three auxiliary premises: the interests of people are best secured when the interested persons can themselves stand up to defend these interests; the general prosperity of society is promoted in proportion to the amount and variety of personal energies enlisted in expanding it;[53] and the improvement of human affairs is a function of active and discontented characters, not passive and satisfied ones.[54] By evaluating together the criterion of the good government and the three additional premises, Mill concludes:

> The maximum of the invigorating effect of freedom upon the character is only obtained, when the person acted on either is, or is looking forward to becoming, a citizen as fully privileged as any other. What is still more important than even this matter of feeling, is the practical discipline which the character obtains, from the occasional demands made upon the citizens to exercise, for a time and in their turn, some social function. . . . If circumstances allow the amount of public duty assigned him to be considerable, it makes him an educated man. . . . Still more salutary is the moral part of the instruction afforded by the participation of the private citizen, if even rarely, in public functions. He is called upon, while so engaged, to weigh interests not his own; to be guided, in case of conflicting claims, by another rule than his private partialities; to apply at every turn, principles and maxims which have for their reason of existence the common good: and he usually finds associated with him in the same work minds more familiarized than his own with these ideas and operations, whose study it will be to supply reasons to his understanding and

stimulation to his feeling for the general interest. He is made
to feel himself one of the public, and whatever is for their
benefit to be for his benefit.[55]

For the moralization of people and their preferences, Mill focuses on
the acquisition of knowledge and the tendency toward impartiality.
In fact, these are the same requisites, according to the assumptions
of our practice of moral discourse, of valid moral judgment.

This view of democracy, particularly its emphasis on moral development and civic virtue, was central to the anti-Federalist movement
during the framing of the United States Constitution and is today
important in the neorepublican movement in constitutional law.[56]
As Cass Sunstein says, "Adhering to the traditional republican view,
the antifederalists argued that civil society should operate as an edu-
cator, and not merely as a regulator of private conduct. Government
bore the responsibility of inculcating attitudes that would incline
the citizenry away from the pursuit of self-interest, at least in the
political realm."[57] Accordingly, democracy helps develop a distinctive kind of personality, self-assured about the equal standing of each
in the political field, involved with public concerns, and in solidarity
with the plight of others. The expansion of these virtues, it is believed, would help overcome self-interest and strike at the very roots
of factions rather than seeking merely to equilibrate their power.

Despite the attractiveness of this view and the intuitive appeal
of the connection between democracy and some civic virtues, there
is a tension between it and the liberal idea of personal autonomy
which has been understood to guarantee a freedom to pursue any
plan of life that does not harm other people and proscribes state
interference with such a choice. Regardless of the particular ideal
of personal excellence, it is not the mission of the state to enforce it.
In contrast to this tenet of liberalism, this perfectionist view encourages endorsement of a model of personal virtue defined by civic and
communitarian ideals.[58]

For similar reasons, there appears to be an inconsistency in Mill
between his defense of democracy based on its impact on moral
development and his famous "harm principle." That principle prohibits society from interfering with actions of individuals which do
not harm other people and is based on the assumption that it is not
the mission of the state to make people virtuous. Rather, the state's
mission is only to secure that no person undermines the conditions
for the exercise of another's autonomy. The use of democracy to

promote certain valuable traits of character in people ignores this proscription. One might say that democracy only promotes public virtue and, according to the harm principle, the state is prevented from discouraging private vices. But it is difficult to sustain this distinction, since human character constitutes a unitary whole; or to believe that private vices have no impact on public virtues, such as the inclination to take impartial stands. The promotion of public virtues may interfere with private inclinations simply because of the existence of material limitations. For instance, if civic virtue were promoted by the state and activities like political participation were encouraged, people would have fewer opportunities to pursue private interests. They would thereby be prevented from developing inclinations for activities which are psychologically, spiritually, or materially contrary to involvement in public life.

Arguably, there is one way to save Mill's political theory from inherent contradictions. According to this view, the personal autonomy principle would be honored if certain virtues of character were promoted not as an end in themselves and not for their intrinsic merits but as a way of obtaining actions that benefit or avoid harm to other people. In this sense, the promotion of public virtues would not be directed at enhancing the character of individuals as something good in itself but would be a way of promoting collective goods. There is evidence to support this view since, as already noted, Mill argues that virtues such as those promoted by democracy are conducive to collective goods such as prosperity. But this connection is, first, empirically controverted, since many societies have achieved considerable prosperity under nondemocratic regimes: consider South Korea or Pinochet's Chile. More important, a collective good such as prosperity, as is true of all the goods endorsed by utilitarianism, is aggregative and may give rise to the objection that its attainment cannot be the sole justification of actions or institutions. This good may come at the expense of individual rights and the manner in which the goods are distributed.

I therefore think it proper to conclude that perfectionist theories of democracy threaten the principle of personal autonomy and are inconsistent with the dimension of constitutionalism provided for by the recognition of rights. As for the historical constitution, it should be recognized that the preservation of a constitutional practice may enhance the opportunities for developing and exercising civic virtues. With regard to the paradox of the superfluousness of government and its laws, the perfectionist justification of democracy does not provide a clear answer. In some cases, it may well be that the laws enacted through the democratic process, exerting the appropriate virtues, are nonetheless prejudicial to the moral development of some or all of the people.

Dialogic Approaches

The moral qualities of dialogue or deliberation account for yet another conception of democracy relying on the transformation of people's preferences. Despite many versions of this general outlook, all rely on dialogue as a means of containing selfish interests and the power of factions based on them. This constraint is achieved by dialogue's tendency to exclude those positions which cannot be sustained on an impartial basis.

Some of the dialogic views converge with ones discussed earlier. For instance, C. B. Macpherson argues that dialogue serves to develop personal virtues, a collective sense of community and mutual attachment, or is a mode of self-expression.[59] In this respect, the qualms provoked by those outlooks apply to the dialogical approaches. Other views connect the dialogue inherent in democratic procedures with values unrelated to character development. For instance, Bruce Ackerman develops an interesting view according to which the merits of dialogue lie neither in the development of personal virtues nor in the approximation to morally correct solutions, but rather in the achievement of mutually acceptable solutions under restraints of neutrality about conceptions of the good.[60] In a similar view, Rawls introduces the idea of "free public reason". According to him, the role of political philosophy, and of course of practical politics, is to achieve an "overlapping consensus," which is neutral toward differing moral conceptions, including that of liberalism.[61]

To my mind, the structure of a dialogue in which the participants avoid discussing the moral correctness of different solutions is uncertain. It is difficult to envisage what people say to one another if the correctness of different moral intersubjective principles is disregarded, and the parties may not even allude to their respective interests. A dialogue can hardly progress if the participants merely describe what they know from the beginning—that their interests are different and possibly in conflict. On the other hand, it seems to be a matter of chance to reach agreement or mutual accommodation or an overlapping consensus if everybody maintains a different underlying moral conception. While there could be an occasional convergence, differences about the implications of the solution reached would reveal divergences in those underlying conceptions.

In truth, to be neutral about conceptions of the personal good is to adopt a distinctive moral conception of society, namely, liberalism. Since liberalism competes with conceptions such as perfectionism or utilitarianism, it cannot be adopted without examining that conception in the context of public discussion. Finally, I should note that the morally neutral conceptions of democracy based on dialogue seem unable to overcome the paradox of the moral superfluousness of government, since they provide no reason for following the result of the democratic process if that result is contrary to moral prescriptions.

Mixed Views of Democracy

The views I have discussed so far are pure. They either consider all preferences of people as outside the political sphere or subject all of them to a potential transformation through the democratic process. However, there are mixed views that seem to distinguish conditions under which the preferences of people are either left to themselves or subject to transformation. We may discuss them briefly, since the component parts of the mixed views have been explained at length in the preceding sections. The theory of deliberative democracy that I articulate in the next chapter is also, in some ways, a mixed view.

According to scholars like Cass Sunstein, the Federalists' conception, handed down mainly through Madison, was a mixed view.[62] Although the Federalists adopted a pluralist conception about the neutralization of factions through the division of powers and representation, it relied on the merits of civic virtue and dialogue in relation to the representatives themselves. Whereas the Federalists assumed that it would be unrealistic and pernicious to rely on the whole community's political involvement in a dialogic way, at least in the case of a large republic, this was an essential aspect of the adequate working of representative government. Sunstein writes:

> The federalists thus achieved a kind of synthesis of republicanism and the emerging principles of pluralism. Politics rightly consisted in deliberation and discussion about the public good. But the process could not be brought about in

the traditional republican fashion. Such an effort, in light of human nature, would deteriorate into a struggle among competing factions. A partial solution lay in principles of representation. The mechanisms of accountability would prevent representatives from acquiring interests distinct from those of their constituents. Moreover, the separation of powers would ensure that if a particular group acquired too much power over one set of representatives, there would be safeguards to prevent that group from obtaining authority over the national government in general.[63]

Of course, just because representatives are subject to the strictures of dialogue does not resolve questions regarding their lack of legitimacy. One of the main problems that dialogic conceptions must surmount, as we shall see in the next chapter, is how to ensure that all the interested parties participate in the process of deliberation and that they do so on an equal basis. The pluralist conception of democracy does not ensure that the representatives represent all the people affected by the measures they take and that they do so equally. Insofar as there may be serious distortions in this respect, they cannot be overcome by the fact that the representatives operate in a dialogic way. Therefore, this mixed theory of democracy bears the burden of its pluralist component and its nonegalitarian spirit.

Bruce Ackerman defends a different mixed view with his "dualist conception of politics," which he applies to the American system.[64] Ackerman maintains that the system advocated by the Federalists and adopted by the framers in Philadelphia is best understood and justified by differentiating two tracks along which political life evolves. The first track is a higher form of politics, called "constitutional politics," which takes place in the rare moments when the people speak through a process of considerable mobilization and debate. According to Ackerman, constitutional politics took place in the United States with the enactment of the Constitution itself, with Reconstruction after the Civil War, and with the New Deal. The second track is the lower form of politics, called "normal politics," when the people do not speak directly but through various institutions of government. The representation provided by these institutions is problematic because of the division of voices and the questionable connection between each of them and the will of the people. Normal politics therefore enjoys a lower legitimacy and must be subject to the results obtained in the higher track. It is the role of judges through judicial review to preserve the will of the people best expressed in these rare constitutional moments.

Ackerman thinks this division of politics is justified since it is a way of economizing public virtue. It allows citizens to pursue their private concerns in normal times, without imposing upon them an ideal of personal excellence through permanent political involvement. At the same time, it establishes a means for signaling those rare opportunities in which mobilization is required. Consequently, Ackerman presents a theory of constitutional rights emanating from democratic decisions taken in constitutional moments and restraining the expressions of normal politics. This theory is contrasted to a monist conception in which rights depend permanently on a continuous and uniform democratic process, and to a fundamentalist conception according to which rights constrain any democratic expression.

Although Ackerman's theory clearly acknowledges the historical dimension of constitutionalism—the preservation of the constitutional practice—there are some doubts about both its explanatory and justificatory import which are not easy to overcome. First, it is not clear why he speaks of "dualism" or "two" political tracks when one might point to a continuum of many different degrees of legitimacy depending on the degree of mobilization and debate. Issues like abortion or discrimination provoke protracted debate and mobilization, even if they are not comparable to Ackerman's few examples that have a definite impact on the legal system. Could it be that the people are given only three opportunities—the founding, Reconstruction, and the New Deal—to speak their minds directly in over two hundred years of eventful history?

The democratic legitimacy of some of the constitutional moments to which Ackerman refers is rather dubious. With regard to the well-known formal democratic deficiencies of the enactment of the United States Constitution, it is hard to see that those deficiencies were resolved by informal debates and widespread mobilization. For instance, were women and blacks part of these debates? Ackerman might respond that he is merely reconstructing the views of current American officials, mainly judges, about the origin of democratic legitimacy. That may be true, but if so, one should try to free them from their obvious mistakes. In addition, the image of the people mobilized and excited with public spirit in dramatic moments can be dangerous for democratic legitimacy. What is the space for open, rational discussion in those moments? Is the equal weight of all the participants relatively guaranteed? For me, the epistemic merits of democracy are better displayed in less romantic and more calm moments. The democratic legitimacy of a constitutional moment is also questionable since there are normally obstacles for enacting the will of the majority. These obstacles signal, in Ackerman's view, the gravity of the moment. Therefore, a minority in favor of the status quo often has veto power. If these obstacles were suppressed, we would have in fact a monistic system.

Ackerman purports to solve the "temporal difficulty"—the fact that a democratic decision taken by people long dead might trump the will of people currently living—but the answer seems inadequate. It relies on the different quality of both expressions of will because of the different degrees of mobilization and debate. Nevertheless, a high quality of a debate with zero value in terms of self-government should not counteract a debate of a quite low quality that maintains some connection with the preferences of the people to which it applies.

With regard to the justification of judicial review, the dualistic view also is problematic since there is no reason why "the will of the people" must be preserved by countermajoritarian officials and not by those closer to the preferences of current majorities. Indeed, it is a quite shocking example of ideological positivism to submit judges to the will of the people in constitutional moments whatever the content of that moment. If freedom of expression or religion were abolished at the constitutional level, judges would have to abide by the new order or else resign.[65] Therefore, dualism does not acknowledge properly the counterweight provided for by the ideal dimension of constitutionalism—the recognition of rights as exerted upon the democratic process.

In this chapter we have reviewed in a quite cursory way some of the conceptions justifying democracy that most often are appealed to by scholars and political actors. These views of democracy have been classified according to one important criterion: whether they separate morality from politics or whether both realms are intertwined. In other words, the theories have been distinguished in terms of whether the merits they ascribe to democracy are independent of the moral transformation of people's interests or rely on that transformation. The different views of democracy that I have discussed not only presuppose quite contrasting philosophical assumptions but also have very different institutional implications.

The theories in question have shown flaws of different kinds. Some flaws are internal to each theory and have to do with imprecisions and inconsistencies that each of them presents. Many of the flaws presented by the first family of theories relate to their inability to overcome problems of collective action. Other flaws consist in their inability to develop values with which democracy has always been associated, particularly the values of equality and liberty. There are also flaws which arise from the failure to meet the challenges that emerge from the development of the previous chapters: overcoming the paradox of the superfluousness of government and its laws; properly acknowledging the counterweight of rights to democracy; and recognizing the value of preserving legal practice as another constitutional counterweight to democracy. Of course, the theories reviewed do not present the same flaws in the same degree, and some of them are quite able to meet many of the challenges mentioned. Nevertheless, all of them are unsatisfactory in important respects.

In the next chapter, I shall try to defend a certain variety of a deliberative conception of democracy—one which is based on the epistemic power of the democratic process—which I hope is free from the flaws that we have uncovered here.

Chapter Five

The Foundations of the Deliberative Conception of Democracy

In the preceding chapter, I reviewed different conceptions of democracy and divided them according to whether or not they attempt to isolate politics from morality. I argued that all the conceptions are flawed. In this chapter, I shall try to articulate the theory best able to overcome those flaws.

The theory I defend is dialogic.[1] While some dialogic views preserve the separation between politics and morality, my conception views these two spheres as intertwined and locates the value of democracy in the moralization of people's preferences. For me, the value of democracy is of an epistemic nature with regard to social morality. I claim that if certain strictures are met, democracy is the most reliable procedure for obtaining access to the knowledge of moral principles. Yet, this position does not fall into perfectionism, since it presumes a differentiation among moral standards and limits the epistemic value of democracy to those standards that are of an intersubjective nature.

Epistemic Constructivism: Between Rawls and Habermas

In order to explain this deliberative theory of democracy, I must deal with some questions of moral epistemology and defend a constructivist conception of the knowledge of principles of social morality. I shall undertake the defense of such a constructivist view by contrasting two distinguished contemporary philosophers—John Rawls and Jürgen Habermas—who approach what I take to be the correct position but never exactly hit the target. Since their misfires go in opposite directions, the comparison between Rawls and Habermas is highly instructive for finding the correct theoretical course.

The Position of John Rawls

An extended controversy exists surrounding the true meta-ethical stance of Rawls's famous two principles of justice: one extolling the priority of liberty, the other limiting societal and economic inequalities to those that benefit the least favored members of society. This controversy stems from the fact that Rawls appeals to practically all the bases, except the theological one, that have been used throughout the history of philosophy to provide an intersubjective rationale for moral judgments: consent, self-interest, intuitions, and the structure of moral reasoning.[2] The least explicit base that Rawls deploys to ground his principles of justice is the formal presuppositions of moral discourse. Yet, even that line of argument emerges on certain occasions. For instance, Rawls insists that principles of justice must satisfy formal conditions such as universality, generality, publicity, and finality.[3] Rawls says that the role of moral theory is to describe our moral capacity to judge things as just or unjust and to give reasons. He maintains that the conditions of the original position are in fact accepted by us, and he asserts that "each one has in himself the complete form of moral theory." He also describes the derivation of the principles of justice as a case of pure procedural justice.[4]

Once we assume that the basic justificatory ground is provided by the formal presuppositions and constraints of moral reasoning, all the pieces of Rawls's theory begin to fit together. The original position converts itself into a dramatization of those formal assumptions or a device of representation. The hypothetical contract alludes to a presupposition of moral reasoning according to which principles are valid when they would be unanimously accepted by all the subjects concerned under ideal conditions. The recourse to self-interest, when combined with the veil of ignorance, has only the heuristic value of allowing us to determine more easily the restrictions imposed upon our reasoning by the underlying requirement of impartiality. Finally, intuitions may be indicative of value if they are considered expressions of the form of the moral theory that everyone has in himself and thus serve as hints regarding the application of formal presuppositions of practical reasoning to judgments about particular cases.

If this more Kantian view of Rawls's theory were plausible, we would be able to maintain that it includes a certain characterization of moral truth. A moral judgment is true, we could say, when it derives from a principle that would be accepted in the original position or, to put in another way, that would be unanimously accepted under conditions of impartiality, rationality, and knowledge of relevant facts.

Rawls is in no way explicit about the proper method for attaining knowledge of this type of moral truth. At first, it seems that individual reflection is a sound method for obtaining access to the truth in moral matters, at least in the area of justice. Indeed, reflective equilibrium can be understood as a method of reaching that truth. The mutual adjustment of general principles and particular intuitions acts as an indicator of the application of formal presuppositions of reasoning that serve as filters of invalid principles. For instance, the intuition that the pain a person suffers cannot be justified on the basis of the greater pleasure it provokes in another person may be an indication that our practical reasoning assumes a certain measure of impartiality. In turn, this intuition indicates that we take into account the separability of people, resulting in a disqualification of utilitarianism and its aggregative principles.

Although individual reflection seems to permit, within Rawls's theory, access to moral truth, this does not mean that the exchange of opinions with others has no value. Certainly, we benefit from the results of the reflections of other people since we all share, at least in part, the same presuppositions and conceptual schemes and have similar possibilities of access to facts through observation. At most, Rawls would probably maintain that one must guide oneself by the result of one's own reflection, since he seems to adopt, like Kant, the concept of autonomy which includes the idea that in morals each is his own epistemic authority.

When Rawls deals with justifying democracy understood as majoritarian rule, he exhibits his epistemic individualism more clearly. Rawls maintains that "there is nothing to the view . . . that what the majority wills is right."[5] He rejects the possibility of applying Condorcet's theorem for justifying the conclusion that as more people support a solution it is more probably correct, maintaining that this requires that each opinion be more probably correct than incorrect and that the votes of different people not be mutually influenced. According to Rawls, none of those conditions is necessarily present in a democratic procedure.

Rawls recognizes that discussion among many people has beneficial effects, since it restrains our partiality, broadens our perspective and knowledge, and allows us to detect mistakes of reasoning. It is not clear, however, to what field this benefit of collective discussion can be applied. Rawls observes that there must be an area of morality in which discussion and majoritarian decision have some relevance for the rightness of solutions. Still, he oscillates between giving those discussions either constitutive value or epistemic value, or no value at all.

The Position of Jürgen Habermas

In discussing Jürgen Habermas, I shall concentrate on one work, his long essay "Discursethik-Notizen zu einen Begrundungsprogramm" (Discourse ethics: Notes on a program of philosophical justification), which presents with uncommon clarity the outlines of his position about the foundations of ethics.[6] Habermas uses the work of Peter Strawson[7] to show that the justification of moral judgments and the blame based on them is part of a social practice pervading life and interpersonal exchanges.

Habermas maintains that practical discourse is constituted by communicative interactions through which the participants coordinate their plans of behavior, arguing for or against different claims of validity with the goal of obtaining a certain consensus about them. The bridge principle is not merely a grammatical requirement or a demand for consistency but involves a requirement of impartiality. It stipulates that a moral norm is valid insofar as it wins the assent of the people concerned.[8] Habermas maintains that when we argue to convince others, we necessarily assume a principle of universalization understood as impartiality.[9]

According to Habermas, a skeptic can free himself from that assumption only if he separates himself from the community of those who argue. But there is not a single socio-cultural form of life in the world which is not connected, at least implicitly, to the furtherance of communicative actions, no matter how primitive and uninstitutionalized that form of life may be. If someone were to attempt to separate himself for a long time from the context of action oriented toward understanding, he would subject himself to such isolation that he would become schizophrenic and prone to suicide.

Habermas explicitly criticizes Rawls for assuming that the postulate of impartiality is satisfied when the person formulating moral judgments puts himself fictitiously in the position of each one of the people concerned. While Rawls believes that anybody, including a moral philosopher like himself, can undertake the task of justifying fundamental norms, Habermas maintains that the task of moral argumentation cannot be discharged in a monologic way but requires a cooperative effort. According to Habermas, "the justification of norms and commands requires that a real discourse be carried out and thus cannot occur . . . in the form of a hypothetical process of argumentation occurring in the individual mind."[10]

Habermas also stresses that the idea of impartiality cannot be reduced to an equilibrium of powers. It requires impartial judgment about the interests of all the people concerned. He writes, "Participants in a practical discourse strive to clarify a common interest, whereas in negotiating a compromise they try to strike a balance between conflicting particular interests."[11]

These assertions of Habermas's align him with a position I have previously deemed "epistemic constructivism." According to that position, the validity of moral judgments is established not by the *results* of real discourse but by its *presuppositions*, though those results are a reliable way to know the presuppositions. This seems to be confirmed when Habermas says, "Practical discourse is not a procedure for generating justified norms but a procedure for testing the validity of norms that are being proposed and hypothetically considered for adoption."[12]

Other statements of Habermas's, however, place him in a more radical position that might be called "ontological constructivism." This position holds that it is the validity of moral judgments—not merely the knowledge of that validity—that is constituted by the result of real discussion when it satisfies certain constraints. Thus Habermas says, "In discourse . . . content is subjected to a process in which particular values are ultimately discarded as not being susceptible to consensus." Habermas states also that "the principle of discourse ethics . . . stipulates [that] only those norms can claim to be valid that meet (or could meet) with the approval of all affected in their capacity as participants in a practical discourse."[13] The transference from discourse to action, he argues, cannot be demonstrated by extracting from the presuppositions of discussion, in an *immediate* way, fundamental moral norms. Rather, the fundamental norms of law and morals should be considered in need of justification in practical discourse. Given that historical circumstances vary, each epoch throws its own light upon the fundamental ideas of practical morality. The moral theoretician may participate in discourse as an affected party and as an expert, but he may not direct those discourses *by his own account*. A theory yielding substantive principles, like Rawls's theory of justice, ought to be understood simply as a contribution to the discourse among citizens. As Habermas's interpreter Stephen K. White asserts, "What justice demands in given social and historical settings cannot be legitimately decided in advance of an *actual* argumentation or discourse among all concerned."[14]

In sum, Habermas agrees with Rawls that there are formal presuppositions, such as impartiality, which are decisive for the validity of moral principles. But, whereas for Rawls they are formal presuppositions of monologic moral reasoning, for Habermas they are rules of a social practice of intersubjective discourse. For Rawls, the validity of moral principles is given by the satisfaction of the requirement of impartiality. Habermas, on the other hand, requires a de facto consensus to be constituted through the employment of the rule of impartiality. Finally, whereas Rawls seems to think that one can reach the conclusion that a moral principle is valid by means of individual reflection alone—though discussion may play an auxiliary role—Habermas clearly thinks this impossible. For Habermas, only collective discussion, "the cooperative search for truth," is a reliable avenue of access to moral knowledge.

The Ontological and Epistemological Theses

It is possible to distinguish at least three ontological tenets about the constitution of moral truth and at least three epistemological tenets about the knowledge of it. Let us examine first the three basic ontological tenets, calling them O1, O2, and O3:

O1. Moral truth is constituted by the satisfaction of formal presuppositions inherent in the practical reasoning of any individual, in particular the presupposition according to which a moral principle is valid if it is acceptable to everybody under ideal conditions of impartiality, rationality, and knowledge of the relevant facts.

O2. Moral truth is constituted by the satisfaction of formal or procedural presuppositions of a discursive practice directed at attaining cooperation and avoiding conflicts.

O3. Moral truth is constituted by the consensus which actually results from the actual practice of moral discussion when carried out according to some procedural restrictions on arguments.

Let us now consider three epistemological theses:

E1. Knowledge of moral truth is attained solely by individual reflection. Discussion with others is a useful auxiliary of individual reflection, but in the end we must inescapably act according to the final results of the latter.

E2. Intersubjective discussion and decision is the most reliable procedure for having access to moral truth, since the exchange of ideas and the need to justify oneself before others not only broaden one's knowledge and reveal defects in reasoning but help satisfy the requirement of impartial attention to the interests of everybody concerned. This does not, however, exclude the possibility that through individual reflection somebody may have access to the knowledge of correct solutions, though it must be admitted that this method is far less reliable than the collective one, because of the difficulty of faithfully representing the interests of others and being impartial.

E3. The method of collective discussion and decision is the only avenue of access to moral truth, since monologic reflection is always distorted by biases of the individual in favor of himself or of the people close to him due to contextual conditioning and the insurmountable difficulty of putting oneself in another's shoes. Only actual consensus achieved after a broad debate with few exclusions, manipulations, and inequalities provides a reliable access to the demands of morality.

Rawls maintains thesis O1 as the characterization of moral truth. In *A Theory of Justice*, the social practice of moral discourse is not absolutely relevant to the rules defining the validity of moral principles. Rawls supposes, like Kant, that "the form of moral theory" is something that "each one has in himself." The rules of monologic discourse do not seem to be relevant for constituting moral truth. In later works, not explored much here, Rawls seems more attracted to giving social practices higher priority in the derivation of moral principles, though he does not distinguish between the practice of moral discourse and other practices of a democratic culture. In this way he seem to fall into a conventionalist position.[15]

Habermas's position with regard to the constitution of moral truth is O3, since he maintains that there are no valid moral principles except those achieved as a result of a moral discussion carried out with due observance of the requirement of impartiality. I have called this approach ontological constructivism. At other points, however, Habermas comes closer to thesis O2, according to which the validity of moral judgments is established by the presuppositions and not by the results of moral discussion.[16]

With regard to the epistemological question, there is no doubt that Habermas subscribes to E3 and rejects E1 and E2. He believes, in effect, that moral knowledge is only attainable through the actual discussion of all the people concerned. In no case can moral truth be obtained—as is maintained by E2—through individual reflection. At most, individual reflection can only result in a contribution to collective discussion.

In contrast, I believe that the most plausible theses about the constitution and the knowledge of moral truth are O2 and E2. These are the intermediate theses between Rawls and Habermas. In the ontological sphere, I think Rawls and his mentor, Kant, are seriously deficient in not incorporating in their outlook the social practice of moral discourse. Inclusion of this social practice would allow them to take into account a strong point stressed by relativism about historical variations in the mode of moral argumentation, without going into the blind alley in which we find ourselves when we admit the relativization of substantive moral judgments. Furthermore, when we focus our attention on a social practice, we have an empirical basis from which to infer the rules and criteria that are in fact presupposed in that practice. Such an approach is all the more plausible once we take into account that such a practice has manifest and latent functions—such as achieving coordination through consensus on some principles—and that the formal presuppositions are adapted to those functions.[17] Finally, it is particularly important to take as a bedrock the actual social practice of moral discourse if one must admit, as we are compelled to do, that discourse has evaluative presuppositions, such as the principle of autonomy.

With regard to thesis O3, maintained by Habermas, I believe that it ends up falling into the relativist confusion between validity and observance. Some actual consensus may be disqualified under the postulate of universalization. And if the postulate of universalization were rich enough to allow for only one principle as a basis for consensus, this would imply recognition of O2, since the valid principle would be determined before its actual consensual adoption. The more basic problem is that O3 does not seem to reflect the phenomenology of moral discussion, which consists, as Rawls and Habermas emphasize, not in expressing personal interests but rather in advancing claims of validity or principles. The participants in the discussion could not defend proposals as valid if that validity depended by definition on the *result* of the discussion. It is also meaningless to *offer* a principle for discussion and decision if there are no reasons that support it. In sum, O3 has a tendency to endorse a conservative conventionalism with regard to the results of discussion and to see its operation as a mere clash of interests.

Thesis O2 incorporates instead the best of both worlds. Like O3, it benefits from the empirical basis that flows from the fact that it is a social practice. The circularity of reflective equilibrium is broken without being tied to the contingent results of actual consensus. The fact that moral truth is defined in relation to the presupposition of moral discourse and not by its actual results allows us to explain argumentation as a means to conform these results to those presuppositions. Presuppositions include substantive principles such as that of autonomy, from which more specific moral judgments can be deduced. Formal rules, such as impartiality, serve as filters for principles and foster a dynamism that enables the enactment of other norms.

If we move now to the epistemological level, we notice that E1, the position Rawls defends, involves quite serious problems. If individual reflection were our only way to have access to moral truth, why should we follow the prescriptions of an authority—even if democratically legitimate—when these prescriptions oppose the results of that reflection? Also, what is the relevance of that authority when its prescriptions coincide with the conclusions of our moral reflection? These doubts contain the roots of either philosophical anarchism or an enlightened dictatorship, depending on whether the individual reaching conclusions by his own reflection has the force to impose them on others. It is not by chance that many Rawlsian jurists favor broad judicial power to review laws democratically enacted. As Michael Walzer says, judges are the new philosopher-kings under this kind of theory.[18] This difficulty in passing from the autonomy of morals to the heteronomy of law is not overcome by simply saying that our individual reflection provides reasons for observing another's prescription, since it does not always provide those reasons and sometimes may suggest an opposite prescription.

These disadvantages of E1 give support to E3, the position of Habermas. E3 asserts that we have reasons to observe the results from collective discussion and decision, since it is the only reliable method for finding out correct solutions. Thus, individual, non-moral, philosophical reflection would indicate that the only method of moral knowledge is collective discussion. This would be true because of the advantages provided by the exchange of ideas—our knowledge is broadened and mistakes more readily detected. The chances of achieving impartiality are also improved. If we start from the hypothesis that no one knows a person's interests better than that person himself, then impartiality is solely secured through the participation of those concerned in the collective procedure of discussion and decision.

But these advantages of E3 are neutralized by all too obvious setbacks. In the same way that E1 leads to moral elitism, E3 seems to lead to moral populism, since it supports the position that a solution supported by all or the majority is automatically correct. It is obvious, however, that the majority sometimes is very wrong. Also, E3, like O3, does not adequately reflect the phenomenology of moral discussion. If it were impossible to find moral knowledge by individual reflection, Rawls could make no contribution to collective discussion. Also, no one could demand that the result of a collective discussion be revised if that result were the only available presumption of moral truth.

Thesis E2 solves these problems of E3 without suffering the defects of E1. According to E2, the procedure of collective discussion and decision constituted by moral discourse (and even by its imperfect surrogate, the democratic decision-making system) is the *most reliable* method of approaching moral truth. It is not the only one, however. It is possible, though generally improbable, that through individual reflection a person may adequately represent to himself the conflicting interests and can thereby arrive at a correct—that is, impartial—conclusion. It is conceivable that an individual reaches more correct conclusions in isolation than by collective discussion. This possibility explains the contribution that each one can make to discussion and why he can legitimately demand that the discussion be reopened. The probability that correct solutions are reached by individual reflection increases when referring to the preconditions for the validity of the collective procedure. This is the subject matter of a priori rights, which is more restricted than the content of Rawls's first principle and which, in my opinion, constitutes the only moral question whose solution by democratic laws can be reviewed by judges or, in the last resort, be the object of civil disobedience.[19] Given that the collective procedure is generally more reliable than individual reflection and that the former would not be operative if we always decided whether to abide by results according to our individual reflection, an obligation to observe that which has been collectively decided is plainly justified.

In sum, the combination of O2 and E2, constituting an intermediate position between Rawls and Habermas, is the most plausible meta-ethical theory. This is the position I call "epistemic constructivism."

The Epistemic Value of Democracy

Unanimity appears to be the functional equivalent of impartiality. If all those who may be affected by a decision have participated in the discussion and have had an equal opportunity to express their interests and justify to each other a certain solution of the conflict, this solution is almost always impartial and morally right as long as everyone has accepted the solution freely and without coercion.

This theory presupposes the premise, accepted by Mill, that no one is a better judge of one's own interests than oneself. This premise, in turn, presupposes the meta-ethical propositions regarding the principle of personal autonomy, which holds that the interests of individuals should be determined by their choices. It also implies certain empirical propositions concerning the enhanced accessibility of the agent to her choices and wants.[20]

A solution proposed by an individual, within moral discussion, to overcome a conflict may be contrary to her interests. She may, for instance, be mistaken about causal relations involved in the satisfaction of her interests. She may also make logical mistakes. This possibility is not completely dispelled by the fact that the very process of discussion may help to overcome logical or factual errors. However, the outcome of the process of discussion is highly likely to be impartial, and hence morally right, if it has been unanimously accepted by all the people involved in the conflict.

When moral discourse is institutionalized and replaced, due to pragmatic considerations, by a regimented surrogate such as majority rule, one must examine whether that surrogate still guarantees, even if to a lesser degree, the requirement of impartiality.

Clearly, a solution to the conflict supported by a majority and not by all the people involved in the conflict may be very partial. A majority may ignore completely the interests of the minority. In fact, opposition to a minority may by itself motivate the majority's actions. In this way, democracy as majority rule appears to be the archetypal mechanism for taking partial decisions. If true, democratic decisions could only be justified by reasons that have nothing to do with their moral correctness.

To deal with this problem, we should begin by examining the actual transition from the original, noninstitutionalized practice of moral discourse to the regimented surrogate of democracy as majority rule. Suppose we live together in a condominium and have gathered together to discuss a conflict of interests. Let us imagine that the elevator must be repaired, and those living in the lower floors who seldom use it are not interested in sharing the costs. At first, each of the participants of the discussion will try to convince the others on the assumption that a unanimous consensus can be reached. Even if it is clear from the beginning that those who oppose sharing the costs of the repair are in the minority, both groups will try to convince the members of the other to try to reach unanimity. But at a certain point, some of the participants will think that a decision must be reached. They may be tired; it may be quite late in the evening; and they may think that the arguments have been exhausted. The main consideration forcing a decision will be that a tacit rather than explicit decision in favor of the status quo — not repairing the elevator — may be taken. Therefore, somebody will propose that there should be a vote. At that point, the majority's wishes should govern. Observe that the passage from the requirement of unanimous consensus to majority rule — which is one of the defining marks of the democratic process — takes place not merely because of the impossibility of unanimity but because of the need to reach a decision at a certain time. Otherwise, an implicit decision in favor of the status quo will always be taken. The introduction of a time limit to end the discussion and to vote crucially differentiates the informal process of moral discussion from its institutionalized surrogate, democracy as majority rule. Therefore, democracy can be defined as a process of moral discussion with a time limit.

In changing from the requirement of unanimity at a certain moment to the requirement of majority at that moment, the participants may decide to vote in order to prevent a minority in favor of the status quo from winning. Interestingly, the minority may feel there is nothing wrong with imposing their views. In responding to them, one cannot say simply that it is better to have a decision supported by a majority than one supported by a minority. It cannot be merely that the majority is closer to unanimity, since the functional equivalence between unanimity and impartiality does not seem to depend on a mere quantitative question. Even when there is only one vote opposed to the solution proposed by all the others, that vote may be crucial to the presumption of impartiality. Suppose, for instance, that in our elevator example the solution proposed by all but one was that this individual must pay the whole cost of repairing the elevator.

Rather than relying on a purely quantitative analysis, the passage from unanimity to majority rule must be based on the idea that impartiality is better preserved by that passage than by any other surrogate of unanimous consensus. In fact, a process of moral discussion with a certain time limit within which a majoritarian decision must be taken—the definitional core of democracy under the normative view I am articulating—has greater epistemic power for providing access to morally correct decisions than any other collective decision-making procedure.

Knowledge of the Interests of Others

The epistemic theory of democracy depends on certain hypotheses. One is that the lack of impartiality is often due, not to selfish inclinations of the actors in the social and political process, but to sheer ignorance of where the interests of others lie. In countries in which there have been frequent dictatorships, it is well known that not all dictators are mean, egotistic monsters, though unfortunately some are. Some dictators are genuinely concerned with reaching morally right decisions, but more often their impartiality fails them in light of the difficulty in representing the interests of sectors of society far removed from their own social background.

This mistaken appraisal of the interests of a particular social group is often due to a perfectionist ethic holding that the interests of people do not necessarily coincide with their choices. The thought is that these interests could better be ascertained by people more knowledgeable about factual issues and morally acquainted with models of human excellence. As I discussed in Chapter 3, one may reject this perfectionist outlook for reasons independent of democracy, but it is convenient to note that a minority's process of decision making promotes this perfectionist vision. If only a few individuals decide what is good for the group as a whole, why should they not be able to decide what is good for each individual?

At other times, a dictator's mistaken assessment of the interests of others is due not to the assumption of a perfectionist stand but rather to factual misapprehensions. The dictator may generalize wrongly on the basis of the interests of people like himself. He may ignore the factual circumstances of the lives of unrelated and strange individuals, or he may be wrong about the values that these people hold, particularly those values which are relevant to their choice of life plans and of ideals of personal excellence.

A dictator or a minority may try to conduct an investigation to minimize the possibility of committing these errors. Even in doing so, the dictator may still not include all the people concerned in a democratic process of collective discussion and decision. Defining the interests of people is not so much a question of knowledge as a question of choice. Therefore, if individuals have no occasion to make a choice that would give a preferential order to their interests, they themselves may be unable to define that order. An investigation conducted by the dictator about the interests of people may provide quite wrong results, since the people have no occasion to choose but are asked to reconstruct their desires.

A dictator's investigation into people's interests will be even more distorted by the fact that interests change when people know the interests of others. For instance, some people tend to imitate others, many of whom do not have confidence in their own wisdom but trust the judgment of certain others. Others realize that if they continue with their choice, a problem of collective action will arise due to the preferences of others. This realization then leads them to change their preferences to avoid self-frustration. Altruists, for example, might find that their own interests clash with others' and therefore change their choices so that the interests of others can be satisfied.

Even compared to adjudication, democratic discussion and decision best ascertain the interests of other people. While a judge is subject to rules of appointment and procedure designed to secure her impartiality, this guarantee of impartiality applies only to the parties involved in the judicial process. It does not apply to other people who may be affected by the standard the judge is applying. Therefore, that standard should not be binding in other cases unless it is formed through a process in which all the individuals affected can participate.

The Quest for Justification

Part of the exchange in a discussion preceding a majoritarian decision involves the mutual relating of each other's interests. Yet if this were all, the participants in that process would simply be expressing descriptive judgments that have no justificatory power whatsoever. If speech-acts performed in democratic discussion by elites or representatives only described the content of their interests, it would be difficult to explain how the discussion could progress and to understand the point of these reciprocal psychoanalytic confessions.

I want to defend here a vision of democracy in which bargaining and expression of emotions play a role but are subservient to argument in promoting the epistemic power of the majoritarian decision-making process. Admittedly, without the help of emotional factors and of negotiations on the basis of self-interest, rational debate and subsequent majoritarian decisions would not tend to be impartial solutions. Nevertheless, these forms of participation have a beneficial impact on the moral value of democracy only through argumentation.

Under my view of the democratic process as a surrogate of the informal practice of moral discussion, all participants are required, as in that practice, to justify their proposals to the others. If their interests are stated, they must be shown to be legitimate. This view presupposes the existence of a line—thin but important—separating those statements in a discussion that we take as real and genuine and those that are phony or that obviously do not comply with underlying rules of an authentic discussion. For instance, knocking on the table with a shoe, as Nikita Khrushchev famously did in a United Nations session, is not to argue. Obviously, genuine arguments must be distinguished from valid ones; otherwise a discussion could not start without immediately ending.

It is not my purpose to articulate all the conditions that make a statement a genuine argument without necessarily making it a valid one. Perhaps those conditions can be summarized under the observation, alluded to by Jon Elster, that there should be a prima facie appearance that the statement in question expresses a normative proposition which could be accepted from an impartial point of view.[21] I would like only to mention rapidly some of the cases where statements clearly do not have this appearance and thus would be rejected as arguments in any genuine discussion. They include:

1. the mere expression of wants or description of interests. If I simply say, "This is what I want" in backing a certain solution to a conflict, I risk the immediate reply, "And so what?"

2. the mere description of facts, such as a tradition or custom, that a human authority has enacted, or a divinity has ordered (for instance, "In this condominium we always have proceeded in that way"). Such a description could serve only as an intermediate premise in a process of argumentation, since the authority of a tradition or of a law-giver may always be put into question.

3. the expression of normative propositions that are not general, in the sense that the cases to which they apply are accounted for with proper names or definite descriptions. I cannot justify a proposal for ending a conflict just by saying, as an ultimate argument, "This is wrong when it is done to *me*" or "This is wrong when it is done in *this* condominium."

4. the expression of normative propositions one is not prepared to apply to cases which are indistinguishable from the present one on the basis of properties relevant to the propositions themselves. This is the requirement of universalizability, interpreted as a condition of pragmatical consistency.

5. obvious practical inconsistencies. For instance, a statement would not be accepted as a genuine argument if it were incompatible with a statement made by the same individual in another conflict. Similarly, the statement would be rejected if it did not conform to actions performed by the individual making the statement.

6. the expression of normative propositions that do not seem to take into account the interests of individuals. We reject ridiculous attempts to justify proposals for solving conflicts, such as "This course of action would benefit the elevator." A similar fate should befall less ridiculous attempts of justifying a certain proposal in some conclusory way, such as "This will be good for the condominium as a whole."

7. the expression of normative propositions that do not purport to be moral, that is, acceptable from an impartial point of view, but are only prudential or aesthetic and thus cannot provide reasons for resolving a conflict of interests among different people.

Some of these conditions for a genuine argument in the process of moral discussion and democratic debate might be disputed.

Others might surely be added to the above list. But the important thing to realize is that some conditions defining the genuine character of an argument without defining its validity must be assumed for any discussion to take place.

Of course, one might argue, as Jon Elster does, that any self-interested position can be concealed under apparently impartial normative propositions. For instance, in a wage dispute between trade unions and entrepreneur groups, the former will surely resort to egalitarian values, whereas the latter will allege libertarian ones. Therefore, the constraint of producing genuine arguments in support of one's position may be incapable by itself of generating a tendency toward impartiality.

Nevertheless, I believe these rules are a real constraint on the defense of self-interest. Together with the other factors, they contribute to a dynamic of acceptance of impartial solutions. The experience of moral discussion, whether informal or institutionalized, shows that people often refrain from putting forward self-serving positions when the only statements that occur to them would not be seen as genuine arguments because they fall under some of the above rules. Also, it often occurs that people formulate a statement and then modify it in the face of rapid rejection as a nongenuine argument on the part of other participants.

All these constraints contribute to the progress of the discussion toward the applicability of criteria of impartiality—by individuals unmoved by self-interest or unaffected by proposed solutions. If, in our example of the discussion between the members of a condominium, it were allowed as a proper move to say, "This is what I want," "This is convenient for me," it would be impossible for the discussion to progress. Thus, the neighbors whose interests are not affected by any particular solution or who have a natural tendency to be impartial would not know how to resolve the dispute. Instead, if the self-interested neighbors are obliged to frame their arguments in the form of "Those who do not benefit from a service are not obliged to pay for it" or "A condominium is a scheme of cooperation in which everybody pays for everything whether he directly benefits from it or not," there are many foreseeable ways in which the discussion may progress and in which unselfish participants may be convinced. Participants might remember that some of the obviously self-interested parties have used the opposite principle on another occasion in which their interests were reversed. Or, for instance, they might think that all the occupants would have accepted living in a more communitarian environment if they had been asked before the conflict of interests arose.

The Detection of Factual and Logical Mistakes

Intersubjective discussion helps detect mistakes of facts and logic. Often a proposed solution is unjust not because it conceals selfish motives or because the person proposing it fails to represent the interests of others but because he ignores certain relevant facts or commits some logical fallacy. In these cases, it is possible that other participants in the discussion can detect those pitfalls and point them out so that the speaker may correct them.

One might say that there is no guarantee that the majority is more correct about facts or logic than the person who proposed the rejected solution. One might add that an isolated individual or enlightened minority often is aware of a truth that the majority refuses to acknowledge. Experts in science or art, for instance, might be more reliable in certain areas than the participants in a collective process of discussion and decision. Finally, it might be argued that people who are interested in a certain outcome have a tendency to misrepresent facts and logic in a self-serving manner.

These rejoinders are valid, but I am not defending a consensual or majoritarian theory of truth about factual, logical, or philosophical issues. I am only defending a consensual or majoritarian theory of knowledge of certain sorts of moral issues. For instance, I am not submitting my own view of democracy to majoritarian assent. I am indeed suggesting something much weaker and, to my mind, more obvious. Specifically, I am arguing that discussion with others most often contributes to detecting factual and logical errors, because, in the end, factual observation and the use of rules of inference are the product of widespread capabilities, and most people do not commit the same mistake. Even when the minority is often correct about a factual issue, the dynamics of true knowledge tend to go from the minority to the majority, not the other way round.

Emotional Factors

There is also an affective dimension of communication that has a very important role in moral discussion and in its democratic surrogate. However, this role is auxiliary to the epistemic value of the process of argumentation and collective decision.

Certainly, the presence of some emotional factors in moral discussion and democratic process can work against the discovery of moral truth. The phenomenon of "mass psychology" obviously reflects this fact. Often the judgment of individuals is quite transformed by uncontrolled emotions transmitted from one person to the other in a gathering of people. Additionally, the charisma or rhetorical ability of some compared to the shyness or awkwardness of others may well make even impartial parties uncertain as to who has the stronger arguments. For those who take seriously the idea of discovering moral truths through intersubjective discussions, we need mechanisms for curbing these dynamics.

The existence of these dynamics should not, however, obscure the fact that there are important ways in which emotions assist in the progress of a genuine process of argumentation. They lead us into the process of moral discussion in the first place and move us to convince others of the rightness of our positions. There is obviously an emotional element entailed in our effort to justify our actions and attitudes to other people, mainly to those who may be affected by them.[22] Emotions also play a role in assessing the interests of others. We must represent vividly to ourselves what is at stake for others in a certain conflict, and this requires an emotional process of identification. The assumption of the moral point of view—the assumption of impartiality—requires putting ourselves in the place, or "into the shoes," of fellow human beings, which involves the intellectual faculty of imagination and the emotional attribute of human sympathy.

Last, emotions contribute to the process of argumentation through the informal sanctions of blame and social isolation levied against those who commit evident mistakes or self-serving faults in the process of argumentation. These mistakes occur when statements do not represent genuine arguments; when arguments are merely superficial ways to disguise self-interested positions; when a person is not prone to justify his or her position to the rest; when a person is inconsistent with stands taken on other occasions; and when a person is committing apparent logical or factual errors. Of course, the desire to avoid social blame is a powerful motive for abiding by the rules of argumentation and trying to look as impartial as possible. Obviously, the easiest way of appearing to be impartial is by actually being impartial.

Bargaining Underlying the Democratic Process

Bargaining, also present in the democratic process, does not confer an independent value on it. Bargaining may, however, contribute to the epistemic value that argumentation and majoritarian decisions enjoy.

It should be noted first that bargaining on the basis of sheer interest often seriously threatens the democratic process. When individuals and factions compete on the basis of their respective strengths, values like equality are endangered; rights are not secured; problems of collective actions arise; and most of all there is no ground for presuming that the outcome of the process is just. This warning deserves serious consideration, and democratic advocates must continually defend the democratic process from factions attempting to press their interests through bargaining. To meet this challenge, it may be necessary to reorient the bargaining process to serve as a genuine procedure of argumentation and majoritarian decision.

If we adopted a procedure in which the triumphant position was the minority's view, we would be content with convincing only a few people, regardless of the interests of all the rest. On the other hand, if the discussion concludes only when the support of the simple majority is obtained, the participants of the discussion try to convince as many people as possible, and that requires them to take into account the interests of as many people as possible. Obviously, nobody is content simply to convince only a minority of the participants in the discussion. But even to have convinced a majority is not satisfactory, since at any moment prior to the vote the majoritarian coalition could disappear because some are convinced by the opposite approach or are enticed by groups of the minority coalition. Thus, politicians exhaust themselves in convincing more and more people, even when the polls tell them they already have majority support.

It is also important to evaluate the bargaining process that underlies the process of argumentation. In order for the democratic process to function properly, a particular minority may not always be isolated due to a factor that causes others to leave them behind regardless of the result of a bargain. Such a minority would constitute a frozen minority, since it always remains outside the majority. Irrational factors producing frozen minorities may include race, religion, and gender. In a working democracy, it is essential that the majority never be a definite group of the population but only a construction which refers to individuals who change constantly according to the issue at stake.

In sum, oddly enough, bargaining, with its accompanying threats and offers, may help achieve impartiality in the process of argumentation. It forces participants in this process to attend to as many interests as possible, offering solutions that satisfy those interests, for fear of losing the favor of the majority. When even a few persons' interests are unattended to, it is a threat for those holding the support of the majority, since a last-moment rush of support on behalf of a few dissenters could spread among the participants of their coalition.

The Collective Tendency Toward Impartiality

In the above analysis, I have focused on the factors in the democratic process that can lead the individual toward impartiality. It now needs to be stressed that this tendency is actually realized at the collective level within a process of collective discussion and majoritarian decision. This is due to two factors: the impact of Condorcet's theorem and an aggregation of satisfied interests.[23]

Condorcet's theorem states that if we assume that each member of a decision-making panel has a tendency to adopt the right decision, the probability that the decision is right also increases as the number of the members of the panel increases. As Lewis Kornhauser and Lawrence Sager say, this formal theorem may be illustrated by considering each person's decision as the draw of a marble from a bag with marbles of two colors: white for the correct decision and blue for the incorrect one, mixed in the proportion of the probability that each person reaches the correct decision.[24] As long as the proportion of white marbles exceeds half of the total amount of the bag, the more draws there are, the more likely that more than half of the marbles drawn will be white—that is, that the decisions are correct.[25] When we increase the number of people who participate in the decision, it is more probable that the decision is right, assuming that people have a tendency to make correct decisions. A corollary of the theory holds that decisions by simple majority rule are more probably correct for small groups than the decision of the most competent member of the group.[26] We can also assume that the more people support a decision, the more likely it is to satisfy their interests.

To begin with, we must resist at least one oversimplified assertion about the relationship between majority rule and impartiality. It would be wrong to assume that if unanimous consensus is a functional equivalent of impartiality, the closer we get to that unanimity, the closer we are to the ideal of impartiality. In fact, the failure to reach unanimity by only one vote may reflect an extreme deviation from impartiality. Nevertheless, there are cases in which the closeness to unanimity is an indication of approximate impartiality. When more votes support a certain solution, we can assume that interests of more people are satisfied than when the solution is supported by fewer votes. We can assume that each voter in that situation at least thinks her own interest is satisfied by the solution she proposes.

By itself, closeness to unanimity does not show the rightness of a solution. Consider again the criticisms raised against the utilitarian aggregation of preference satisfaction. Often the interests frustrated are protected by rights which cannot be overridden by the collective increase in satisfaction. Indeed, there are cases of insurmountable conflicts of rights. Such cases become more frequent when we assume that rights are violated not only by actions but also by omissions. In these cases, one should defer to the right of a higher order relative to the value of autonomy, regardless of the numbers of people involved on each side of the conflict.

Sometimes the rights in conflict may be of exactly the same order. In these cases, there is no way of avoiding infringement of the principle of the inviolability of the person. The aggregative principle of personal autonomy is the only one that controls the outcome. Therefore, when there is a conflict of rights of the same order which cannot be overcome in another way, the morally correct outcome is that which maximizes the satisfaction of interests protected by those rights. In the next chapter we shall examine the institutional arrangements necessary to put into effect this conception of representation. In this limiting case, perhaps quite frequently encountered, the majoritarian support for a decision is indicative of the rightness of the decision through the presumption that more of the interests at stake are satisfied by that decision.

The Reach of the Theory

The epistemic capacity of collective discussion and majoritarian decision to detect morally correct solutions is not absolute but varies according to the degree of satisfaction of underlying conditions of the process. The conditions include that all interested parties participate in the discussion and decision; that they participate on a reasonably equal basis and without any coercion; that they are able to express their interests and to justify them on the basis of genuine arguments; that the group has a proper size which maximizes the probability of a correct result; that there are no insular minorities, but the composition of majorities and minorities changes with the issues; and that people are not extraordinarily excited by emotions.

When the conditions promoting the epistemic value of democracy are not satisfied, democracy does not achieve this value. Not every process called "democratic" enjoys the conditions necessary to give it epistemic value. Consider the mob gathered in a square and approving by acclamation the proposal of a leader. The degree of epistemic value varies with the degree of satisfaction of the above-mentioned conditions. Therefore, this view of democracy not only partially justifies existing democracies which satisfy only in part the prerequisites for their epistemic value, it also serves as a charter for reforming democracies in order to enhance their capacity for acquiring knowledge of morally right solutions.

The epistemic value achieved by democracy must be compared with alternative available procedures for collective decision making. The epistemic value of democracy may well be very low but still higher than any other alternative for taking a collective decision. In particular, the epistemic value of democracy must be compared with the epistemic value of our own individual reflection on intersubjective moral matters. This value in general is quite low in light of the difficulty each of us has in representing vividly the situations and interests of people very different from ourselves. It is extremely unlikely that we can match the knowledge of the interests of others achieved by the concerned people themselves when defending their interests in a collective setting. Naturally, each of us is generally prone to rationalizations and to logical and factual mistakes that disguise, sometimes unconsciously, our own partiality. The democratic process must, therefore, be very far from ideal in order to justify an assertion that our own isolated individual reflection can more reliably achieve impartial solutions. If this is generally true with regard to our own reflection, the same applies to the isolated reflection of others, such as a dictator or the leaders of an aristocracy.

The epistemic value of democracy flows from the process of decision and discussion in general and not from any decision in particular. I do not believe that the majority is always right, nor can I endorse the demagogic slogan *vox populi, vox dei.* There may be many democratic decisions which surely are wrong, where our own individual reflection would have led to a more impartial solution. Often, it is obvious that the interests of some have been ignored and that the majoritarian decision is partial. But the general epistemic value of democracy provides a reason for observing the democratic decision even when our individual reflection tells us with certainty that the decision is mistaken. If we ignored the result of collective discussion and majoritarian decision each time our isolated reflection told us it was wrong, we would be giving priority to this reflection, observing the majoritarian decision only when it coincided with our own thinking. This would clearly contradict our conclusion that the democratic process is generally more reliable epistemically than the isolated reflection of any individual. Accordingly, we must observe the outcome of the democratic process even if we are sure that it is wrong, insofar as the conditions which ground its epistemic value are fulfilled.

This does not mean that, individually, we cannot disagree with the majority. In objecting to epistemic collectivism, I have acknowledged that it is possible to have access to moral truth by a process of individual reflection. However, this possibility seldom deserves more than asking for the reopening of the debate and continuing to defend the position rejected by the majority. The general epistemic value of democratic procedures gives exclusive reasons for observing its results even if in any particular case we doubt the moral wisdom of the decision. Otherwise, the democratic process would be undermined and the conclusion that it is more reliable from the epistemic point of view than alternative procedures would be frustrated in practice. Furthermore, it is important to stress that the epistemic value of the democratic process of discussion and decision is restricted to certain subject matters. This value does not arise, for instance, in the context of scientific or, in general, factual issues, even though there is some benefit in these domains from the process of discussion. There is no presumption in favor of scientific and general factual assertions just because they are supported by a majoritarian opinion. The same applies to religious and philosophical matters. I do not rely for the defense of my view of democracy on the support of the majority of my readers (besides, I am not very hopeful of obtaining it).

Nor is democracy to govern whole dimension of morality. This dimension is constituted not by intersubjective moral principles, such as the prohibition to kill or the permission of progressive taxation, but by self-referential or personal moral ideals. The latter distinguish themselves by evaluating actions for their impact not on the interests of other people but on the quality of the life and character of the agent. These are, for instance, ideals which refer to one's own sexual life, diet, attitude toward one's native country, business, and so on. As we saw in Chapter 3, the principle of personal autonomy prohibits the state from interfering with the free adoption or rejection of these ideals. Similarly, the democratic process has no epistemic value with regard to these personal ideals. Consequently, the state, even when acting democratically, cannot produce laws that provide us with epistemic reasons concerning these ideals over and above those provided by our own individual reflection.

The democratic procedure generating epistemic value is not an "ideal speech situation" but is meant to be quite realistic. Consider the earlier discussion concerning the condominium. Everybody has roughly the same opportunity to present their interests and to try to justify them. There is no permanent minority caused by some feature which is the basis of discrimination, and there are no extraordinary emotions disturbing the possibility of judgment.

Nonetheless, this kind of situation differs greatly from that confronted by the government of most modern industrial nations. These polities are far larger. The differences between the inhabitants are considerable, and there barely exists time for all citizens to express and defend their interests. The factual issues involved in the appraisal of interests are often extremely technical. There is a deep and complex interrelationship between groups making a decision and other contemporary, previous, or successor groups. The formation of factions defending crude interests seems unavoidable, and the bargaining process on the basis of self-interest appears unstoppable.

In assessing the adequacy of real democracies, attention must be paid to representation. For some democratic theorists—those who do not make the value of democracy depend on the people's interests—representation is a blessing. Representation not only resolves the impossibility of direct communication and the technicalities associated with large polities, but also neutralizes the power of factions. Representatives enjoy some isolation from the battles of crude interests and may thus help equilibrate them without allowing the monopolization of any one group of them.

Under my view of democracy, representation is at best a necessary evil. The intermediation of representatives in discussion and decision might benefit the process from the point of view of higher technical knowledge, but it weakens the awareness and consideration of the interests of people involved in different conflicts. While such awareness is crucial for the attainment of impartiality, representatives, who generally belong to more or less definite sectors of society, may very well lack the experience in ways of life that determine other preferences. Moreover, the intermediation of a representative, like that of an agent, always involves the possibility that she will put forward her own interests in managing the business confided in her. Nevertheless, the intermediation of the representative may be unavoidable, since the persons directly concerned may lack the time, expertise, and power to make their voices heard.

How could a conception of representation be framed that minimizes the evils involved in it? First, representation could be conceived of as a delegation to continue the discussion from the point reached by the electors during the debate leading to the choice of representatives. During the electoral campaign, representatives would pledge to defend particular values and ideas in a discussion between themselves and, as far as possible, with the people whose votes are being courted. Debate in the electoral campaign would reach a point at which it would be required to stop due to the need to vote. The result of the elections would mean the triumph of some of the positions put forth to the electorate. If the representation is indivisible—as in a presidential election—the representative should be obliged to implement that position and to continue his own reflection from that standpoint, trying to use his own technical knowledge to arrive at specific ways to implement the views he was elected to represent. If the representation is divisible—as when a collective body is elected—the body should seek to reflect the support that each position received among the electors and the number of representatives disposed to support that position within the collective body. These representatives should continue their collective deliberation from where the electorate left it at the end of the electoral campaign, also trying to achieve further specificity of the positions in question by engaging in discussion and drawing upon the necessary technical knowledge.[27] Sometimes it may be necessary to recall the representatives so that the common people can discuss the issues at stake directly and decide by themselves what should be done. As we shall see in the next chapter, it is imperative to look for some forms of direct democracy under the deliberative conception of democracy that I am defending here.

Political parties also act as intermediaries in the democratic process and may help to materialize further this view of representation insofar as the parties are organized around ideological stands, systems of values, and models of society, and not on the basis of pure interests. As I said earlier, the epistemic value of democracy requires that people participate in the democratic debate not only to present their interests but also to justify them on the basis of normative propositions, which should be general, universally applicable, final, and acceptable from an impartial point of view. It is obvious that in a modern polity this poses a difficulty, since it is hard for millions of people to become amateur moral and political philosophers trying to articulate principles that justify the solution they propose for a current conflict. Political parties may simplify this task enormously, offering to the electorate a menu of ideological stands that try to harmonize conflicting interests that can be defensible from an impartial point of view. This crucial service deteriorates when parties simply serve as obvious representatives of economic or social groups and make little effort to try to justify the interests of those groups impartially.

Another major problem concerning implementation of my view of democracy involves the question of inclusion. Who should a democratic polity include in order for the process of collective discussion and majoritarian decision to preserve its epistemic value? The theoretical answer under the view of democracy defended in this chapter is quite clear. The polity should include as full citizens all those whose interests are at stake in a conflict and may be affected by the solution adopted through the democratic process. Of course, there is a practical question of how to delimit that involvement, since most policies adopted by a country, particularly if the country is powerful, may affect the interests of far away people. One might object to foreign interventions based not on moral soundness but on their display of epistemic elitism on moral matters. Those interventions substitute the judgment of the government of a foreign country for that of the people who are directly affected by a certain measure.

Under this view, decentralization may be necessary not only for allowing possibilities of direct democracy but also for ensuring that only those whose interests are affected will participate in taking the decision. On the other hand, some kinds of centralization—for instance, through confederations—could be needed where a certain policy or measure has effects that impinge on interests of people subject to different jurisdictions. Similarly, it may be necessary to use changing gradations of citizenship. Some decisions may affect only some subgroups of that polity, while other decisions may affect subgroups that also comprise members of other polities.

The problem of inclusion is also related to the question of the capacity for citizenship. By holding an interest that cannot be known as well by a third person, one satisfies the principal reason for allowing citizenship. Of course, the person in question must have the minimum capacity to identify that interest, to put it forth, and to try to justify it to the others. This allows the usual exclusion of minors and mentally disturbed individuals, though perhaps they should be represented in the political process, just as they are represented in other activities in which their interests are involved. On the other hand, it would not be justified, for instance, to make exclusions based on the commission of crimes. In the same way that capital punishment should be banned on the grounds that it excludes somebody from the process of moral discourse,[28] the commission of a crime cannot justify excluding representation of the criminal's interests in the political process. The criminal's voice should be heard in the task of justifying a certain solution.

The Superiority of the Epistemic View of Democracy

This view of deliberative democracy and its epistemic value has numerous advantages over competitors reviewed in the preceding chapter. I shall try to show this by probing how this conception of democracy fares when confronted with the problems that were not properly solved by the alternative views: the apparent paradox of the superfluousness of law, the dilemmas of collective action, and the acknowledgment of the counterweights of the two other dimensions of constitutionalism (specifically, the recognition of basic rights and the preservation of a continuous legal practice).

The Paradox of the Superfluousness of Government

Under the epistemic view, the laws enacted democratically constitute not substantive reasons but epistemic ones. Therefore, laws—always reducible to factual circumstances—do not by themselves provide reasons for justifying actions and decisions. Nor does this view deny the importance of autonomous reasons—principles accepted because of their validity or intrinsic merits, not because they were enacted or endorsed by some authority. The significance of laws enacted democratically, according to this view, is that they provide reasons for *believing* that there are reasons for action and decision. The democratic laws are not in and of themselves reasons for acting and deciding.

Because democratic laws provide epistemic reasons for believing that there are moral reasons for actions, there exists a sharp contrast between democratic and nondemocratic governments. The latter generate no epistemic value and therefore their laws are not reasons for believing that there are moral reasons for actions. With regard to nondemocratic regimes, there is no presumption of justice that justifies one's suspension of her own reflection. Laws enacted by authoritarian governments are fully subject to the paradox of their superfluousness for practical reasoning. Only as a matter of a continuing practice do they have any significance for practical reasoning, and it is very unlikely that there are moral principles justifying the preservation of this sort of practice.

This conclusion is extremely relevant for countries that have experienced authoritarianism in their recent past and that still have laws enacted by the past dictatorship on the books. In Argentina, for instance, the "doctrine of *de facto* governments" developed by the Supreme Court said that such laws outlived the regime that created them, even though they could not be treated the same as democratic ones. From 1983 to 1989, state agencies took the view that these de facto laws should not be recognized if their moral content is obnoxious.[29]

The epistemic quality of democratic laws certainly varies according to how far the process of collective discussion and majoritarian decision has complied with the conditions grounding that value. When those conditions are not fully satisfied, the epistemic reasons provided by those laws are weaker and the competition with the epistemic quality of individual reflection may have a different result.

Collective-Action Problems

Many problems of collective action, including the prisoner's dilemma, the assurance game, the chicken game, and the battle of the sexes, arise because the participants in the situation are moved by self-interest. A suboptimal result, generally defined on the basis of the Paretian criterion of efficiency, is achieved, and therefore the interests of the participants are frustrated, just because the dominant option for each participant is a noncooperative one. Theories that justify democracy based on a dynamic determined by the actors' self-interests promote a model of interaction that often generates collective action problems. For instance, a democratic process molded on the pluralist conception of factions that struggle for their interests may initiate an inflationary process. The rational action for each group is to push for the increase of their wages or prices, with the result that everybody is prejudiced by the ensuing inflation. The discussion-focused view of democracy limits the probability of collective action problems insofar as the democratic process succeeds in attenuating the pursuit of that self-interest. In the above example, if some of the parties are constrained by the process of argumentation from pressing for laws increasing wages or prices in view of the collective harm perceived from an impartial point of view, then perhaps the threat of inflation can finally be averted.

The view of democracy that emphasizes its deliberative character also better handles problems of collective choice, like those detected by Arrow's theorem, than views explaining democracy as an aggregation of preferences. Arrow's paradox arises only if there are three or more options. This condition does not apply when a democratic process is seen as an aggregation of judgments justifying a certain balance of preferences, as opposed to a mere aggregation of judgments expressing those preferences.[30] Judgmental deliberation implies deciding between only two options: the truth or falsity of the judgment which is the object of decision. What must be decided, for instance, is whether capital punishment should or should not be established. Of course, there could be a whole chain of those judgments in a tree-like fashion. After deciding, for instance, that capital punishment should be imposed, then it is necessary to decide whether it should be by shooting or by electrocution. But every decision is binary, since in the end that which is being decided is the truth or falsity of a justificatory judgment. This is shown by way of posing questions in a referendum ("Is it true or false that shooting is the most humane way of carrying out capital punishment?"). This raises, of course, serious problems of setting the agenda and ordering the questions.

The Relation to the Ideal Constitution of Rights

Several of the views previously considered confront a serious problem of reconciling the substantive ideal dimension of a constitution—the "constitution of rights"—with the ideal procedural dimen-

sion of that constitution—the "constitution of power." Many conceptions of democracy are quite paradoxical in this respect. Typically,
they are each defended as the only model of authentic liberal democracy that respects individual rights. Ultimately, however, they offer
quite a weak justification of those rights. In fact, the substantive
values that these theories assert in order to justify democracy, such
as the preservation of freedom through the avoidance of tyranny,
could undermine the particular democratic model being defended,
as when those values suggest solutions different from those resulting from the democratic process.

The deliberative view of democracy based on the epistemic value
of the process resolves this tension between procedure and substance. There can be no tension between the recognition of rights
and the operation of the democratic process, since the value of
the democratic process arises from its capacity to determine moral
issues such as the content, scope, and hierarchy of rights. Therefore,
one does not confront the situation faced by other justifications of
democracy. Specifically, the value of the procedure cannot be outweighed by the results achieved through that procedure, since the
value of the procedure lies in producing results which are presumably valuable. Similarly, the democratic procedure is not contingent,
and we are not exposed to the demonstration that those good results
may be produced by other procedures. The results are presumed
to be good just because they are produced by that procedure. Consequently, the tension between the value of the procedure and the
value of the results simply dissolves because of the essential connection between the two.

A similar relation exists between the ideal constitution of rights
and the ideal constitution of power, that is, between the substantive and procedural ideal dimensions of the complex constitution.
The epistemic value of deliberative democracy overcomes the magnified conflict between these two constitutional dimensions, since
they are located at different levels and cannot compete with each
other. The ideal constitution of rights is the end product that we
tend to achieve. Its materialization in a certain society is what
makes the ideal constitution of power valuable, and the rights established constitute reasons for justifying actions or decisions. In contrast, the ideal constitution of power is the best means of gaining
access to the knowledge of the substantive ideal constitution and
of the justificatory reasons that it provides. The materialization of
the ideal constitution of power only provides reasons for believing

that certain rights are established by the substantive constitution. Rather than a tension between the ideal constitution of rights and the ideal constitution of power, the relationship more closely resembles that between watering the lawn and subsequently having green grass.

To some it may seem that I prefer the ideal constitution of rights over the ideal constitution of power. The former is the end, the latter only an instrument. In reality, however, the priority is reversed. We must establish the ideal constitution of power, since the ideal constitution of rights follows as a result. I recognize that it would be an expression of epistemic elitism to determine constitutional rights prior to or apart from the democratic process. Accordingly, discussion of rights in Chapter 3 should be taken as mere proposals to be considered within the democratic debate. The debate should not be fictitious or imaginary but a real one in which real people participate, as is presupposed when democracy is ascribed an epistemic value. The attempt to exclude from consideration any right from the deliberative process seems unwarranted. After all, for the same reasons that we resort to discussion of moral issues, we should utilize discussion in ascertaining rights. Besides, if we accept a strong conception of rights, comprising not only negative but also positive correlative obligations, almost all moral questions are associated with basic rights. Thus, to exclude rights from the scope of democracy potentially would leave the field of operations for democratic procedure completely empty. This would lead to the conclusion, defended by constitutionalists such as Alexander Hamilton, that a bill of rights is superfluous and antidemocratic.[31] Hamilton assumed that the constitution of power would create a bill of rights if we simply achieved the right political organization.

This cannot, however, be the whole of the matter. The epistemic value of democracy requires fulfillment of certain prerequisites without which there is no reason to defer to the results of democracy. Those conditions include the free and equal participation in the process of discussion and decision; the orientation of the communication toward justification; the absence of frozen and insular minorities; and the existence of a proper emotional setting for argumentation. Some of these prerequisites for democracy's epistemic value can be seen as the basis of a bill of rights, since they are goods that people must be given. These rights, prerequisites for the proper working of the democratic process, may be deemed "a priori rights."[32] Respect for these rights promotes and provides the epistemic value of democracy. Conversely, if these rights are not respected, for instance, by democratic decisions, a person engaged in practical reasoning has no reason to defer to the result of the process. He may resort to his own individual reflection, which has already told him that there is a right which the collective process has not respected.

The open-ended nature of a priori rights creates significant problems. As we saw in Chapter 3, social rights are the natural extension of classical individual rights as soon as we acknowledge that those rights are violated by omissions as well as by positive acts. Therefore, the freedom and equality which are preconditions of the democratic process are not only undermined by actions like threats or actual violence but are also frustrated by failing to give people equal means to participate effectively in the process of deliberation and majoritarian decision. The right of freedom of expression, which is of course an a priori right, requires not only freedom from censorship but also positive access to the means of communicating with others. If the public debate requires one to stand on a soap-box, one must have access to a soap-box. If it requires a microphone, one needs a microphone. If it requires radio and television, one must have access to broadcast time. Similarly, persons who are uneducated, seriously ill, or without proper housing cannot participate fully, or at least equally, in the process of collective deliberation and majoritarian decision.

It seems that if we make provision of all these resources preconditions for democracy's epistemic value, there will be very few questions for democracy itself to answer. Most political decisions consist in the proper distribution of these kinds of resources. If rights are interpreted in a broad way, by acknowledging that they may also be violated by omissions, democracy is deprived of most of its likely subject matter. Here we again have a conflict between procedure and substance and seem once more to be heading toward the paradox of the superfluousness of law, democratic law.

The paradox can be averted, however, because the epistemic view of democracy provides a way to achieve a balance between the prerequisites of democracy and its actual operation. We must not try to make the democratic procedure so perfect, by strengthening its preconditions to the maximum, that its scope of operation shrinks so much that it embraces almost nothing but coordination problems like the direction of traffic. If so, we would lose the most reliable epistemic procedure for gaining access to intersubjective moral solutions. The knowledge of a priori rights would be inaccessible to us if the democratic procedure of which they are prerequisites were epistemically sterile.

Therefore, we must acknowledge that the epistemic value of democracy is not all or nothing but gradual. The lack of full satisfaction of a priori conditions may deprive democracy of some degree of epistemic value, though not all. But the system may still enjoy considerable epistemic value. While the exact measuring point may be hard to determine, the dividing line should be correlated to the comparison between democracy and other procedures for taking collective decisions. If the failure to satisfy an a priori right makes the democratic process so epistemically weak that it is inferior to our own individual reflection, we must proceed, if possible, to do what is necessary to fulfill that a priori right even by nondemocratic means. But if the deterioration of the value of democracy due to the nonfulfillment of some a priori right is not so egregious that it is inferior to our own reflection, we should defer to the result of that process and trust that the process will provide for the fulfillment of the right in question. There is a certain baseline below which the democratic process has lost all capacity to improve itself. Above the baseline, democracy replenishes itself, working for the fulfillment of its own preconditions. The baseline, I repeat, is fixed by comparison with alternative methods of decision making, including our own reflection.

Although the epistemic view of democracy involves a tension between a priori rights as preconditions of the democratic process and the results of that democratic process, this tension is crucially different than the one confronted by other theories. Under other theories, it is the value of rights that confers value on democracy. When democracy fails to recognize those rights, it has no value, and when it does, it is irrelevant, since we already knew the rights which gave it value. Under my view, however, democracy's value consists in its reliability for discovering those rights. Nevertheless, some rights acquire epistemic value, since they are preconditions of the epistemic value of democracy, but their own epistemic value is a reflection of that of democracy itself. If the satisfaction of those rights does not allow democracy to operate, they do not acquire epistemic value. Under these circumstances, democracy may operate with a low epistemic value but at a value higher than that of other epistemic methods, justifying incomplete satisfaction of the a priori rights in question. Democracy can be balanced against some rights, and the theory provides guidelines for comparing the democratic process's epistemic quality and scope with other methods.

The Preservation of the Constitutional Practice

In discussing the tension between democracy and the preservation of a constitutional and legal practice, I compared the historical constitution with the ideal one that establishes a valid set of rights and a legitimate organization of power.[33] I argued that the preservation of the legal practice founded by a certain constitutional event is valuable insofar as it can be legitimated by autonomous moral principles. But one cannot act in pursuit of those principles if it is not within the context of such a practice. Not all theories of democracy that I reviewed, however, account for the value of preserving a generally legitimate legal practice or provide for ways coherently to integrate this value with the democratic process.

The ideal constitution of power cannot lead to the ideal constitution of rights without the interposition of a historical constitution. The ideal constitution of rights is inferred not from a hypothetical procedure but from the operation of a real process of decision and discussion. Therefore, the only possible tension exists between the ideal constitution of power and its materialization through a historical constitution which can be closer or further away from the former's prescriptions. When the democratic procedure established in the historical constitution adequately approaches the ideal constitution of power, the historical constitution of rights presumably coincides with the ideal constitution of rights. This identity is not absolute, however, since we may deploy a different ideal constitution of rights to criticize the real one as part of the permanent debate about its moral validity. At the same time, we must recognize that the configuration of rights in the historical constitution has a rebuttable presumption in favor of its coinciding with the ideal one.

The democratic process may, however, undermine the continuation of the legal practice. Some democratic decisions may fundamentally challenge strong expectations created by past decisions. It may be anticipated that future decisions will not take current ones into account but will adopt a completely different path. This weakening of the legal practice may determine the effectiveness of democratic decisions or the decisions taken by other legitimate procedures, such as adjudication. A democratic decision may thus weaken legal practice. Therefore, one must ask whether a person engaged in practical reasoning may disregard the democratic decision in extremely serious cases. Consider, for instance, a fully democratic decision that goes clearly against the text of the constitution, or against a principle that has been consistently endorsed by thousands of other democratic decisions.

This conception of the democratic process, relying on the impartial contemplation of everybody's interests to give it value, must account for the change of interests along time. People may well change their minds. More important, people themselves change continuously. Some die or emigrate and others immigrate or are born. We need a continuous voting method to account for the changes of people and their preferences, and even more a way to integrate the result of the new votes with those taken in the past and future. Moreover, there is a problem of partially overlapping interests in that the decision taken by a certain town of a certain nation in some way affects the interests of a neighboring town, though not enough to justify that its inhabitants also participate in the decision. We need to account for the votes of neighboring groups.

This need to integrate into our practical reasoning different democratic results obtained at different times and different places is perfectly congruent with the need to preserve the legal practice founded by a certain successful constitutional event. The legal practice is continuously fed by democratic decisions imbued with epistemic value and moral principles. Thus, a moral basis may be inferred not just for a specific, present decision but also for those decisions taken in times and places surrounding that specific decision. These principles should also be applied to evaluate the legitimacy of the whole practice constituted by successive democratic decisions. If the present decision endorses a principle that completely disregards relevant past or future decisions, the person engaged in practical reasoning can try to construct a moral principle that takes into account not only the present decision but also the content of other decisions. By doing so, that person acknowledges that the epistemic value of democracy requires consideration of interests expressed in adjacent times and spaces in preserving the constitutional convention.[34]

Therefore, there are two reasons for concluding that the view of democracy based on its epistemic value explains better than any other the relationship between the ideal and historical constitutions. First, this view implies an almost automatic congruence between the rights recognized by the constitutional practice and the ideal set of rights, insofar as the real democratic process is not too far removed from the ideal one. Second, the view provides reasons for qualifying the result of present democratic decisions that undermine the constitutional practice, taking into account other democratic decisions made within the context of the same practice.

In this chapter, I have tried to present a theory of the value of democracy which differs radically from most of the ones reviewed earlier. Unlike utilitarianism, the economic theory of democracy, elitism, pluralism, and consent theory, the deliberative conception of democracy sees democracy as deeply intertwined with morality and relies on its power to transform people's preferences into morally acceptable ones. Unlike the doctrine of popular sovereignty, perfectionism, or dialogic conceptions that do not rely on the epistemic value of the democratic process, the view of democracy defended here tries to respect a set of strong liberal assumptions.

The deliberative view of democracy grounded on its epistemic value emerges once we simultaneously confront the problem of moral cognition and try to avoid the extremes of Rawls's world of individual reflection and Habermas's populism. My position implies that the consensus reached after an exercise of collective discussion must have some reliability as to the knowledge of moral truths. But that reliability cannot completely exclude any trust in our own individual reflection in order to express our arguments in the discussion.

Even if this epistemic constructivism is considered viable, the harder step is transferring the epistemic value of the informal process of moral discussion to institutionalized democratic procedure. In the next chapter I shall examine the institutional arrangements which, in my view, would maximize the value of deliberative democracy under the epistemic justification provided in this chapter.

C h a p t e r   S i x

• • • • • • • • •

Establishing Deliberative
Democracy

In the last chapter I tried to put forth, more tentatively than it may at first seem, a theory of democracy that differs radically from most of those presented in Chapter 4. Like some of the conceptions reviewed in Chapter 4, mine relies on the capacity of democracy to transform people's interests and preferences. The way democracy turns selfish preferences into impartial ones is on the basis of dialogue. But I differ from others because I insist on the epistemic value of the consensus achieved through dialogue. In contrast to Habermas, I do not conceive of consensus, even when achieved under ideal conditions, as constitutive of just solutions, nor do I believe that the collective enterprise of discussion is the exclusive way of knowing those just solutions. My claim is only that deliberative democracy is the most reliable method for reaching those ends.

I think that the strongest objection to this kind of epistemic view of democracy comes from political practice. Ultimately, we must resolve the practical objections relating to the existence of widespread, abhorrent inequalities and staggering relative poverty within democratic polities. If the democratic process actually has an inherent tendency toward just solutions, allowing us to rely on its enactments in our justificatory reasoning, how can we explain the unjust distribution of resources produced by the democratic process? Consider, for instance, the striking contrast we notice along Fifth Avenue in Manhattan. One might say, in light of these inequalities, that liberal democratic constitutions are not "constitutions of liberty," paraphrasing the title of Friedrich von Hayek's famous book, but "constitutions of poverty." It might be alleged that the freedom enjoyed by some under democratic constitutionalism is achieved at the expense of the freedom of those who do not have enough resources to satisfy their most basic needs. It does not seem that democratic polities are more just than authoritarian ones from the social and economic perspective. Some data supports that assertion, but in the end it is not fully convincing.

From this perspective, our study of the theory of deliberative democracy might be considered as an exercise in legitimate utopianism. Legitimate utopianism sets forth an ideal model of society that is perhaps unattainable but does not treat as equivalent all situations which do not fulfill the model. It orders those situations according to how far they are from satisfying the elements of that ideal model. In the case of democracy, the order depends on the degree to which the conditions that give the democratic process its epistemic value are fulfilled and on institutional arrangements allowing different degrees of satisfaction of those conditions.

To counter the challenge grounded in the reality of politics, we must show a correlation between an ordering of social contexts and an ordering of political arrangements reflecting different degrees of satisfaction of the needs of their citizens. This ordering of political arrangements would involve variables related both to productivity and to distribution of resources. Of course, this method of correlation would face diverse conceptual and empirical problems. For instance, the same institutional arrangements may produce quite different degrees of satisfaction of the conditions underlying the epistemic value of democracy depending on historical, cultural, and psychological factors. We would have to define the very notion of human needs in order to determine different degrees of development.[1] We would also need to determine how to value the different distributions in each polity. How would a more extensive freedom unequally distributed compare to a more equitable distribution of a lesser amount of freedom? I shall not tackle the breathtaking difficulties entailed in answering this kind of question but shall assume that these difficulties can be overcome.

My ambition in this chapter is of another nature. I shall address another dimension of the practical challenge to the epistemic view of democracy. This one is more common to the constitutional lawyer, the political scientist, and the practical politician. It comes when the objection is raised that, given the empirical features of real contemporary societies, no possible institutional arrangements can satisfy the conditions underlying the epistemic value of democracy. If this were true, it would make this view of democracy utopian in the bad sense—a dream that has no connection to reality. As part of my undertaking, I will explore some institutional structures that are relevant, under certain empirical conditions, to deciding whether a particular democratic process is closer to or further away from the ideal model. With regard to each aspect of the institutional structure we are going to review, I shall point out the deficiencies that often cause the democratic process to fail to produce morally acceptable results.

Direct Democracy

Political representation can be either a valuable asset or a necessary evil. For a pluralist, representation is an intrinsically valuable institutional mechanism, since it creates an equilibrium between the pressures of different self-interested groups through the intermediation of a political class. Therefore, pluralists generally shy away from direct democracy, fearing that it leaves the field open for the untrammeled manipulations of factions over those normally ignorant of the complications involved in making serious political decisions. In the deliberative conceptions of democracy, the use of a small group that makes decisions affecting a larger group implies a hiatus in the process of deliberation. That hiatus must have a negative impact on the reliability of the process.

The epistemic justification of democracy adopts the second view of representation rather than the first. Mediation through representatives is one of the main distortions of democracy that pulls it away from ideal moral discussion's maximum epistemic value.

For the moment, I begin with the conventional view that some degree of representation is necessary in a large polity given the impossibility of face-to-face discussion at the national level, the complexity of current political issues, and the need to respect personal autonomy. Respect for personal autonomy implies that considerable time must remain for citizens to pursue personal interests. Where democracy is a substitute for moral discussion, representation should be a delegation to continue the discussion the citizens have begun. Discussion should be continued from the consensus reached in the electoral process so as to achieve more detailed conclusions with regard to the implementation process. But what needs to be emphasized is, as I said in the preceding chapter, that representation is a necessary evil, and direct democracy should be mandatory whenever possible. Direct democracy enhances the epistemic quality of democracy and assists in making the historical constitution approach the ideal one.

There are many standard methods of direct participation for citizens in fairly large polities. A *plebiscite* consults the citizenry about a particular measure, such as an international treaty or a loss of sovereignty. A *referendum* seeks the population's endorsement or rejection of a proposed or existing statute or constitutional amendment. An *initiative* is a way through which citizens, above a certain number, petition for the consideration of a legislative measure. A *recall* consists in petitioning by a number of citizens, also above certain threshold, so that a certain official may be removed from office.

Due in part to the influence of populists in the late 1880s and 1890s, several states and towns in the United States adopted procedures of initiative, referendum, and recall.[2] The constitutions of many Western countries—Switzerland, France, Italy, Spain, Canada, Australia, Uruguay, Brazil, Chile—establish different possibilities for direct popular participation. There have been occasions in many countries when a significant question was solved by a popular consultation. Consider the plebiscite that legitimized the withdrawal of France from Algeria in 1958; the advisory referendum through which the British people were consulted in 1975 about remaining in the European Community; the plebiscite through which Gen. Augusto Pinochet tried unsuccessfully to extend his rule in Chile in the late 1980s; and the popular consultation to which President Raúl Alfonsín of Argentina subjected the ratification of the treaty with Chile in 1989.

The benefits and risks of these methods of direct participation by common citizens in centralized decisions have long been the object of much controversy. Plebiscites and referenda at the national, provincial, and local levels may be the only way to overcome the pressures of interest groups or the inefficiencies of politicians.[3] Of course, plebiscites and referenda should be carefully regulated and should never be used to expand executive power. While one may praise direct participation, it is very difficult to make it operative against well-known risks of manipulation and take-over by factions.

Hitler and, more recently, Pinochet, for example, tried to manipulate plebiscites to their own advantage. Informal means of participation may also be taken over by fanatics or interest groups. Fanatics have a better chance to dominate informal means of participation, since they have intense, sharply focused interests, unlike ordinary citizens, who have so many interests and commitments that they cannot justify spending their time in interminable discussions.[4]

Many of the arguments for and against direct democracy are reviewed in Thomas E. Cronin's research on the subject.[5] Opponents of these methods frequently argue that common citizens are not sufficiently well informed and intellectually prepared to grasp the complex issues sometimes involved in these decisions; that their opinions are often manipulated by groups having access to the media and money to launch a propaganda campaign; that methods of direct democracy undermine the confidence of a political class and its continuity; and that these methods frequently infringe the rights of minorities and manifest deeply ingrained prejudices.

Cronin analyzes these arguments with equanimity and concludes that although direct democracy involves dangers, these dangers have generally been overstated. For instance, although referenda and initiative have occasionally expressed biases against minorities, they have not infringed any more than legislatures may have done. He asserts that "direct democracy measures in recent years have not generally had the effect of diminishing minority rights."[6] Similarly, Cronin responds to the worry that voters are not competent to tackle complex issues:

> Citizen-voters have responded more responsibly than critics anticipated. Although unusual measures and a number of discriminatory issues have found their way onto state ballots over the past eighty-five years, they have rarely won support from the voters. Part of the explanation is that voters are able to make good judgments—especially when an aggressive press, community and state officials, and other leaders make it their civic responsibility to help shape public opinion. . . . The process is not foolproof, yet bad legislation probably gets approved about as often in the initiative and referendum process as it does through the legislatures.[7]

One can distinguish technical aspects of a policy from normative ones. Whereas experts should provide technical advice to a decision maker—be it a legislature, the people at large, or an individual person—every normal and mature individual is able to judge the normative aspects of a policy. Likewise, Cronin denies that legislatures get weaker by a society's resort to direct democracy.[8] He acknowledges, however, that the procedures can be manipulated. The use of huge amounts of money by certain interests groups in campaigns, the unequal access to the media, and manipulation of the way in which issues are set forth and signatures obtained may distort the results. He proposes, therefore, a set of regulations for carrying out direct democracy. Cronin also opposes initiatives and referenda at the national level, since too many national issues involve defense or foreign relations, which would require significant continuity over time.

One ultimately comes away from Cronin with less enthusiasm for direct participation, not because he recognizes its dangers if left unregulated, but because the advantages he finds in it are much less impressive than its supporters proclaim. For instance, he says:

> Direct democracy processes have not brought about the rule by the common people. . . . Direct democracy devices occasionally permit those who are motivated and interested in public policy issues to have a direct personal input by recording their vote, but this is a long way from claiming that direct democracy gives a significant voice to ordinary citizens on a regular basis. That early claim was considerably overstated. A related claim was that direct democracy devices would lessen the influence of special interests. These devices may have done this in some respects, but special interests are still present and can still afford highly paid, high-caliber lobbyists. . . . On the other hand, direct democracy devices have sometimes allowed less well-represented interests to bring their messages before the public. . . . Ultimately, however, single individuals unwilling to join groups and form coalitions are unable to use direct democracy processes. . . . Direct democracy was also supposed to stimulate educational debate about important policy issues. It does, yet the debate usually lasts only five or six weeks. . . . The most unfortunate deficiency of this claim . . . is that the side with more money too often gets to define the issue and structure the debate in an unbalanced way. Whereas a town meeting gives all sides an equal chance to speak, money and court rulings permitting unlimited spending promote a system in which the better-financed side can, and often does, outspend the other by a dramatic margin.[9]

Despite these disappointments, Cronin lists several valuable advantages. They include providing escape valves for popular discontent, enabling better control of corrupt officials, and allowing voices not normally taken into account to be heard. These methods, however, do not dramatically change the nature of the political process and enhance its epistemic value to heights that prevent the most widespread forms of injustice.

This analysis leads us to ask whether it does not reveal a weakness in the epistemic justification of democracy. If this epistemic justification were correct, there should be an obvious gain in justice each time the process of democratic discussion and decision moves closer to the original process of moral discussion. If representatives are eliminated, we should expect that distortions in achieving impartiality would wither away. Even when Cronin is positive, he is not as overwhelmingly favorable as would be suggested by the epistemic theory of democracy.

We must pause to consider the differences between the methods of direct democracy and the process of the original practice of moral discussion. While direct democracy involves a direct expression of the voters' opinions regarding issues or the performance of officials, it does not reflect a genuine discussion. The participants simply answer yes or no. The epistemic view of democracy relies primarily on the process of collective deliberation and validates majoritarian decisions only as an essential mechanism for pushing that deliberation in the direction of impartiality. It differs from populist views of democracy that simply emphasize the value of the majoritarian method of decisions, no matter how that majority is achieved.

In a discussion, the participants themselves set forth the questions, express where their interests lie, and try to justify those interests to others. A discussion is not a mere sum of individual reflections operating in isolation but a collective process in which the position of each participant gets increasingly focused in reaction to the arguments of others. The reflection of each is enriched by that of the others.

None of this occurs in a referendum, initiative, or recall, where common citizens only get the messages that politicians manage to send through the media. At best, the members of the public only reflect privately about the different positions presented. The participants in these forms of direct democracy almost never have the opportunity to raise questions and objections to the proponents of the different positions. Exposure to the positions of others and to criticisms provoked by one's own position should generate a tendency toward impartiality. Nevertheless, this does not take place to a considerable extent in a "one-way" conversation where politicians or leaders of different interest groups do all the talking and the voters merely respond monosyllabically.

Given these considerations, traditional methods of direct participation in the centralized decisions of a polity are not accompanied by dramatic improvements in the general tendency toward more just solutions. Those improvements can only be expected if much more of the original process of moral discussion is replicated in the political process. Therefore, we must ask whether this is possible in a large and heterogeneous polity facing complex issues typical of modern industrial and postindustrial societies.

Some ideas have been proposed for introducing more genuine aspects of direct democracy in the political process of modern nations. Among the ideas commonly proposed is the use of modern technology, such as interactive television or computer networks, to enhance the exchange between the political or social leadership and common citizens. Such technology may possibly even permit an instant expression of the final opinion of those citizens. However, the extent to which the exchange of questions, arguments, objections, can take place among millions of people is quite uncertain.

Some theorists have proposed sampling small groups of people who reflect the tendencies and interests of the larger citizenry and asking this group to perform the roles of the public. For instance, Robert Dahl suggests selecting a "populus" for setting the agenda of political discussion and deciding different aspects of those issues.

> Suppose an advanced democratic country were to create a "minipopulus" consisting of perhaps a thousand citizens randomly selected out of the entire demos. Its task would be to deliberate, for a year perhaps, on an issue and then to announce its choices. The members of a minipopulus could "meet" by telecommunications. One minipopulus could decide on the agenda of issues, while another might concern itself with a major issue. Thus one minipopulus could exist for each major issue on the agenda. A minipopulus could exist at any level of government—national, state, or local. It could be attended—again by telecommunications—by an advisory committee of scholars and specialists and by an administrative staff. It could hold hearings, commission research, and

engage in debate and discussion. . . . The judgment of a minipopulus would "represent" the judgment of the demos. Its
verdict would be the verdict of the demos itself, if the demos
were able to take advantage of the best available knowledge
to decide what policies were most likely to achieve the ends it
sought. The judgments of the minipopulus would thus derive
their authority from the legitimacy of democracy.[10]

In a similar vein, James Fishkin has proposed forming panels of citizens selected randomly in order to discuss certain public issues with
candidates to elective offices.[11]

These ideas should be explored and implemented to test the assumptions made about the representativeness of the sets of people
chosen to represent the larger group. Nevertheless, it should be
stressed that they are another form of representation, based on randomness, and not a form of direct democracy in the strict sense.
The epistemic capacity of this form of representation depends on
the power of randomness, and yet there is no reason to think that
randomness by itself would produce a distribution of interests and
opinions reflecting larger society. At the very least, there must be
an earlier segmentation of the demos according to the number of
people within categories such as social class, gender, race, and religion. However, once we depart from pure randomness, the danger
of political manipulation becomes more serious.

I think we must be bolder, at least in our imagination, about
getting closer to direct democracy. It seems fairly clear to me that
the most pure form of democracy should emerge from a process of
political decentralization which would produce political units small
enough to make possible a process of face-to-face discussion and
collective decision. In and of itself, this is not so fanciful, since there
are many current examples of direct democracies in towns and small
cantons—mainly in the United States and Switzerland. More fanciful, I would say, is the idea that the most important political issues
facing a nation may be decided through popular assemblies. My proposal would require that issues like abortion, criminal codes, taxation, social services, education, and police protection be transferred
down to the level of small political units, where all those concerned
could actually meet and discuss the issues. This would also increase
the possibility of people choosing the polity to which they want to
belong.

Today we are witnessing a globalization of many issues, including trade, basic human rights, defense, and the fight against terrorism and organized crime. As these important subjects are transferred up to supranational bodies, such as the European Council of Ministers, the remaining concerns are issues of social morality dealing with unending conflicts of rights and resource distribution. Once a priori rights are secured by supranational organizations and highly contested political issues like defense or foreign relations become greatly constrained by the emergence of continental if not universal organizations, it is possible to allow nationalists and localists to have their way in defining the scope of the demos in which conflicts of interests can be decided.

Ultimately, the impartial solution of these issues requires empathy for the interests of others. This empathy occurs to the greatest extent in small communities. Perhaps it is not coincidental that as certain issues are globalized, localism tends to emerge precisely in the regions in which the globalization process is most advanced, such as Europe. Liberals have not adjusted their reflexes to this new reality and do not appreciate that globalization makes localist tendencies much less dangerous than they were decades ago. For instance, a European Community formed by units such as Scotland, Catalonia, the Basque country, Croatia, and Slovakia is not so prone to conflicts, discrimination, and persecutions as long as those units share a common framework of rules and institutions.

Of course, this level of decentralization is not sufficient for direct democracy, since it does not permit face-to-face discussions. We must still decide how to implement it in very small units as well as in bigger ones. Moreover, we must continue to explore new ways of popular participation. Public hearings should be utilized when conflicting interests between different sectors of the population are at stake. Recipients and employees of public services—such as schools, hospitals, transportation, and energy suppliers—should share in their administration and control. Similarly, we must address the issue of the range of democratic decisions, raising the question of whether there should be democracy in the workplace and how it should be conducted. There is an underlying ideal that all should have a say and some control in work-related decisions. While workers have influence through their power to quit, it is fairly obvious that this power is generally less than completely free insofar as the choice between acceptable jobs is normally quite restricted for most people. These extremely complicated questions necessarily involve the justice and efficiency of the economic system within which the economic unit at stake operates. It would require another full study to delineate even the rudiments of a theory of workplace democracy.[12]

The Problem of Political Apathy

Various authors have proposed diagnoses and prescriptions for the "crisis of democracy"—apathy. For instance, Samuel Huntington, Michel Crozier, and Joji Watanuki, who clearly endorse the pluralist or elitist view of democracy,[13] believe the crisis is caused by an overload of popular demands that the system cannot satisfy. They advise curtailing mechanisms of expressing those demands. In contrast, C. B. Macpherson, who endorses a populist conception of democracy, thinks that the crisis of present pluralist democracies is produced by inequalities caused by lack of participation. Macpherson's therapy consists in increasing citizens' intervention in politics.

My position is that the causes and solutions of the crisis of democracy cannot be detected without a conception about what makes democracy valuable. Otherwise, we might end up fortifying something at the cost of its value. Political apathy in significant sectors of the citizenry is obnoxious to democracy, since relevant interests and opinions will not be considered. Increased political involvement should not overload the system with insatiable demands but may give people a sense of responsibility in voicing concerns. After all, when concerns are raised, the people must look for resources to satisfy them. Participation attenuates the abyss between government and society, felt even in working democracies, which makes government alien and aloof.[14]

The goal of increased political involvement has often been rejected for implying a perfectionist view of democracy where an ideal of civic virtue is forcefully imposed. This critique is, in part, true. The solution, however, is not to give up on participation but to select mechanisms that do not absorb all the free time of citizens. By the same token, we should not suppose that requiring moderate citizen involvement risks perfectionism.

Involvement can be required for several nonperfectionist reasons. First, a democratic government is a public good. As such, it is unfair to enjoy its benefits as a free-rider. Second, to participate in public discussion and decision is essential for protecting the interests of others who are similarly situated. If I am a music lover and there is a dispute about whether a public building will be devoted to a music hall or to a basketball stadium, I would be greatly harmed if other music lovers remained politically passive. To make these music lovers participate in the process would not be perfectionism but would prevent that harm. Third, participation may be required as a legitimate form of a nonperfectionist paternalism, since voluntary participation can create a prisoner's dilemma where each refuses to assume the costs of participation because of the negligible gain of voting in a large group. The poor and less educated, for whom participation is most costly, reason in the same way. Thus, their interests are not represented in the political process, with the consequence that the final solution is greatly partial against them. As in all situations in which collective-action problems arise, there is no way out by individual decision. Instead, it requires either a general change of self-interested motivation, which ends up frustrating itself, or external coercion. In the political process, this dynamic feeds on itself, because the nonparticipation of certain groups results in the absence of attractive political options. In this way, the tendency not to participate is reinforced.

It is sometimes argued that there are no significant differences between the political opinions of voters and nonvoters, and therefore that voters represent nonvoters.[15] But this argument is questionable. According to Robert M. Entman, for instance, the data indicate that the current electorate does not represent the entire public. He believes that knowledgeable nonvoters are significantly more liberal than both knowledgeable voters and ignorant voters. He writes, "Contrary to the popular conclusion in political science, voters probably do not fully represent those who stay home. Nor do election outcomes accurately reflect what would happen if everyone voted."[16] For these reasons, I have defended the preservation in Argentina of the present system of compulsory voting, a system shared by countries such as Italy and Australia.[17] It helps solve the collective-action problem, which otherwise may frustrate the interests of many participants and distort the tendency of the democratic process to create impartial solutions. Abstentionism may in fact cause deterioration of the democratic process, since it is harmful not only to the very people who decline to vote but to all citizens.

The arguments against obligatory voting do not seem to be particularly strong. Unlike other compulsive ways of making people politically involved, compulsory voting cannot provoke the charge of perfectionism, since the time and effort necessary to vote in a thinking manner are not so excessive as to impede people in developing their plans of life or pursuing personal matters. Also, compulsory voting does not preclude expressing displeasure with politicians and parties—a legitimate aim of abstention—since one can always express that displeasure by voting so that the ballot is not imputed to any party or candidate. Finally, if somebody has a special reason, based perhaps in their ideal of the good, not to vote—such as in the case of some religious sects in Israel—one can always conscientiously object and seek a special exemption from the general obligation.

Under certain political and social conditions, extensive popular involvement in the political process may pose serious dangers for the stability of the democratic system. The continuity of the constitutional practice may be threatened. The improvement of democracy's epistemic quality should be hailed, but it may endanger the preservation of constitutional practice, which, unusually enough, is a necessary condition for the effectiveness of democratic process. In the end, democracy may defeat itself not just because of decisions taken but also because of the impact of those decisions on the prerequisites for the democratic process—the continuity of the constitutional practice.

This point can be illustrated by examining the case of Argentina. Universal, secret, and obligatory voting was introduced in Argentina by law in 1912 and applied from 1916 to the present. This law completely changed the political landscape of the country, putting an end to more than fifty years of dominance by a social and political class that coexisted peacefully with two conservative parties. In the past, this alliance had manipulated the electoral process by various forms of fraud, particularly by preventing or discouraging most people from voting. However, the mandatory voting law multiplied by approximately three times the numbers of people who voted in general elections. After its enforcement, right-wing parties could never again win over the Radical or the Peronist parties in open and free elections.

This may seem to be an inevitable result of democracy, but it also had the effect of putting democracy in jeopardy. Once the social and economic establishment was unable to gain access to power through legitimate methods, it resorted to coups d'état to seize power. This hypothesis seems to be confirmed by the fact that soon after the introduction of obligatory voting, the country entered a period of political instability that lasted for half a century, with military coups overthrowing almost all elected governments. The coup leaders could rely on the support of corporatist formations representing the landowners, industrialists, and bankers.

The impact of high degrees of popular participation on the stability of the democratic system may also be responsible for one of the perennial problems of the presidential system of government. Fred Riggs remarks that as participation increases in presidential systems, the contradiction is more acute between the interests of those capable of funding a presidential campaign and those of the voting majority. In contrast, parties in parliamentary elections representing the interests of the poorest sectors of society are capable of generating wider participation without straining the system. According to Riggs, the presidential system works smoothly when turn-out is low. He writes: "Norms and motivations based on parliamentary democracy are more apt for stimulating a broad participation than the norms of a presidentialist republic. Or, to present a negative example, the participation of the masses is less threatening for the survival of a parliamentary regime than for that of a presidentialist one."[18]

This risk is compounded by the threat that increased popular participation poses for a minority that economically benefits from the status quo. This risk is greater when there is no effective protection of property rights against democratic decisions possibly impinging on an existing property distribution. Karl Polanyi describes how the United States and Britain dealt with the conflict between democracy and property:

> When in the 1920s the international system failed, the almost forgotten issues of early capitalism reappeared. First and foremost among them stood that of popular government. . . . The more viciously the labor market contorted the lives of the workers, the more insistently they clamored for the vote. The demand for popular government was the political source of the tension. Under these conditions, constitutionalism gained an utterly new meaning. . . . The American Constitution, shaped in a farmer-craftsman's environment by a leadership forewarned by the English industrial scene, isolated the economic sphere entirely from the jurisdiction of the Constitution, put private property thereby under the highest conceivable protection, and created the only legally grounded market society in the world. In spite of universal suffrage, American voters were powerless against owners. In England it became

the unwritten law of the Constitution that the working class must be denied the vote. The Chartist leaders were jailed; their adherents, numbered in millions, were derided by a legislature representing a bare fraction of the population, and the mere demand for the ballot was often treated as a criminal act by the authorities.[19]

Jennifer Nedelsky has shed light on the Federalist strategy in the United States "to try to remove the most fundamental and most threatened issues from the contested political realm by designating them 'law.'" She writes that "with property as one of the chief subjects of judicial review, the Supreme Court could call upon the traditions of the common law to support their assertion that the issues at hand were fundamentally legal, not political."[20] Similarly, electoral apathy, not easily overcome once established due to collective-action problems, protects the status quo in the United States and preserves the stability of the whole system.

When no mechanism functions to protect vested interests from the operation of the democratic system, as happened in Argentina, the stability of the system may be endangered.[21] In the Argentine case, the introduction of universal, secret, and mainly obligatory voting made it impossible for parties in favor of the status quo to win a clean and open election. When one considers that the Argentine Supreme Court has been quite ineffective in defending a strong right of property against the advances of progressive and populist governments, it is understandable that elite groups sought alternative avenues of access to power and supported repeated coups d'état.

In order to preserve democracy, a dynamic must be created that will preserve the preferred option of relevant groups. This has been illuminated, with special attention to the Latin American context, by Adam Przreworski. He writes: "Democracy is consolidated when it becomes self-enforcing, that is, when all the relevant political forces find it best to continue to submit their interests and values to the uncertain interplay of the institutions. Complying with the current outcome, even if it is a defeat, and directing all actions within the institutional framework is better for the relevant political forces than trying to subvert democracy. To put it somewhat more technically, democracy is consolidated when compliance—acting within the institutional framework—constitutes the equilibrium of the decentralized strategies of all the relevant political forces." He adds that compliance depends on the existence of a probability of winning in future political competition. Conversely, this implies that "if some important political forces have no chance to win distributional conflicts . . . [they] will turn against [it]." It is therefore critical that "democratic institutions . . . give all the relevant political forces a chance to win occasionally in the competition of interests and values."[22] In Argentina, the perception of the political and social establishment that it did not have a chance to win legitimate elections may have created the stormy political dynamics between 1930 and 1983.[23]

These dynamics can be schematized in the following way: While an inequality may be reduced in an alternative state of affairs (the second situation), the party benefited by the greater inequality of the first situation may threaten to move to still a third situation in which the other party is still worse off than in the first. This disadvantaged person may have no other option than to attempt to move to still another state of affairs (the fourth situation), in which she is even worse off than in the first, and of course than in the second, but better off than in the third.

In the case of Argentina, the situation before the application of the mandatory voting law in 1916 was of a restricted democracy. One could say that the application of that law provoked a change toward almost a full liberal democracy. In turn, the displaced conservative groups have reacted since 1930, particularly during the "infamous decade" from 1932 to 1943, to produce a movement toward authoritarian regimes. These regimes involved highly unequal forms of representation. All sectors, even the dominant economic and social groups, suffered a loss of representation in comparison to the situation of the restricted democracy. After 1945, the popular sectors reacted, achieving a populist democracy which insured better representation than under both authoritarian regimes and restricted democracy, but worse representation than provided by full liberal democracy. From 1955 to 1983 there was a permanent oscillation between authoritarian regimes, restricted democracies, and populist democracies. Only after 1983 have we had the most serious attempt to reestablish a full liberal democracy.

As this example shows, the attempt to have a better form of democracy may ultimately result in a more degraded form of democracy or even to authoritarian regimes, since many people are threatened by the political participation of the least-favored sectors of society. That is one reason why democratic systems have not produced the just social states one would expect from the epistemic value they offer. In improving the value of the process through a more extended participation, we must be careful not to produce social reactions that may undermine the whole democratic process. Despite these risks—which must be considered, since they endanger the continuity of the historical constitution—the achievement of high levels of participation should be the permanent aim of political and judicial action.[24]

The stability of a political system, even when it implies the preservation of the historical constitution, should not be achieved at any cost. As we saw in Chapter 2, the practice that is the historical constitution is only the reference for an intermediate premise of justificatory practical reasoning. Ultimately, the practice must be justified by moral principles constituting the first premise of that reasoning. The central thesis of the preceding chapter is that the democratic process is the most reliable epistemic way for determining those intersubjective moral principles as long as those affected by decisions participate in a direct and reflective way. The goal must be full participation, otherwise the epistemic quality of the democratic process will remain weak and the democratic constitution will invariably be a "constitution of poverty."

Collective Communication and the Quality of Public Debate

Another dynamic diminishing the epistemic value of democracy, found throughout the modern world, is the poor quality of public debate. Discussion of principles of political systems, of general views of society, and of solutions to deal with social problems is often replaced by pictorial images of candidates, extremely vague statements of positions, and emotive appeals. The lack of seriousness in the whole process makes candidates, once elected, feel unobliged to follow the result of public debate.

This impoverishment of collective discussion is caused in large part by the presidential system of government, an aspect I shall address specifically in a later section. This system has the tendency to focus electoral campaigns on individual persons who are candidates for the unipersonal center of power, instead of focusing on public ideals or substantive proposals. The personality of the candidate, his or her family life as well as tastes and hobbies, are more important than positions on the size of the public sector, unemployment, or social security. It is true that something similar is also happening in parliamentary systems such as those in Britain or Spain, prompting discussion of more presidentialism in those systems. But the degree of this distortion in parliamentary systems is less than in presidential systems.

The presidential system has yet another impoverishing effect on public debate. The system allows a candidate to be elected president by a simple majority of votes. This poses the very serious risk of a president beginning his mandate with very little consensus, as was the case with Salvador Allende in Chile and Arturo Illia in Argentina. To address this problem, the system may contain some mechanism, such as a run-off or the electoral college, to guarantee that the victor receives an absolute majority, but that will increase the risk of polarization and bipartism where parties transform themselves into great coalitions without definite substantive content. An extreme example involves Uruguay, where the *ley de lemas* (literally, the "law of slogans") provides that each faction of a party can present candidates in general elections. Those factions that enjoy higher levels of support can absorb the votes of the other factions. The same effect is produced in open primaries, where people not affiliated with a party and without any commitment to its ideas vote in the party's internal elections for candidates. In such a case, the presidential candidate represents a party which is a coalition without a definite set of ideas. His own message must be as unsubstantive as possible in order to reach a wide range of social and cultural sectors. Otherwise, he cannot obtain the broad support needed to remain competitive. Hence, we get vague statements, an emphasis on emotive aspects, and contradictory promises.

The dynamics are significantly different in a parliamentary system. There, even if the election is dominated by a few personalities, any person in parliament, particularly if part of the majoritarian block, may end up as chief of government or as a member of the cabinet. At the very least, the possible candidates constitute leaders of the party and their personalities are much less relevant. This helps keep the public's attention on the party's ideology.

Parties in a parliamentary system are not adversely affected by substantive commitments. On the contrary, these commitments might be the only way of maintaining an identity and attracting those who desire representation of those ideas in parliament. The polarization and confrontation provoked by the binary nature of presidential politics is avoided, since a party that acquires a few seats in parliament may have a decisive role in forming a government. This also enhances principled discussion in parliament and the cabinet, since the governmental policies are determined by the consensus reached among parties of different ideological stances.

The deterioration of public debate in society is determined not simply by the dynamics of the presidential system but also by the mass media, particularly television, which so dominate the political process. Television transforms almost all events and debates into superficial spectacles prepared to entertain, giving rise to the political phenomenon that Giovanni Sartori has aptly described as "video-power." [25] These shows are intended not to illuminate public controversies and to make people reflect seriously about the substantive positions of different candidates or about the implications of the disputed policies, but to shock spectators with the latest scandal, to present political figures like glamorous stars, and to direct attention to the ridiculous or melodramatic. A premium is attached to anything that can be synthesized in an image or a slogan. Of course, this does not favor serious moral debate. As Robert Entman says, "The media feed a spiral of demagoguery, diminished rationality in policy making, heightened tendency toward symbolic reassurance and nostalgic evasion of concrete choices, and ultimately misrepresentation of the public." [26]

The deterioration of public discussion is also caused by lack of access to mass media. Equitable access is essential for the epistemic quality of public discussion, since mass media is the modern equivalent of the Athenian agora. It is the medium in which politics is exerted. When the mass media is almost completely in private hands—and of an oligopolistic character—the distortion is similar to what would have been produced if the agora had been replaced by a private theater, entrance to which was at the pleasure of the owner.[27] Of course, the situation is not improved if mass media is controlled by governmental entities, which in turn are controlled by the party controlling the government.

These considerations require careful evaluation of possible systems of distribution of access to the means of public communication. One distributive mechanism is the market. One advantage of the market in distributing opportunities for expression is clear in view of the value of personal autonomy. The market avoids the risks of perfectionism and discrimination in satisfying preferences, since it is a decentralized mechanism allowing resources to flow to the satisfaction of the most intense and widespread preferences, regardless of who is speaking or the content of that speech. The market also ensures that each individual is held responsible for her own preferences and interests, since each individual must assume the cost of satisfying those preferences. The market yields considerable pluralism. Any attempt to restrain an idea automatically creates an incentive for propagating it, since it converts the expression of that idea into a product in demand with insufficient supply.

Notwithstanding these advantages, the market has its limitations in achieving the good of enriched public debate. For instance, the market is not often neutral concerning preferences that are incompatible with the expansion of the market itself. Besides, those who can communicate their political ideas through private mass media are only those who have enough capital to control the media and buy the corresponding time. As Owen Fiss says, the market restrains the presentation through mass media of questions of public interest in two different ways. First, the market privileges select groups because of their economic power, creating programs and articles which are sensitive to their points of view. Second, the market allows profit and efficiency concerns to influence decisions about editorial or programming policy.[28] Also, Entman criticizes the market as a means of providing access to mass media:

> Even if journalism did feature analyses of ideas from many perspectives, or of historical context and trends rather than yesterday's ephemera, a proper "marketplace of ideas" could not be a market at all. In a real market, producers supply what consumers like, and stop supplying what they do not like. If news producers followed this practice, the media would supply only the popular ideas, an obvious insult to the free press ideal. Suppliers in the marketplace of ideas are emphatically not supposed to behave the way producers in real markets do. If they did, novel notions would not circulate widely; only low-profit (or non-profit) media could afford to tell unpopular truths in an unpopular style, since for mass-targeted media, unpopular is, by definition, unprofitable. Mass circulation media would say largely the same fashionable and expected things. It is unfortunate that journalism in the real competitive economy resembles this portrait more than it does the chimerical ideal.[29]

These disadvantages of the market mechanism for providing access to public communication justify a review of alternative mechanisms. One such alternative for distributing opportunities for expressing ideas is the political system. The advantages and risks of this mechanism for maximizing free expression and enriched public debate also emerge quite clearly. If we assume that the institutions charged with that task possess a democratic origin, one may expect an egalitarian and pluralist distribution of the opportunities for expression. But there is, obviously, a tendency among those who exert power to perpetuate themselves in it. Thus, there is often favoritism and corruption in granting spaces to express political opinions. This tendency may be attenuated by creating bodies that are independent of the administration, such as the British Broadcasting Corporation. It is always difficult, however, to avoid political influence while striving efficiently to manage the means of communication in the effort to enrich the political process and contribute to the self-development of the citizens.

The advantages and disadvantages of different methods of distributing opportunities for expression suggest the option of combining them so as to maximize their assets and minimize their deficiencies. Given that the sources of discrimination and distortion of these mechanisms are different, their combination in a *mixed* system allows for those who are excluded to find in other options appropriate channels of expression. The combination of mechanisms implies not only the coexistence of public and private property but also the convergence of diverse public and private agents who can interact at different stages of communication. For instance, the mechanism of direct state decisions may have an impact on the private media through the provision of spaces devoted to collective issues, or through subsides that encourage expression of minority views. In turn, the market may have an impact on the public media through some limited advertising or the acquisition of some spaces. A mixed system maximizes pluralism and neutrality, since the decisions concerning the allocation of opportunities of expression are as decentralized and participatory as possible. To realize this goal, control of the mass media must be distributed among diverse political units. Moreover, participation in that control by individuals and organizations—both formal and informal—should be promoted.

The deterioration of public debate is also caused by the ways in which electoral campaigns are conducted. Nothing is gained in democratic terms by the extremely emotive, commercial-like advertisements that characterize modern political campaigns. On the contrary, much is lost in terms of irrationality and the possibility of corruption, since the immense cost of campaigns must be borne by private interests. One ought to consider the use of voluntary agreements to get candidates to consent to the terms of a campaign, limit the extension of it, and proscribe advertisements that contain only names and slogans instead of ideas and proposals. Clearly, the way money is raised for electoral campaigns in most Western countries considerably harms the quality of the deliberative process and adversely affects its tendency toward impartiality.[30] Since candidates increasingly depend on private sources of funds—mainly due to the reliance on television—many possible candidates are excluded from the race or forced to give up at some stage. This dynamic greatly influences the commitments that the remaining candidates undertake with interest groups, shapes the way they present their views, determines who are the targets of their proposals, affects the issues they put forth in the public debate, and reduces participation by marginalizing a public ever frustrated by the sense that politics is beyond their influence. Some Western democracies have regulated private funding of electoral campaigns—as has been attempted in the United States after the Watergate scandal—but it is probable that nothing short of an absolute prohibition of private funding and the use of public financing combined with mandatory access to the media can overcome the grave distortions that the present system involves for the epistemic quality of the democratic process.

Decentralization: The Problem of Dispersed Sovereignty

Pluralism seeks a democratic system in which nobody is allowed to speak for the whole people. Popular will is dispersed through several temporal, spatial, and functional dimensions. With regard to the temporal dimension, there is the divide between the expression leading to the constitution, interpreted by institutions such as the supreme court, and current expressions in present elections and legislative enactments. Of course, laws themselves respond to expressions of will voiced at different moments, as different organs are elected at different times. In Argentina, half of the House of Representatives is elected every two years, and the deputies have a mandate lasting four years. Spatially, in countries with federal organizations, such as the United States and Argentina, the will of the people is dispersed into national, state, and local representatives that deal with different but often overlapping issues. Functionally, popular sovereignty is dispersed through different bodies and officials that must react positively or negatively to the same decisions. In a presidentialist system, they include the president, the house of representatives, the senate, and judges, particularly the members of the supreme court. While these functions are formally distinguished, the legislative role of the president has increased enormously in contemporary presidentialist systems, making that person the formal or informal source of most successful legislative enactments.

Pluralism celebrates this dispersion, on the theory that it helps avoid tyranny. To the pluralist, the dispersion of sovereignty impedes any faction from monopolizing power by representing itself as the voice of all people. Neither the majority nor any minority is able to control all the loci of power when there are so many and they are so separate from each other. This benefit, however, is achieved at the cost of a considerable weakening of the epistemic value of democracy, since there is no direct connection between the conclusion of democratic dialogue and a justification for acting according to that conclusion. Even if we assume the legitimacy of representation, one must decide how to transform a will expressed at such different temporal, spatial, and functional levels into a decision representing the conclusion approved by the majority after a process of open and ample debate. Consider the problem of abortion. The solution of that problem will include an extremely complex procedure where, in the United States, many governmental dimensions will interact. These dimensions include governors and state legislatures (elected at different times), the president, the Senate and the House of Representatives (both elected at different times by dissimilar procedures), as well as judges, particularly the Supreme Court. In fact, the Supreme Court may well limit state and federal action in light of a constitutional interpretation based on the will of people living two centuries ago.

There is no guarantee that the results of this cumbersome mix of different decisional centers reflect the present, majoritarian conclusion of all the people concerned following a free and open debate. Perhaps the governor of a particular state was elected two years ago after a strong campaign against abortion, but the legislature adheres to a pro-choice position pursuant to a popular debate or a recent election of its members. Perhaps the majority of senators from less-populated, conservative states support restraints on public funds for abortion, whereas the House members, representing past majoritarian judgments for free choice, support the use of federal funds for abortions. At the same time, the president may have been elected notwithstanding his strong stance against abortion. However, the

Supreme Court now has a majority, thanks to recent appointments by a former president, which believes that the founders were in favor of a right of privacy which includes abortion at least in the first stages of the pregnancy. Whether the result of all this mess is that a particular citizen of a particular state may or may not legally resort to abortion seems to be a matter of almost pure chance and without significant connection to the result of public debate by any one relevant group.

Many people think that as more "volitions" influence the solution, the solution will more closely reflect the will of those expressing their volitions. In reality, the accumulation of volitions makes it more difficult to reach a decision. According to general rules, the lack of decision means that the status quo prevails. This puts a premium on preserving the status quo unless the majoritarian wave is strong enough to overcome it. For many conservatives, the status quo is per se a morally permissible position and the only thing that can counter it is a majoritarian consensus for change. But this priority for the status quo regardless of whether a majority seeks to preserve it is difficult to justify when it is obviously unjust. One may argue that this dispersion of sovereignty creates a highly passive government which was meant to protect a status quo in which, among other things, a given distribution of private property prevails.[31]

Where the social structure includes strong corporatist formations or entrenched interest groups, as is true in many Latin American countries, this passivity caused by the need to accumulate many volitions for making a decision weakens democratic power.[32] Therefore, the result is the opposite of that sought by pluralism. While it is difficult for corporations and factions to acquire control of state power when the centers of decision making are dispersed, they may acquire that control during authoritarian periods when the decision-making centers are concentrated. In turn, the dispersion of sovereignty makes it extremely hard for the democratic government to take that control away from such factions.

The spatial dimension of dispersed sovereignty presents less serious theoretical problems, though the practical difficulties for overcoming it are enormous. This dimension involves the degree of decentralization of the political unit in question. If the votes of all the citizens of that unit converge at some level but are diversified at others, the polity has a kind of federal organization. In the United States, there are at least three different domains in which democratic politics is carried out: the local, the state, and the national.

The adoption of a federal system of government in the United States—and in Argentina, Brazil, and Mexico, following the U.S. model—entails a complex organization of political power. There is a division between the central government and the component units. The authority of these decisional centers is exercised directly upon the people and upon objects located in their respective territories. Of course, the federal power overlaps with that of each state. Each government is comprised of legislative, executive, and judicial branches. When there are conflicts within the spheres of competences between the central and state governments, the central one prevails. This implies the use of a dual system of government with two mutually exclusive areas of power in which power holders have equal footing.[33]

Some other federal systems display a quite different structure. For instance, the Canadian federal organization establishes in article 91 of the Constitutional Act of 1867 that all powers not given to the provinces belong to the central government. There are, in addition, two special times for the central government to assume powers. First, the government may legislate in matters normally considered provincial in emergencies such as war, invasion, and famine. Second, the federal parliament may legislate concerning issues that affect the operation of central institutions. With the constitutional reform of 1982, different powers, mainly in the economic sphere, were transferred to the provinces, while the central government committed itself to supporting public services. To give another important example of a different federal structure, the system established by the West German Constitution of 1949 (now extended to the East) has been called a system of "cooperation" rather than a dual system. Federal statutes are applied by the states, or Länder, which have ample power to interpret them. In that sense, the excutive power over federal statutes is ordinarily vested in the Länder. But there is no division of the judicial power, which is central. The constitution forbids the Länder from legislating in areas considered federal. With regard to concurrent legislation, the Länder may legislate insofar as the federal parliament does not do so. The local law maintains its force in all which does not contradict the federal one. A series of agreements evolved for cooperation and consultation between the federal government and the Länder, and in 1969 they were constitutionalized.

Finally, we should note the unique model of decentralization found in Spain. The powers of the "autonomous communities" are not established in the Constitution of 1978, which only puts forth a framework of possibilities within which an "organic" statute, enacted by the national parliament for each community, defines the faculties or powers attributed to it. The possibilities are set forth in article 148. The constitution also provides that after five years the communities may expand their competences, up to the limits of article 149, which sets forth subjects that belong exclusively to the central government, such as regulation of the conditions guaranteeing the equality of the Spanish people, nationality, immigration, foreign relations, defense, and administration of justice. Article 150 allows the national parliament to delegate its powers to the communities. The first phase of implementing this system attributed broad powers to Catalonia and the Basque country. An impasse owing to the difficulty of defining the breadth of powers of other communities lasted until 1981, when the different political parties agreed gradually to generalize the autonomy of the communities.

The evaluation of different systems of federalism in the context of the epistemic theory of democracy is a very complex task. Perhaps, more than any other issue, these systems largely depend on the historical and sociological background of each country. Distortion caused by the spatial dispersion of sovereignty and the obstacle to collective deliberation caused by the size of the unit in which decisions are made might be solved by modifying the federal structures in which distortion is most evident. One such reform would be to create deep decentralization, so that crucially important issues are discussed and decided at the provincial or even the local level. This could be done if public services such as secondary and university education were handled by states or provinces. The same may be done in relation to substantive legislation, such as the criminal and civil codes, as occurs in the United States but not in Argentina and other federal countries. Of course, decentralization would facilitate collective discussion of those issues, highlighting the peculiarities of each province or town. Cooperation between the different provinces might lessen as a result, however, and the social and economic differences between them might widen.

A second set of reforms to the historical constitution could overcome the distortions of representation at the national level. Bicameralism, including the use of a senate, was a wonderful invention in countries like the United States, where it was rightly assumed that, in its absence, people living in some regions would face discrimination. But in many situations this is no longer the case. The existence of a senate in which residents of less-populous political units have the same representation as those living in the more populous ones seriously offends the principle of "one person, one vote." This principle is at the core of an individualistic vision of democracy projected by the ideal constitution.

One alternative is to adopt a unicameral parliament like New Zealand's. A drawback, however, is that a special forum is sometimes needed to air regional interests. Another possibility is to modify the composition and functions of the senate so that it specializes in issues which are of direct concern to the autonomy of provinces or states. Also, the senate could have a veto power only in relation to legislation directly involving individual rights. Most statutes approved by the house of representatives would therefore be enacted automatically as long as they were not vetoed by the senate within a certain time. This would remove the senate's ability to block initiatives enjoying popular support reflected in the house of representatives.[34]

The third kind of reform is inspired by a different kind of federalism than in the present system. Instead of dividing issues into federal and provincial concerns, an often complex division which frequently weakens cooperation, this other kind of cooperative federalism divides the processes of decision and implementation. Many solutions could be adopted at the provincial level by the legislatures or through popular consultation. Then, the senators and representatives of each province could implement those solutions at the national level.

This process would constitute something analogous to the mechanism of democratic centralism defended by C. B. Macpherson.[35] It would encourage collective deliberation in small political units by those directly concerned about important issues. The decision reached in the local community would be reflected by representatives of the majority and minority, in proportion to their number, at the provincial level in deliberation with representatives of other local communities. In turn, the representatives of the majority and minority positions reached at the provincial level could discuss these matters in the national parliament with the representatives of other provinces. Once a decision was taken at the national level, a process in the opposite direction could then be established with regard to the implementation of that decision. This process would achieve something similar to what Habermas calls "implementation discourse," in which the local and factual conditions for implementing a measure are taken into account. While utopian in its aspirations, this sort of federalism, in which the three levels of government cooperate in reaching and implementing a decision, more closely resembles the federal system used in Germany than that in the United States.

Electoral Systems and the Problem of Imperfect Mediation

Under the deliberative form of democracy, representation is seen as an evil. That evil is nevertheless necessary, given the size of modern polities, the scarcity of time citizens can devote to public issues, and the complexity of many decisions. The most generous way to conceive of representation under the epistemic view of democracy is as a delegation to continue the deliberation that has taken place among the citizens before the representatives have been elected. The discussion should be continued on the basis of the platforms approved by the electors when choosing those representatives.

Even when representation is confined in this manner, however, it still reflects the ambivalence between the two conflicting views of representation. On the one hand, there is the "agency" view of representation, defended by thinkers like Burke, according to which representatives are agents of the electorate. On the other hand, there is the "reproduction" view of representation, supported by Mill and other philosophers, according to which representative bodies must mirror the larger electorate, reflecting the distribution of interests and opinions of those being represented. The first view requires electors to identify their representatives, who are then accountable to support their opinions and interests. The second view demands a symmetry between the represented group and the representative bodies with regard to relevant features such as ideological commitments and interests.

Under the view of representation as a delegation to continue collective deliberation, these two views of representation converge. Under the Burkean theory, which holds that representatives are individually the agents of the electorate, they are obliged to defend the principles and values the voters approved of when choosing them. But the representatives must deliberate so as to come as close as possible to the deliberation that the electors themselves would have carried out. But the best way to ensure this dynamic is to have a body which is a highly accurate sample of the values and interests of the larger unit. For the deliberation of the representative body to enjoy an epistemic value approaching the level of deliberation that the whole group would have enjoyed, representatives must be committed to the opinions of their electors and they must collectively reflect the composition of the whole electorate.

Under this conception of representation, a parliament or assembly is the most representative institution. An elected president, for instance, only maximizes one aspect of representation, the facility of electors to identify their agent. Nevertheless, as we shall see in the following section, the president is unable to account to different sectors of the electorate or to reflect contrasting ideologies and interests. Furthermore, only a collective body can continue a deliberation which starts from positions receiving different degrees of support from that electorate. For those reasons, a parliamentary government is superior, since it is more directly and continuously responsive to the results of discussion in society at large.

It is fairly obvious, however, that parliaments and congresses in modern democracies fall short of this vision of reproducing the ideal deliberation that the whole society would undertake if it were practicable. The popular image of legislatures in most Western countries, particularly in Latin America, is of places where politicking and verbosity reign, lobbyists function behind the scenes, and inefficiency and sluggishness are omnipresent. To some extent, this image is unjust and results from the lack of comprehension of the need to obtain consensus through discussion and negotiations. Still, some of the deficiencies are real and stem from the composition of parliaments and the way they function. Mechanisms which secure efficiency and openness should be adopted, such as approving laws in parliamentary committees, publicizing committee meetings, and enacting a law approved by one house if the other does not act within a certain amount of time.

Behind the problems of a parliament loom the problems of political parties. Many of the deficiencies in parliament reflect the deficiencies of parties. Political parties everywhere have converted themselves into mediators in the democratic process. There are even constitutions, such as the German one of 1949 in its article 21, that recognize their indispensable role in forming the popular will. In theory, political parties are necessary vehicles for conducting public discussion on the basis of principles, social ideals, or models of society and for counteracting the power of factions that unite people on the basis of crude interests. Even when a party is associated with some interest or social class, it must justify that interest on the basis of principles that would be accepted from an impartial point of view. A party must at least pretend that its interests coincide with the common good. When a citizen votes for a party, he or she saves a good deal of deliberation by adhering to some view of society and to substantive proposals that can be evaluated with others. In practice, as Jean Blondel maintains, all parties are both aggregative of interests and expressive of ideals.[36] The proportion of these two dimensions varies from system to system and from party to party.

Nevertheless, the proportion of interests to ideals seems to have become quite imbalanced in many polities. Political parties in most democratic countries display increasing distortions, which turn them further into corporatist groups defending their own interests. As already noted, the presidential system creates a polarization that makes big parties amorphous coalitions with diminishing definition in terms of public ideals. Membership in a party becomes more a matter of family tradition, personal loyalty, and sport-like competition than a question of substantive commitments. Similarly, most political activity inside the parties is devoted more to internal competition than to the analysis of national problems. Despite the fact that candidates are elected by open general elections, there is the feeling that the options are greatly restrained by internal party politics. All these deficiencies, experienced in many democratic countries, require deep transformations in the structure of the parties.

More important perhaps than modifying internal parliamentary procedures and party structures are revisions in the electoral system. We should begin by considering the issue of district size. The district may be the whole nation, as in Israel or Holland, or it may consist of smaller political units like states established for reasons apart from the elections. It could also be an ad hoc district formed simply for purposes of the elections, ensuring that a certain number of representatives are elected by each district. With regard to the method of allocating seats, there are two main systems from which to choose. One system is the majoritarian one, implying that the party which obtains a simple or an absolute majority of votes, in the first or a run-off election, wins all the seats in the district. In the proportional system, seats are adjudicated to the parties in the proportion of the votes obtained in the district. A proportional system contemplates that the district elects various representatives.[37]

There are certainly many variations of these systems. One such variation is the vote of preference which allows the voter to determine the order of the candidates in the party list in a proportional system. There is also the alternative vote in the majoritarian system, which allows the voter to express a second choice in case the first choice does not pass a certain threshold. There are also mixed systems that combine these two main ones. For instance, the German electoral system gives each elector two votes, one for the representative of the single member district to the Bundestag, elected by simple majority, and the other for a party list of candidates representing a larger district—normally one of the Länder—elected by proportional representation.

A comparative analysis of electoral systems shows that no one system satisfies all the minimum requirements. These requirements include sensitivity to the ideological composition of society; a close relationship between represented and representatives; noncontroversiality in its application; manageability of the resulting collective body; and attenuation of the confrontation between the parties and powers of the state. The proportional system fairly represents all important shades of opinions expressed by the electorate, thereby converting the parliament into a mirror-like representation of the ideological geography of society. However, the proportional system has a serious setback in that there is very little relationship between representatives and represented, since each citizen votes for a long list of candidates proposed by the party to represent the whole region. The voter may know only the first one or two names on the list. Citizens therefore do not feel they can address their representatives, and representatives feel less responsible to their electors than to the party leadership that chooses them. On the other hand, the majoritarian system, involving a single representative for each district, though optimal with regard to creating a close relationship between represented and representatives, has well-known deficiencies. These deficiencies include the difficulty of drawing the districts in a neutral way; the unfairness to third and fourth parties not usually represented in proportion to their votes and their subsequent withdrawal from the system; and the parochialism of candidates, who must be more attentive to local problems than to national ones. While the proportional system makes it hard for one representative to think of herself or himself as an agent, the majoritarian system fails to satisfy the view of representation as reproducing the represented group. In a majoritarian system, the legislature will not reflect the distribution of opinions and interests existing in the electorate.

The advantages of these two systems can probably be combined to neutralize their disadvantages in a mixed system. There are at least two possibilities. The first is the German system, which divides the house into two parts, one elected by districts and the other by proportional representation. The second allows citizens to move down the list of representatives and pick from that list so that candidates begin to look for special constituencies.

All these concerns require much more extended discussion and empirical research. The main point remains: Since parliaments and political parties are the primary channels—besides direct popular participation—through which deliberative democracy works, their deficiencies account in crucial ways for the weakness of the whole system. These deficiencies largely explain the poor moral results of the democratic process, despite its alleged epistemic value when it approximates the informal practice of moral discussion.

Presidential vs. Parliamentary Government and the Creation and Maintenance of Social Consensus

There is a continuum of democratic regimes, ranging from pure parliamentarianism to hyperpresidentialism. In the pure parliamentary system, popular consensus has an impact on the formation of parliament, which then decides who shall head the government. With regard to the head of state, he or she obtains the position on a hereditary basis or is appointed through some indirect procedure in which parliament plays the decisive role. In the presidential system, popular consensus has two expressions that have a separate impact on the formation of the legislative and executive organs. Both the legislature and the executive are elected by the people. In the mixed system, the executive has two functions, as head of state and head of government; the head of state—say, the president—is popularly elected and the head of government—the prime minister—is chosen by the parliament.

Another variable for defining a system refers to the extent to which diverse expressions of popular opinion, where there are more than one, are mutually coordinated. In the pure presidential system, there is no coordination in forming the legislative and executive organs, though there are certainly mechanisms to coordinate their decisions. Presidentialism may be attenuated where congress confirms appointments or has the power to censure those appointed, or even the president himself. In the most common mixed system, one branch of the executive—the government—is formed through the coordinated decision of the head of state and parliament. Additional coordination exists when the head of state affects the formation of parliament through the power to dissolve it and call for new elections. Usually, parliament does not have the analogous capacity to censure the president, though some have proposed presidential resignation if the president loses parliamentary elections.

In another mixed system, never tried in practice, the head of government—not the head of state—is popularly elected but is still subject to parliamentary censure. If the head of government is censured, however, parliament must also dissolve itself. Similarly, if the head of government wants to dissolve parliament, he or she must also stand for a new election. In the pure parliamentary system, there is no coordination between several expressions of popular opinion. Some way of coordinating the government with parliament is required, however, since the former, though appointed by the latter, may acquire different degrees of independence, according to the censure process or informal mechanisms such as the party and electoral systems.

In other works, I have put forth functional arguments, associated with values of stability and efficiency, against the presidential system of government in general and Latin American hyperpresidentialism in particular. I have stressed that a pure presidential system can suffer from a lack of subjective legitimacy. Often, a president may have very little popular support when elected only with a bare simple majority of the votes. This slender margin may conflict with the sense of mission that the presidency generally infuses in the person who takes hold of it. Thus, a president may attempt profound transformations without the necessary support. This took place in 1970 in Chile with President Allende. He was elected by less than 30 percent of the votes but embarked on deep social and economic reforms. The election was thrown to the House, since no candidate had obtained a majority, and then a coalition of left-wing parties selected Allende. The usual remedy for this difficulty is to establish a second electoral race between the two main candidates, a run-off, or what the French call *ballotage*. Generally, however, this remedy is ineffective, since it produces an artificial and circumstantial majority that vanishes as soon as the election is over. This took place with the election in 1990 of President Fernando Collor de Mello in Brazil.

Moreover, even when the president is elected with a broad genuine majority, the rigidity of the presidential system allows the president to lose popular support during his term and thus requires him to govern without the necessary consensus. This was obviously the case with President Raúl Alfonsín of Argentina after the parliamentary election of 1987. His party lost the election, and as a result he faced two more years in office with increasing opposition from Congress and a lack of credibility in society at large.

Additionally, presidentialism can be dysfunctional when a political, social, or economic crisis arises because of the lack of effective escape valves. The impeachment of a president is a very difficult operation, as demonstrated by the few cases in which it has been successfully carried out in the United States and Argentina. Impeachment requires accusing the president of the grossest misbehavior or commission of a crime and can only be carried out with some support from the party of the president. This is generally tantamount to political suicide for that party, since it must accuse its leader of gross misbehavior. Short of impeachment, the president may respond to pressure by removing a member of the cabinet or the whole cabinet. But that is generally not enough to renew the credibility of the government, since the perception is that the president has ultimate responsibility for the policies considered inadequate. Therefore, the system lacks the capacity to create a "fuss" that might be able to cool a political situation that has become overheated. In a parliamentary system, the fuss may mean nothing more than the dissolution of parliament. In presidential systems, a fuss must involve the whole democratic structure. Thus, the system collapses—or is overthrown—when powerful social sectors perceive that a break is the only way to preserve wider social structures. This has been the unfortunate historical experience of Latin America.

The presidential system of government also implies a personalization of power that weakens the institutional structures. Most expectations and pressures are concentrated on one person. Any problem affecting that person—for example, loss of popularity and credibility, or physical or psychological ailments—necessarily reflects upon the whole institutional structure. It is very difficult to replace the president against his will, and an early resignation (as happened with President Alfonsín in July 1989) is perceived as an abandonment of responsibilities. The vice president often is not an appropriate replacement, because he is chosen more for political reasons than for considerations of presidential succession. Besides, the personalization of power involved in the presidential system increases the possibility of authoritarian abuses and corruption, since the halo of untouchability surrounding the president provokes a reverence for the head of state which often interferes with the proper operation of republican controls.

The confrontation between parties generated by a presidential system also constitutes a dysfunctional feature of that system. As Juan Linz has pointed out, the "zero-sum" nature of presidential elections is caused by the indivisibility of the central seat of power among the parties.[38] A dynamic of confrontation becomes most apparent when the parties are well organized and disciplined, a condition especially fueled by proportional representation. While in the United States and Brazil do not have proportional representation, it is present in Argentina and Peru, and the consequences are apparent. Politics becomes an "all-or-nothing" competition—since the presidency controls almost all power, including the distribution of public positions. Therefore, the party in opposition tries to undermine as much as possible the credibility of the president in order to diminish the reelection prospects of the reigning party.

This dynamic of confrontation produces gridlock between the various branches of government when those branches are controlled by different parties. When these parties are disciplined, it is extremely difficult for a president to get approval for his or her initiatives from a congress dominated by the opposition. This took place with President Alfonsín after he lost the parliamentary elections of 1987. It also served as a reason for President Alberto Fujimori of Peru to close Congress down in 1992. Conversely, when the party of the president dominates congress, the legislature generally becomes submissive. This undermines congress's role in controlling the administration, since the all-or-nothing dynamic encourages parties to close ranks around their leaders.

Finally, presidential systems also suffer from the difficulty of forming the interparty coalitions required to overcome deep crises or confront corporatist pressures. This is a product of the inability to share presidential power and the small incentive for opposition parties to occupy cabinet positions that rely on the president. Opposition leaders know that if they accept a position in the cabinet, their parties will suffer from the erosion of popularity that normally besets the government in power. President Alfonsín experienced this when he was cornered by trade union interests connected with the Peronist party. Alfonsín tried to negotiate with union leaders, including some in his own cabinet, but they were immediately isolated from the Peronist party and trade union members.

While the above arguments have been primarily functional, many of the moral reasons regarding the justification of democracy also undermine the presidential system. The presidential system fragments public discussion into two different expressions—the election of the president and the election of the legislative assembly. These elections may take place at different times. In the United States, when the president is elected there is also an election for seats in the House of Representatives, but the House is renewed every two years, while presidential elections take place every fourth year. Thus, a House member may be elected in a year with no presidential election.[39] The division of the expression of popular sovereignty is praised by pluralists in one respect: No person can legitimately invoke the voice of the people. But a price is paid: The overlapping of voices muffles the message. As a result, no one has fully heard and accepted the conclusion reached in the electoral debate.

Occasionally, there is an exception that allows the people to feel that the president is speaking for them. This takes place when the president is elected by a real landslide. In Argentina, consider Perón in 1973 and, to a lesser degree, Alfonsín in 1983. In those cases the president begins his mandate with great popular support—often even more approval than expressed in the election, since popularity usually breeds more popularity. But a new problem arises, one of maintaining that support. The president, elected for a certain term, may well feel he is not bound to follow the consensus reached in the electoral process. Often, the crude reality of government makes him retreat from the easy promises made in the campaign. Remember George Bush, who uttered the famous phrase "Read my lips" and promised not to increase taxes, but later did.

Also consider the much more serious case of President Carlos Menem of Argentina, whose stances on economic issues during the presidential campaign of 1989 gave little hint of the changes he would make once in office. The privatization program he launched once in office was a sharp departure for Menem's party. Similarly, one could not have foretold that Menem would give pardons to the military after promising to let justice do its job. A presidential candidate knows that once elected he will not be made accountable for unfulfilled promises and so finds it easy to make them.

A parallel process takes place in the people at large. The citizens know they will not be asked to confirm or reject their mandate for several years. Therefore, a sense of irresponsibility ensues. The norm then becomes widespread criticism of government, and no one provides positive alternatives or positions.

More important than the loss of consensus is the difficulty in reconstructing that consensus within a presidentialist system. The long presidential term prevents a call for new presidential elections even when the president has suffered a catastrophic loss of popularity and credibility. Some Latin American presidents have been supported by only 5 percent of the population as measured by polls. There is no way for popular opinion to find new expression in the principal seat of power, since it is almost impossible to remove the incumbent. Also, the president very seldom is inclined to resign voluntarily, as Alfonsín did in Argentina in 1989. The president typically believes he has a mandate that transcends contingent public opinion and knows that resignation almost always implies political death.

Nor can popular support be reconstituted in congress. First, there exists a relative absence of representativeness reflected in the senate's regionally biased structure and in electoral defects that are expressed in the composition of the house. Second, congress has limited power to initiate political action but a clear power to obstruct the president. Obstruction is the most likely course of action when at least one house is dominated by an opposition party. Given these conditions, it is almost impossible for a president to get support from legislators outside his own party, since they are subject to discipline from their party leaders who seek to discredit the president in order to increase their own chances in future elections.

For these reasons, the presidential system as it operates in many countries, mostly in Latin America, does not ensure that the popular will resulting from public debate is permanently reflected in the formation and working of government. This conclusion implies a considerable departure from the conditions granting epistemic value to the working of democratic government, and may also explain its poor moral results.

In contrast, a parliamentary system (such as in England, Germany, and Spain) or a mixed system (such as in France, Portugal, and Finland) tends to reflect in a much more flexible way popular support in the operation of government. Although parliamentary systems have difficulties of their own, the main problem is not the oft-cited tendency for governmental instability, since this tendency can be overcome by devices of "rationalized parliamentarianism." Such devices include "constructive censure" that prevents the majority from bringing down a government if there is no majoritarian support for a new one. Moreover, it is important to remember that instability in a particular government is sometimes the best insurance against the instability of the whole democratic system.

In my view, parliamentary systems have two main limitations. First, it is impossible to break ties between the main parties. This may make the main parties subject to undue pressures from small ones (as has happened in Israel), since the small parties will be called in to break the tie. Second, and more important, the formation of a government in a parliamentary system is in the hands of the parliament and thus is a step removed from the electorate. This may encourage a popular belief that the government results from political maneuvering in the secretive halls of power.

Mixed systems may avoid the difficulties of both pure presidential and pure parliamentary systems of government. In a mixed system, such as France's and Portugal's, the president is the center of power so long as he enjoys enough popular support to make a parliamentary censure of him impossible or too risky. When the popularity of the president begins to wear thin, he will have to negotiate with the representatives of his own party in parliament even before a parliamentary election. In that case, the prime minister and his cabinet acquire independence from the president and become more responsive to a parliamentary majority, even when formed by the same party of the president. If the president loses popular support, it will be reflected in the next parliamentary election, since the whole assembly is elected for four years in the middle of the presidential four-year term. Therefore, the president may have to negotiate with the opposition in parliament to form a government that could be considerably independent from the president. In fact, the formation of a new government may help protect the president, since it may have the effect of reconstituting his prestige and beginning a new cycle of electioneering.

The most important feature of the mixed system is that it coordinates expressions of popular sovereignty reflected in the parliamentary and in the presidential elections at different times. It adjusts the structure of government to those expressions so that the government will be supported permanently by the popular understanding resulting from continuous public debate. The disadvantage of this mixed system of government is that it separates the official who has popular legitimacy, the nation's president, and the official who is the highest responsible party in government, the prime minister or head of government. As Juan Linz has emphatically maintained, this may cause political trouble, since the president may resort to that legitimacy in order to exceed the limits of his formal powers and to place undue pressures on the government.[40] This risk may increase dangerously in a context like Latin America if the president is head of the armed forces. In the French system, the president also has important powers concerning defense and foreign relations. These enhanced presidential powers create ambiguities in the division of responsibilities between the president and prime minister, not only because the president has the power in these areas but because they are impossible to separate completely from areas such as economic management and internal security, which belong to the prime minister. In social contexts less politically civilized than France, this confusion of roles may be a serious cause of political tension.

This sort of confusion can be overcome in a mixed system in which the functions of head of state and chief of the government are sharply separated. The head of state only receives symbolic functions or powers transcending day-to-day politics. In a mixed system, the head of state is appointed by a special majority of parliament, while the head of government is popularly elected. The popular election of the head of government does not prevent parliament from voiding the election by censuring or dismissing the head of government. This creates a problem for the system, since the popular legitimacy enjoyed by the head of the government may conflict with the threat of parliamentary censure. It seems that popular sovereignty is frustrated if the official elected by the voters to head the government can be dismissed by a parliamentary scheme. The way out of this difficulty is to require parliament to subject itself to new elections if it brings down the government. Similarly, if the president dissolves parliament, he or she would be obliged to resign and be exposed to a new election. In this way, the coordination between the two organs of popular sovereignty and the integrity of popular will is preserved, since the electorate is the final arbiter of the conflict between its representatives.

Clearly, questions related to the best form of government are highly speculative and depend to a great degree on the historical, sociological, and cultural features of each context and on empirical data concerning the functioning of these different arrangements. The main point of the exercise undertaken in this section, however, is to answer this important question: Why does the democratic process produce such unsatisfactory results from a moral point of view? These results may well be explained by the fact that the system of government chosen is not the best for promoting, preserving, and reflecting the popular understanding that may be reached through a process of collective deliberation, even when the process itself is not significantly distorted. In turn, this discussion reveals that the weakening of the epistemic quality of democracy, a reality of modern political life, may be partially overcome if cautious but significant institutional transformations are undertaken.

The Use of an Entrenched Constitution

The temporal dispersion of sovereignty also affects the epistemic quality of the democratic process in light of the problem posed by the present binding power of decisions taken in the past. It is clear that majoritarian decisions acquire a democratic deficit with the passage of time. As the interests of people change and the people themselves change, there is a progressive weakening of the presumption that the prior decision reflects a solution in which the interests of all those concerned were considered. With time, the prior decision no longer reflects new interests of people or the interests of new people.

Since we cannot have an "instantaneous democracy" that adapts decisions to the continuous emergence of new people and interests, we must rely on some idea of tacit consent that could explain how decisions taken in the past bind people in the present. If the earlier decision is not reversed, one can assume that there is a majority in favor of it, or at least in favor of not bearing the cost of changing the situation. This assumption vitally depends on it being easy for a majority that opposes the status quo to change it. Therefore, the requirements of special majorities should be avoided. It also follows that there should be procedures to help people evaluate past decisions in terms of current interests. This goal could be achieved, for instance, by a procedure by which courts could request legislatures to reconsider old pieces of legislation that appear on their face to be particularly unjust.

There are strong arguments justifying the binding power of past majoritarian decisions on present majorities. Stephen Holmes has expressed the idea that constraints on majority rule adopted in the past can actually expand the power of present majorities in certain ways.[41] One way consists in undertaking a voluntary precommitment. Consider the autopaternalism practiced by Ulysses, who bound himself to the mast in order to resist the lure of the Sirens. As Holmes himself says, however, one should be careful in extending to a collective group a conceptual framework that applies to one person. After all, the majorities are formed at different moments by different people, and thus it is hard to speak of autopaternalism. Some cases of heteropaternalism could be justified, however, where there is a risk that a person's unconstrained will would harm her own subjective interests. Still, it is difficult to imagine the risks to which a present majority is subject that explain why its decisions should be constrained by a decision taken by another majority at an earlier time which did not face the same risks. In his explanation, Holmes resorts, like Ackerman, to the alleged superior quality of the majority's decision as expressed in the constitution. This explanation, as I have already indicated, is dubious in light of the democratic deficiencies arising from the simple fact that a constitution enables a group in power in the past to bind a present majority.

Holmes makes a more persuasive argument when he points out that not all decisions may be taken at once. Therefore, present decisions must be taken on the basis of some past decisions. He states: "It is meaningless to speak about popular government apart from some sort of legal framework which enables the electorate to have a coherent will. For this reason, democratic citizens require cooperation from regime-founding forefathers. Formulated somewhat facetiously: without tying their own hands, the people will have no hands. Decisions are made on the basis of pre-decisions."[42] Despite the intuitive power of this appeal to the need to decide within certain parameters established in the past, the basis of the argument is rather obscure. Why cannot the present majority decide everything?

For democracy to have epistemic value, its procedures must allow for discussion and majority decision. It is unclear why a past majority is in a better condition to establish the right procedure. While there is no majority rule without first establishing a correct procedure that makes certain decisions authoritative, there is no way to entrench that procedure without questioning the authority of the majority to decide what is best. If one believed that the procedure established in the constitution was right, one would celebrate the fact that no simple majority could reform it. Similarly, if one believed it to be wrong, one would regret the inability of the majority to reform it.

The appeal of Holmes's argument may well be a product of other circumstances that I discussed earlier in connection with MacCormick's understanding of the constitution as a convention. There I acknowledged that no majority enjoys authoritative power unless it is part of a collective practice. Even today's constitution only represents one successful effort among others that have failed to establish that collective practice. A majority by itself cannot always establish a new practice, and it must often rely on the existing practice to be able to rule. Similarly, the majority, unlike a monarch or aristocracy, is not an individual or a set of individuals. Rather, the majority is an abstraction which is formed by different sets of hands raised in answering different questions. Some of the people whose hands made a majority for one question could be in a minority for another issue. People can also vote differently if an issue is joined with other issues. In addition, a majority may change because people change or their ideas or interests change. An equilibrium must be achieved that both allows for shifting majorities (since no majority should dominate other majorities) and provides for stability so that the majority is not frustrated. Moreover, insofar as democracy protects interests that can be justified on the basis of impartial principles, its functioning should take into account the fact that interests are not instantaneous but extend into time. Many interests are for things to happen in the future. It is therefore to everyone's advantage that once those interests have been legitimized by public discussion and majority decision, society guarantees their fulfillment despite the change of people and their interests.

These observations preclude any sharp advice. Since there are no conclusive theories presently about the weight of past decisions and the justification for entrenching them, the best one can do is to proceed with caution. I would not recommend, for instance, making the procedure for constitutional reform the same as for normal law. At the same time, I would certainly adopt a less rigid procedure for amendment than the ones used in the constitutions of the United States and Argentina.[43]

One might argue that my view of democracy is utopian in the bad sense, since modern democracies do not display the institutional features which are required by the epistemic theory of democracy. But this is not the case. Imperfect as they are, current democracies—mainly in Western Europe—display to a considerable degree the features of open and free discussion and popular participation that provide majority decisions with epistemic quality. Certainly, the degree to which they possess those features is incomparably higher than in other systems throughout the world. Still, distinctions should be made among these democracies, depending on how far they fall from the informal practice of moral discussion, and the epistemic theory of democracy indicates the scope and direction of reform.

Once we acknowledge a certain degree of utopianism—be it

legitimate—we must ask about the strategy of change. How can we get the historical constitution closer to the ideal? Along with formal and explicit reforms of the institutional design—which can be very difficult to achieve—our attention swiftly turns to the judiciary. We look to the judiciary to recognize a better system of rights or a better organization of power. This, however, places courts in the throes of a terrible tension. Courts must balance the claims of the historical constitution and those of the ideal one, and they must also balance the two features of the ideal constitution—respect for democratic procedures and enforcement of substantive rights. In the next chapter, I will examine this challenge and ask how judges should act in promoting deliberative democracy within the framework of a complex constitution.

Chapter Seven

· · · · · · · · · ·

Judicial Review in a Deliberative Democracy

The power of courts to review the constitutionality of legal norms enacted by democratic organs is one of the central features of constitutional or liberal democracies. The idea was introduced by Chief Justice John Marshall's opinion in the famous United States case of *Marbury v. Madison.*[1] The doctrine expanded in a similar form to many Latin American countries. For instance, it was accepted in Argentina for the first time by the Supreme Court in 1887 in the case known as *Sojo.* It came to Europe after World War I in the Austrian and Weimar constitutions of 1918 and 1919 in the form a special constitutional tribunal (largely the creation of the philosopher Hans Kelsen). Following World War II, ideas of judicial review returned to the Continent again, embodied in varied forms in almost all the constitutions of the era, including those of Italy, West Germany, France, Portugal, and Spain.

Notwithstanding its crucial place in defining a constitutional democracy, the justification of judicial review is rather mysterious. This mystery is attested to by the number of works devoted to the subject. Judges, particularly those in higher courts, such as a supreme court or a constitutional tribunal, do not generally enjoy a direct democratic origin, since they are not elected by popular vote but are appointed. Furthermore, these courts are not typically subject to a periodic renewal of their mandate, nor do they respond directly to public opinion and discussion. The supreme courts in the North American style—the model for most Latin American countries—consist of members chosen by the president, sometimes with confirmation of the legislature, and enjoy life tenure, unless a justice is impeached for misbehavior. The constitutional tribunals of the European style are made up of persons who are appointed by political bodies and remain in their position for a specific period, generally a quite extensive one. While the European courts may have a closer connection with the democratic process, they still differ in significant ways from legislative bodies or heads of government. Therefore, in both the American and European systems of judicial review, doubt arises as to why the judiciary—this aristocratic organ —should have the last word in determining the scope of individual rights, conflicts of powers between the branches of government, and the rules regarding democratic procedures. Such an important role for judges challenges the traditional view of a division of powers where judges simply apply the decisions of the democratic organs, without analyzing the merits of such decisions.[2] Alexander Bickel labeled this problem "the *counter-majoritarian difficulty* of judicial review."[3]

In the last chapter, I suggested that deliberative democracy is the best procedure for understanding and realizing individual rights. From this position, I argued that the ideal dimension of the constitution concerning rights could emerge from the ideal organization of power if this organization could ever be achieved in actual constitutional practice. Initially, it would seem that such a view would preclude all possibility for judicial review in light of the democratic deficit characterized by the judicial branches of most liberal democracies. This democratic deficit is greater in the United States system than in the Continental European one, placing judges in the United States in an even weaker epistemic position than institutions more directly tied to the democratic process to determine the scope and hierarchy of individual rights, but it is present everywhere.

While the majority may, and often does, infringe on the rights of individuals or of minorities, there is no guarantee that isolated individuals, such as judges, are not similarly tempted, unless their interests happen to coincide with the minority whose rights are in jeopardy. When judges have no direct democratic origin, their decisions do not enjoy the epistemic value that accrues to the democratic process. A judge's perspective is limited to those persons directly affected by the conflict being adjudicated, excluding some of the people who might be affected by the conflict. The judge is entirely alien to the dispute. While noninvolvement enables impartiality when the conflict encompasses only a few people, it is impossible to achieve impartiality when the conflict involves the interests of a multitude of individuals, whose experiences are very different from those of the judge.

The common view that judges are better situated than parliaments and other elected officials for solving questions dealing with rights seems to arise from an epistemic elitism. It assumes that in order to arrive at correct moral conclusions, intellectual dexterity is more important than the capacity to represent vividly and to balance impartially the interests of all those affected by a decision. It is understandable that scholars who celebrate the marvels of judicial review should identify themselves more closely with judges than with politicians and, thus, are inclined to think, as Michael Walzer remarks, that what they deem to be right solutions—their own—would be more readily obtained by judges than by politicians.[4]

The impression that the democratic process cannot satisfy all the requirements of the ideal constitution of rights is so strong, however, that judicial review cannot be dismissed with only a cursory invocation of the merits of deliberative democracy. In what follows, I shall analyze the claim that the argument on behalf of judicial review follows as a matter of pure logic. If this proved true, it would preclude all other normative considerations. However, I ultimately find the logic not as convincing as it appears upon first examination.

The Supposed Logical Necessity of Judicial Review: Marshall's "Logic" and Kelsen's "Problem"

The clearest ground for judicial review was probably advanced at the moment of its invention by Chief Justice Marshall in *Marbury v. Madison*. Marshall's arguments for judicial review exhibit such a pristine clarity and overwhelming cogency that one is tempted to speak of Marshall's "logic." It is still fascinating to study the adept way this military man deployed subtle conceptual distinctions—concerning the validity of norms and different normative strata—that only much later were elucidated by scholars of considerable philosophical sophistication such as Hans Kelsen.

The logical structure of Marshall's reasoning in *Marbury vs. Madison* can be displayed along the following lines:

Premise 1: The duty of the judiciary is to apply the law.

Premise 2: When there are two contradictory laws, the application of one of them excludes that of the other.

Premise 3: The constitution both is the supreme law and defines what other norms are law.

Premise 4: The supremacy of the constitution implies that when it is in conflict with a norm enacted by the legislature, the latter ceases to be valid law.

Premise 5: If premise 4 were not true, the legislature could modify the constitution through an ordinary law, and thus the constitution would not be operative in limiting that legislature.

Premise 6: The legislature is limited by the constitution.

Premise 7: If a norm is not a valid law, it lacks binding force.

Conclusion: If an enactment of the legislature is contrary to the constitution, it is not binding upon the judiciary.

This reasoning seems to to indicate that judges should not apply legislative enactments contrary to the constitution. This rule would apply to any legal system where a constitution is recognized as supreme. Similarly, if judicial review does not exist—as in the British legal system—this logically implies that the system lacks either a written or unwritten constitution! This "logical necessity" of judicial review has rarely been touched upon by constitutional lawyers, who instead have devoted their energies to the legitimacy of that institution. Yet, if Marshall's "logic" is cogent, the effort to explain its legitimacy would be a waste of time, since logical necessity does not need a normative justification.

Upon further examination, however, I believe that Marshall's "logic" is not so valid. The flaws are subtle, so I will try to identify them through an analysis of the ideas of Kelsen when he constructed a conceptual scheme similar to Marshall's. This comparison seems partially appropriate, since Kelsen, like Marshall, greatly influenced the introduction of judicial review in the European legal tradition.

Kelsen is well known for analyzing the structure of a legal system through the image of a pyramid.[5] At the top of the pyramid is the famous *Grundnorm*, or basic norm, which grants validity to the positive norms or laws at the next tier. In turn, these norms—let us suppose they are part of the historical constitution of a country—grant validity to the further norms enacted in conformity to the prescriptions concerning the source, procedure, and content of the former norms. Assuming that these further norms are legislative statutes, the statutes determine the validity of other lower norms enacted in conformity to them—such as administrative decrees and municipal ordinances. Finally, the basis of the pyramid is constituted by particularized norms, such as those embodied in administrative orders, judicial decisions, and contracts. All of this assumes that norms at the lower tiers of the pyramid are enacted in conformity with the prescriptions of general superior norms or laws. If a prescription is enacted without following the requirements established by valid higher norms of the system, it is not a valid norm of that system.[6] A law is valid for Kelsen if it "exists as such," has "binding force", and belongs to the legal system.[7]

When Kelsen deploys this conceptual structure to deal with conflicts of norms or laws that sit on different levels of the pyramid (such as the case of unconstitutional statutes or illegal ordinances), he meets a quite serious difficulty. We may call this difficulty "Kelsen's problem." From all I have said, it would seem that if a statute contradicts a higher norm, it lacks validity. In Marshall's theory, the statute would not exist as law, since it would not belong to the legal system. Nevertheless, Kelsen, unlike Marshall, perceived that this does not accord with the phenomenology of legal thinking. There are many statutes, for instance, which objectively contradict constitutional clauses, but are nevertheless considered by jurists to be valid and binding laws. This occurs, for instance, before the laws are declared to be unconstitutional by a final judicial judgment. Sometimes, an act may be considered unconstitutional only in the situation in which it was so declared. The courts may also be mistaken, declaring constitutional a statute which obviously is not, or giving effect to a law in a legal system where there is no procedure for judicial review.

Certainly, some facets of Kelsen's problem should be distinguished from others. For instance, if there is no procedure for declaring the constitutionality of a statute, the supremacy of the constitution may be put in doubt. This problem can be solved easily. Moreover, when a judge or the superior court commits a mistake as to the constitutionality of a statute, the epistemological problem arises about who determines and how that constitutionality is determined in an objective manner. Nevertheless, taken as a whole, the situations identified by Kelsen show that the notion of legal validity and normative hierarchy underlying the logical argument for judicial review do not seem to coincide with the common view presupposed in legal thinking. For instance, one may believe that the Georgia statute declaring homosexual acts among adults as punishable goes objectively against the liberty protection of the Fourteenth Amendment. However, it is quite different to believe that the statute has no binding force, since the Supreme Court in *Bowers v. Hardwick* declared such a statute constitutional.[8] Most lawyers would not believe that imprisonment under that statute constitutes an illegal kidnapping, even if they believed the statute to be objectively unconstitutional.

Kelsen resorts to two theoretical devices in order to try to solve his problem. The first consists in adopting a subjectivist approach toward the validity of legal norms, maintaining that validity depends on a declaration by judges. This a highly unfortunate theoretical move: If the validity of a legal norm depended not on the objective satisfaction of the conditions established by a superior norms but on a *judicial declaration*, the concept of validity would not be available to the judges themselves to justify their own decision about whether to apply a legal norm. As Joseph Raz says, Kelsen has confused the question of whether a law or legal norm is valid (and whether the decision of a judge to apply it is correct) with the fact that a decision of a judge, correct or not, has binding force and constitutes *res judicata*.[9]

Kelsen offers a second theoretical device—the alternative tacit clause—to solve his problem. It posits that if ordinary legal thinking considers, under certain circumstances, a statute to be valid and binding despite the fact that it contradicts a valid superior norm, we must be assuming that, in addition to the express provisions of the higher law, there is a tacit clause that would authorize the adoption or enforcement of the lower norm despite the contradiction with the higher one. According to this view, higher norms include a disjunction: One of its terms is the explicit stipulation of conditions for the enactment of lower norms and the other is a tacit authorization to enact norms without complying with the former conditions. Kelsen makes clear that the legal system generally privileges the explicit text, establishing sanctions or nullification procedures when the inferior norm or law departs from it. But an inferior norm's conformity with the tacit clause of the higher norm explains why the lower norm is considered valid even when it infringes on an explicit provision of the higher norm.

Unless properly qualified, Kelsen's device of the alternative tacit clause is clearly unacceptable, for it would require us to suppose that a constitution authorizes a state to enact statutes no matter what their content. Given the interdependence of procedure and substance, the alternative tacit clause would encompass not only the substance but also the procedure and the authority established by higher norms. Thus, according, to Kelsen's proposal, any norm or law enacted by anybody, through any procedure and with any substance, would be a valid norm of any legal system, since its enactment would be authorized by the tacit clause of any norm of competence in that system.

The origin of Kelsen's error has been identified by Eugenio Bulygin.[10] According to him, there are two meanings of "validity" that Kelsen does not correctly distinguish and that are relevant in the case of norms that contradict the requirements of a higher norm. One meaning of "validity" refers to *membership of a norm to a legal system,* and the other to *the obligatory nature of the norm in question.* A norm may not belong to the legal system, and it may be, in certain cases, obligatory according to norms of that very system. Consider, for instance, laws of a foreign legal system which, according to private international law, are obligatory in certain cases. The same is the case, according to Bulygin, of unconstitutional statutes: They are invalid in the sense that they do not belong to the legal system, since they do not satisfy the conditions for their enactment established by norms of the system. Nevertheless, they may be obligatory if they are not nullified in the way established by the same system.

Kelsen's confusion is deeper than that attributed to him by Bulygin, however. In my opinion, it stems from the fact that Kelsen is not fully aware that his dominant concept of validity is not that of *membership of a norm to a legal system* but that of the *specific existence of norms or binding force.*[11] Under my view, a norm is valid when and only when one should do what the norm prescribes. In other words, the norm is valid when we are allowed to go from describing the fact that some authority has prescribed "*x* should be done" to the normative proposition that *x* should be done.

To some extent, Kelsen recognizes this sense of validity when he posits the basic norm, for it allows us to describe legal reality as a genuine normative phenomenon and not as a mere sequence of actions of prescribing. When a norm is valid, in the sense that it has binding force, its binding quality is established and the norms that it prescribes should be obeyed or applied even when enactment of those norms is not authorized. But the idea of membership of a norm or law in a legal system requires that the enactment of the norm be authorized by another norm also belonging to the system. Therefore, the central concept of validity in Kelsen's theory—that of binding force—is not coextensive with that of membership of a norm in a legal system, since there are binding norms for a certain legal system which do not belong to it. When Kelsen confronts the critical case of unconstitutional statutes—which indicates that there are valid and binding norms or laws which do not belong to a legal system—he argues that the higher norms tacitly *authorize* the enactment of those binding norms (which thus would belong to the system).

. Speaking more generally, I believe the resolution of "Kelsen's problem" shows the flaw in "Marshall's logic." Just because the enactment of a statute did not satisfy the conditions established by the constitution does not necessarily mean that the statute is not valid in the sense of obligation or binding force. The legal system may include norms that make it, under certain conditions, obligatory to observe and to apply unconstitutional statutes. In fact, even legal systems that widely accept judicial review—such as in the United States and Argentina—routinely require application of unconstitutional statutes that have yet to be declared as such, either because of judicial mistakes or because the right case has not yet come to court. In the Argentine legal system, statutes that have been declared unconstitutional may well be applied and relied upon in those situations outside the context where it was declared invalid. Admittedly, Kelsen's notion of the alternative tacit clause tries to cope with this phenomenon, but there are three differences between Kelsen's idea and my position.

First, norms granting validity to the unconstitutional enactments do not *authorize* those enactments but merely declare that there is an *obligation* to apply and observe the resulting rules. Second, these norms are not necessary components of every legal system but are only contingent parts of some systems. Although they generally have not been explicitly enacted, these norms, rather, are generated in a customary way. They may or may not exist in a system. If they do exist in a system, their content may vary widely. Third, a norm requiring application of an illegal enactment might consider all laws obligatory regardless of their substance or procedure through which they were enacted. In fact, such norms usually require that the norm in question satisfy, along with negative conditions of not being declared unconstitutional by the appropriate court, certain affirmative conditions—specifically, that the norm in question should enjoy a certain "color or appearance of legality."[12] For an unconstitutional statute to be obligatory until declared as such, its unconstitutionality should not be extremely gross and evident but should maintain some minimum appearance of satisfying the established conditions for enacting norms of the legal system.

Let us go back now to Marshall. The foregoing discussion shows that just because a norm is not a "law of the system" (according to the conditions established by the constitution), it does not follow that the norm could not be obligatory according to tacit, but contingent, clauses of the very same constitution. Just as Marshall surely would accept that this is the case when the Supreme Court has wrongly declared a law constitutional or before it has declared the law unconstitutional, those tacit clauses of the constitution could well establish that judges, or even the Supreme Court itself, are obliged to apply the law until it is either abrogated by the organ that enacted it or declared unconstitutional by a different political body. The first occurs in England and occurred in the traditional French system before the Constitutional Council was introduced. The second system, involving the use of a different political body, is closer to the current European model.

Therefore, Marshall's "logic" breaks down between premises 4 and 7 of my reconstruction of his argument. The supremacy of the constitution implies that a law contrary to it is not valid, as premise 4 states, insofar as "valid" means membership to a legal system. If, on the other hand, "valid" means that the application of and obedience to the law is obligatory, it may be true that a law contradicting the constitution is valid. The denial of premise 4—the proposition that a law contradictory to the constitution is not valid—does not necessarily mean, as premise 5 states, that the constitution does not limit Congress and that Congress could modify the Constitution by an ordinary law. Congress may indeed be prohibited by the Constitution from enacting certain laws. Still, if Congress violates this prohibition, the application and observance of the law by the courts and the citizenry may well be obligatory until Congress itself abrogates this law or the Supreme Court acts. Hence, Marshall's conclusion does not follow. It is not necessarily true that a law which contradicts the Constitution should not be applied by the judicial power. Rather, this decision depends on other norms implicit in the system that have been established for this sort of situation.

Marshall might well reply that if a constitution requires judges to enforce statutes which contradict the constitution, that document no longer serves as an instrument for limiting government but instead becomes an ordinary law that can be modified by those who enact the laws. But this reply would confuse a *logical* problem with a *practical* one. It is logically possible that a constitution—like the customary British or former French constitutions—would prohibit the parliament from enacting certain norms, even when no organ is authorized to abrogate or nullify the norms that are enacted in violation of that prohibition. Of course, one must suppose that there is another institution or procedure to resolve questions of unconstitutionality that do not involve judicial review. This procedure may be administered by a political organ or by direct appeal to the electorate, either by some formal institution (a plebiscite) or by a diffuse social understanding that would allow any citizen to disobey the unconstitutional law.

Therefore, it is not true that a system which does not utilize judicial review is a logical impossibility or that such a system negates the supremacy of a constitution. Review is necessary, but it may not be judicial review. The power of judicial review is a contingent arrangement even when the system has a supreme constitution.

Judicial Review as Logically Required by the Recognition of Rights and Democracy

Even if the absence of judicial review is logically compatible with constitutional supremacy, it may not be compatible with our conception of an ideal dimension of rights and organization of power. While judicial review is not logically required by the notion of the constitutional supremacy, it might be required by recognizing an ideal constitution.

It is often said that the democratic process cannot be the last resort for the protection of individual rights, since the main function of rights is to contain majoritarian decisions and protect the interests of isolated individuals or minorities. The idea of a liberal democracy implies a limited democracy and insists that certain rights not be trespassed, even by majoritarian decisions. These rights can be protected by mechanisms—such as judicial review—that lie outside the political process.

Ronald Dworkin makes this type of argument when he distinguishes between policies and principles.[13] Policies define collective objectives—such as national defense or a clean environment—comprising states of affairs the value of which is appraised in an aggregative and not an individualized way. Principles establish rights that protect states of affairs the value of which takes into account distribution and individualization of the goods involved. Principles thus limit the pursuit of a collective objective. In this way, a reason based on a collective objective cannot override a reason based on a right. According to Dworkin, the rationale for making certain decisions through the democratic process is related to policies, since that rationale refers to the need to balance diverse interests. On the other hand, this process does not apply to decisions made on the basis of principles, for they do not rely on a balance of interests and in fact have an atemporal validity. Judges, according to Dworkin, should decide their cases on the basis of principles and not on the basis of policies.

I think, however, that this vision of rights as limiting democracy—as a logical matter—is not plausible. Rights admittedly protect individual *interests*, setting forth barriers to considerations based on the interests of others or the social whole; it is entirely true that if I have a right to x, this right, by definition, cannot be displaced by the fact that the interests of the majority would be promoted if I were deprived of x. But from this proposition we cannot infer that rights are barriers to all majoritarian decisions. There is no logical inconsistency in stating that the only authority competent to recognize and enforce rights is a majoritarian one. While some may argue that majoritarian decisions benefit majoritarian interests, this is a factual and moral question, not one required by the logic of the concept of rights.

Dworkin's thesis must be appraised on a moral and factual basis, not as a conceptual matter. It is to be noted, however, that Dworkin seems to assume that there is an ample space for the operation of policies that establish collective objectives without colliding with rights, a space which is occupied by the political process exempted from judicial control. This can well be questioned if one supports— as I do—a robust theory of rights, according to which those rights can be violated not only by positive acts but also by omissions, since in this case rights occupy almost all the moral space, allowing very little room for policies and thus, according to Dworkin's thesis, for the unrestrained operation of majorities. Dworkin's thesis is also in tension with the view of democracy which conceives of it as dealing with intersubjective moral issues and not merely, as the opposite pluralist vision holds, as a process of aggregating interests.[14]

One may think that judicial review is fully compatible with the recognition of the epistemic value of democracy since judges, when enforcing the constitution, honor the popular sovereignty expressed in that very constitution. This is a common argument which identifies the historical constitution with the highest expression of the will of the people, and therefore asserts that judicial review follows logically from democratic legitimacy. But this argument breaks down, as we saw in Chapter 2, since most of the historical constitutions in force in different countries have not been enacted in a genuinely democratic way. Consider the constitutions of the United States and Argentina. Only a fraction of the population—white, mostly wealthy males—participated in the constitutional process. In those cases where the constitution has been enacted democratically—as in Spain—the durability of that constitution means that the democratic legitimacy fades with time, since the constitution may no longer express a consensus about the way people would solve current social conflicts.

To overcome these objections, some have resorted to a notion of tacit consent. According to this view, the fact that the constitution is not abrogated by modern society shows that it is acquiesced to by it. But, as Bruce Ackerman has noted, the very difficulty of the procedure for modifying an entrenched constitution makes one wonder whether its preservation really signifies majoritarian support.

An alternative theory for establishing a suitable connection between the value of democracy and judicial review would be to argue that the value of democracy requires certain preconditions. When judges interpret the constitution to prevail over ordinary legislation, they are protecting those preconditions. This theory has two versions, one of which clearly fails, while the other is much more promising.

The version that fails is the unsophisticated one which would treat any application of the historical constitution in order to nullify ordinary legislation as a way of preserving the preconditions of democracy. It is obvious, however, that many provisions of the historical constitution seem to be irrelevant to the epistemic value of the democratic process. Moreover, even when they are relevant, they may not be the best way of preserving those preconditions. Therefore, it seems that this strategy of argument leads not to the enforcement of the historical dimension of constitution but to that of an ideal one, which may or may not coincide with the former.

The sophisticated version of the argument for judicial review based on the preconditions of democracy points, at least in the first stage, to the prerequisites for the democratic process to enjoy epistemic value. Epistemic superiority is not something which accrues to the democratic process just because it is called "democratic"; it depends on certain positive and negative conditions that the process must fulfill. Perhaps our intuition in favor of judicial review is associated with those situations in which those conditions are not satisfied, and consequently the political process—be it called "democratic" or not—is no longer epistemically superior to the judicial process. In these instances, we may turn to the judiciary to establish the conditions which endow the democratic process with epistemic value.

Three Exceptions to the Denial of Judicial Review

As a general matter, the epistemic theory of democracy calls judicial review into question. There are, however, three exceptions to this rule. Two of those exceptions are based on conditions that make democratic decisions epistemically reliable. The third is grounded on a condition that makes democratic decisions, which are epistemically reliable, efficacious.

The First Exception: Strengthening the Democratic Process

The democratic process is not a spontaneous activity but a product of rules. Those rules are not arbitrary but are designed to maximize the epistemic value of that process. As discussed before, this value depends on several factors, including the breadth of participation in the discussion by those affected by the decision ultimately taken; the freedom that participants enjoy to express themselves in deliberation; the equality of the conditions under which that participation is carried out; the satisfaction of the requirement that the proposals be properly justified; the degree to which debate is principled rather than the mere presentation of interests; the avoidance of frozen majorities; the extent to which the majority supports the decisions; the distance in time since the consensus was achieved; and the reversibility of the decision. The rules of the democratic process try to ensure that these conditions are met to the maximum degree possible in order to make the enactments of that process reliable guides to moral principles.

The question arises, of course, as to who must ensure that the rules of the democratic process are adequately complied with. That responsibility cannot be delegated to the democratic process, since the monitoring function would simply be influenced by noncompliance with the rules and conditions grounding epistemic value. Therefore, scholars such as John Hart Ely, who take quite seriously the countermajoritarian difficulty, conceive of the judiciary as a type of referee in the democratic process.[15] The central mission of this referee is to see that procedural rules and conditions of the democratic discussion and decision are satisfied.

Why should the judiciary be in a better place than democratic bodies, even with the vices affecting their operations, to detect distortions in the democratic system? The first reply to this objection is that, given that anyone can defer her moral judgment to that emerging from a regularly conducted process of democratic discussion and decision, anyone may determine whether the conditions which give epistemic value to the democratic process are satisfied and to what degree. The power of judges is nothing more than the power of any citizen who is in the predicament of applying a legal norm for justifying an action or decision and who, compelled by the structure of practical reasoning to resort to moral principles, must determine for herself whether the conditions are satisfied for relying on the democratic process to identify those principles. Therefore, judges— like anybody facing the predicament of applying a law to justify an action or a decision—have no alternative but to determine whether the collective process leading to that law has satisfied the conditions of democratic legitimacy, in the same way that they have no alternative but to determine how the law originated.

Second, since the intervention of the judges is by nature unidirectional, their activism in this respect is always directed to broadening the democratic process—requiring more participation, more freedom of the parties, more equality, and more concentration on justification. It would be unthinkable for a judge to nullify legislation on the ground that it was enacted through too broad a process of participation or with too much equality. Admittedly, judges may be, and often are, mistaken in their conclusions about the operations of the democratic system, but the overall effect of a procedural theory of judicial review is to promote the conditions granting the democratic process its epistemic value.

Many of these conditions involve a certain category of rights that comprise the ideal constitution. Those rights may be deemed a priori rights, since they are conditions of the validity of the democratic process and their value is not determined by the democratic process but rather presupposed by it.[16] These a priori rights ought to be, thus, respected by the democratic process as prerequisites to its validity. It is the mission of judges to guarantee that respect.

Certainly, it is quite difficult to determine the range of a priori rights and to distinguish them from those rights that are established by the democratic process itself, the so-called a posteriori rights. Some a priori rights are obvious. For instance, active and passive political rights along with freedom of expression are clearly central to the minimum working of the democratic system. But these rights presuppose others which are even more basic, including protection from assault and from political restrictions on freedom of movement. These are preconditions for free participation in the democratic process.

The a priori status of other rights may be more controversial. Take the case of so-called social or welfare rights. I maintained in Chapter 2 that these rights are not antagonistic to classical individual rights but are the natural extension of them. A classical individual right, such as the right to life, is violated by positive acts but also by failing to provide the resources necessary to protect those rights, such as medical attention, food, and shelter. Once we broaden the definition of individual rights, however, the counter-majoritarian difficulty of judicial review becomes much more dramatic, since all political decisions may affect, by action or omission, an individual right. Even under the procedural theory, the scope of judicial review would be quite broad, given that social and economic conditions of individuals, such as their level of education, are preconditions for free and equal participation in the political process. But this simply provokes again the question of why judges should be in a better situation than those immersed in the democratic process to take extremely controversial decisions about the distribution of goods and the best social mechanisms to carry out that distribution.

There is no algebraic formula to determine the content of a priori rights. Some goods are so fundamental to the proper working of the democratic system that if they are not provided, the democratic process will deteriorate so much that its epistemic value vanishes. If someone is starving, or very ill and deprived of medical attention, or lacks all possibility of expressing his ideas through the mass media, the democratic system is harmed in the same way as if he were disenfranchised. But we must be careful to limit the cases in which we are prepared to interfere with the democratic system for its own protection. If we decide, for instance, that a specific distribution of goods is required as a precondition of the proper working of the democratic system, we prevent the system from having any say about the appropriate distribution. In the end, we could have a magnificent democratic system, from the epistemic point of view, which is only allowed to decide very few things.

We must therefore confront this tension between the strength and the scope of the democratic process. The more we enhance its epistemic quality by expanding a priori rights to provide the goods ensuring freedom and equal participation, the range of matters to be decided by that democratic process becomes narrower. When some threshold concerning the a priori distribution is surpassed, the democratic system, through its tendency toward impartiality, may correct and improve itself by providing people with the preconditions for their equal and free participation. On the other hand, if that threshold is not reached, the weaknesses of the process will be magnified so that the partiality of solutions promoted by unequal or constrained participation will lead to further inequalities or limitations on the participation.

While there is no exact formula for locating this threshold, there is a general guide that a judge, or for that matter anyone deciding whether to justify a decision on the basis of the law, must take into account. That decision maker must determine whether the vices of the "democratic" system are so serious that its general epistemic reliability is lower than that enjoyed by the isolated reflection of an individual. If the vices are that serious, the decision maker must act on the basis of his or her own moral judgment, both in order to solve the case at hand and to promote a course of action that can improve for the future the epistemic quality of the system (often the two things can be achieved by the same decision). Of course, there is no epistemic authority to guide one in deciding whether to defer to the epistemic authority of the democratic system or to decide on the basis of his or her own lights. This decision about the best epistemic process for achieving just decisions must be taken in isolation.

This exception to the general denial of judicial review requires some modification to an earlier conclusion. We have said that the ideal constitution of rights derives from the operation of a historical constitution adjusted to the requirements of the ideal organization of power. Yet there is an a priori set of rights implicit in the ideal organization of power which must be complied with by the historical constitution in order to define the remaining part of that ideal set of rights.

The Second Exception: Personal Autonomy

The second exception to the denial of judicial review arises from a negative condition of the epistemic value of democracy. We have based the value of democracy on the greater reliability of the democratic process, as compared with alternative methods of decisions, for arriving at morally correct solutions. This reliability obviously depends on defining the validity or correctness of solutions in terms of impartiality or the equal contemplation of all interests affected.

As we have seen, not all moral standards or requirements depend for their validity on the satisfaction of the requirement of impartiality. Consider the ideals of being a good patriot, a good soldier, or a responsible parent; of a life devoted to knowledge or beauty; of integrity and honesty; or of religious commitments. All these ideals can only tangentially be associated with the idea of impartiality.[17] In *The Ethics of Human Rights*, and again in this book, I have distinguished between two dimensions of morals.[18] First, there is public, intersubjective or social morality, which consists of those standards that evaluate actions for their effects on the interests of individuals other than the agents. Second, there is private, self-regarding or personal morality, which consists of those ideals of personal excellence or virtue that evaluate actions for their effects on the quality of the life or character of the agents themselves.

As part of this second dimension of morality, we can infer from the general value of moral autonomy implicit in our practice of moral discourse the more specific, and unrestrained, value of personal autonomy. This value consists of the free adoption of ideals of personal excellence and of plans of life based on them. An additional argument for this value of personal autonomy is provided by the self-defeating nature of any policy to impose personal ideals upon people.

The validity of personal ideals does not depend on the satisfaction of the requirement of impartiality. Accordingly, collective discussion and decision are not substantially more reliable than individual reflection and decision for arriving at morally correct solutions in this regard. Therefore, judges have no reason to subordinate their moral judgments to a democratic law that is based on personal ideals of virtue or excellence. There is no epistemic ground which would justify such action. In these matters, only the judgment of the agent himself is relevant. Consequently, a judge, or any citizen who has a basis for conscientious objection, ought to revise and eventually set aside any perfectionist laws and other norms of a democratic origin.

The most relevant basis for disqualifying a democratically enacted law because of its perfectionist nature is the rationale upon which it was been enacted. The value of personal autonomy does not protect particular actions, but simply prevents those actions from being interfered with on the basis of certain reasons. The extreme example of the personal ideal is the situation where someone's ideal is to kill other people. The state or other individuals cannot interfere with that action because they object to the personal ideal on which it is based. The state can only interfere because this personal ideal also implies the adoption of an unacceptable intersubjective moral standard. The reason to set aside perfectionist legislation is that its real ground is the imposition of an ideal of human excellence. Consider laws punishing the possession of drugs even for personal consumption. If the genuine rationale of such a law is to protect unwilling third parties (even if the factual basis of this rationale was erroneous), the soundness of the legislation would be something to be discussed through the democratic process—not the judicial one. But judges could invalidate the law if its objective was to impose an ideal of personal excellence. For these reasons, it is essential to consider the genuine reasons behind legal norms, since they determine the rationality of their application and constitutionality.

This second justification for judicial review has implications for evaluating many controversial judicial decisions. It calls into question, for example, the ruling of the United States Supreme Court *Bowers v. Hardwick*. In that case, the Court upheld a Georgia statute based on perfectionist grounds that proscribed homosexual behavior. Always, the test should be whether the rationale underlying the legislative proscription—whether it concerns homosexuality or possession of drugs or divorce or exemption from military service—involves adhesion to a particular ideal of human excellence or whether the proscription only involves the adoption of some intersubjective moral standard. If the proscription involves the adoption of an intersubjective moral standard, this proscription is only for the political process to determine and to correct. In such a situation, the proscription should not be addressed by the judiciary even when the proscription is wrong.

By restricting the ideal constitution of power to intersubjective moral matters, one may perceive the dominance of the ideal constitution of rights where the recognition of personal autonomy is concerned. The right not to be coerced on the basis of standards of personal excellence is thus a part of the set of a priori rights that condition the democratic process.

The Third Exception: The Constitution as a Social Practice

Unlike the first two exceptions, the third exception to the denial of judicial review is not based on the conditions for democracy's epistemic value. Instead, it is based on making those democratic decisions which have epistemic value more efficacious. The purpose of judicial review is to preserve the social practice or convention within which that decision operates, specifically, the historical constitution.

Remember that what was wrong with the model of legal or practical reasoning developed in Chapter 2 was the assumption that what must be justified is an individual action or decision instead of a collective practice or convention to which the agent must decide whether to contribute or not. In our case, the collective practice is the historical constitution which, once justified in the light of the ideal constitutions of rights and power, serves as a basis for justifying individual actions and decisions. But we saw that the two-stage reasoning must take into account what would be the most realistic alternative for enforcing the ideal constitution of rights and powers if the historical constitution were dismissed. Sometimes, there would be much more frustration of the requirements of the ideal constitutions than if the morally unsatisfactory historical constitution were enforced. Therefore, a "second-best" type of rationality is in order, and respect for the ideal constitutions of rights and power requires us to depart from some of their requirements.

This contingency must be acknowledged by judges. A democratic decision may, even while satisfying the ideal constitution of power and of rights, seriously undermine the convention that makes up the historical constitution. Consider the case in which the democratic decision clearly infringes the text—the most salient aspect of the convention according to conventional rules of interpretation. That democratic decision may be impeccable from the point of view of the liberal and participatory elements of constitutionalism, but it could run counter to the element that preserves the rule of law. While no right would be violated if the democratic decision were respected, the social practice constituted by the historical constitution may be weakened, and as a result the efficacy of democratic decisions writ large may be undermined. In this situation, the judge may justifiably intervene to invalidate the democratic law to protect the constitutional convention that grants efficacy to the democratic decisions themselves. Typically, the judge in this way may be furthering the ideal constitution. Therefore, even when the judicial invalidation of democratically enacted norms seems to weaken the ideal constitution, it actually preserves the possibility of enforcing the ideal dimensions of the complex constitution.

Let me illustrate this use of the judicial power with a case from Argentina. In 1990, President Menem pardoned several military officers who had been tried for human rights violations. But a conventional interpretation of article 86, section 6 of the Constitution of 1853 would have precluded those pardons, since they had not yet been convicted. The constitutional text refers to pardons or commutations of "penalties" for federal crimes. These pardons did not directly infringe on the elements of constitutionalism associated with the ideal constitutions of rights and power; no individual right was directly violated by those pardons.[19] Moreover, Menem, who earlier had been elected by a wide majority, had probably more democratic legitimacy than Congress, which possessed the amnesty power, or a judge who could have acquitted the officers. In my view, however, such a frontal contradiction with the text—conventionally accepted as the coordination point of the constitutional convention—greatly weakened the continuity of the historical constitution and threatened the enforcement of the ideal constitution. Thus, an exercise of judicial review to nullify those pardons might well have been justified.

This third exception to the denial of judicial review creates an inherent dilemma. The nullification of a democratic enactment is done in the name of the ultimate enforcement of the ideal constitutions of rights and power. The immediate effect of that nullification, however, is to ignore the requirements of those constitutions, dismissing a democratic decision and going against the ideal of participatory democracy, notwithstanding the epistemic presumption that its determination of rights is morally correct. Therefore, the judge must necessarily balance the immediate harm to the participatory and liberal ideals of constitutionalism vis à vis the harm that would be caused to those ideals if the constitutional practice were undermined because a democratic decision infringed on it.

Obviously, not all deviations from the historical constitution by the democratic process are so harmful to its continuity as to justify overriding that process. Again, there are no exact formulas for resolving this tension. Ultimately, it is question of judgment whether one is justified in restraining the operations of democracy not to promote democracy directly, as in the first case for judicial review, or to respect its limits, as in the second, but to preserve a practice that lends efficacy to democratic decisions.

Testing the Theory

In order to test the adequacy of this theory of judicial review, let us examine briefly its implications for three of the most important constitutional cases ever resolved by the United States Supreme Court. These decisions are *Griswold v. Connecticut*,[20] *Roe v. Wade*,[21] and *Brown v. Board of Education*.[22]

Griswold v. Connecticut

In *Griswold*, a practically unanimous Supreme Court called the Connecticut statute penalizing the use of contraceptives by married people obnoxious, probably stupid, and even violative of the moral right to privacy. There was a general agreement that the statute violated an ideal set of rights. Most of the Justices would have accepted this moral conclusion, because the statute ignored what I have called the value of autonomy of the person. The main disagreement among the Justices involved what to make of this conclusion. There were three main responses to the statute.

For Justice John Harlan, this moral violation was enough to invalidate the statute. The vagueness of the Fourteenth Amendment required the Court to consider basic values and to intervene to protect the fundamental rights that belonged to the citizens of all free governments. This view comports with my thoughts on the need to resort to those principles of social morality comprising the ideal constitution of rights. This is done when we decide to recognize a certain constitutional practice after confronting its indeterminacies. Justice Byron White agreed with this view, but believed also that invalidating a statute in light of fundamental rights must take into account the rationale of the statute and the instrumental relationship between the end of the statute and the means used to achieve that end. In this case, he found the end sought objectionable.

For Chief Justice Earl Warren and Justice Arthur Goldberg, the

Connecticut statute ran counter to a right of privacy "older than the Bill of Rights." They believed this right could be found in the four corners of the United States Constitution. Warren thought that this right could be found in the penumbra of several amendments to the Constitution, such as the First, Third, Fourth, Fifth, and Ninth, which the Fourteenth applied to the states. This theory provided power to the Court without converting it into a superlegislature. Goldberg emphasized mainly the power of the Ninth Amendment, which, when combined with the Fourteenth, protected fundamental aspects of liberty. These Justices, thus, in the spirit of my argument of Chapter 2, resorted to the need to preserve the historical constitution, in its conventional interpretation, as a ground for invalidating the statute under review.

For Justices Hugo Black and Potter Stewart, the two lines of argument already outlined were not adequate. Black and Stewart agreed with Harlan and White about the moral right to privacy and the obnoxiousness of the statute but insisted that those views were a "subjective opinion." Using my language, they would have said that these opinions evince an epistemic moral elitism. They also rejected the appeal to the constitutional convention, since it was extremely far-fetched to connect the right to privacy to rights of free speech or association. In a spirit that recognized the epistemic value of democracy, they upheld the right of the legislative bodies to make this sort of decision, without being disturbed by the isolated reflection of judges as to the acceptability of this law.

Each of the three groups of Justices resorted respectively to a different component of the complex ideal of constitutionalism: the liberal dimension expressed by the ideal constitution of rights; the conventional dimension expressed by the historical constitution; and the participatory dimension expressed by the ideal constitution of power. Because I have indicated tensions between these three dimensions of constitutionalism and the absence of any formula to solve them, one may believe there is no right answer in a case such as this. But this is not so.

First, it is important to realize that Justices Black and Stewart were plainly right in saying that there was no definite constitutional practice regarding privacy. The text or existing practice at that time was flexible enough to allow for many conflicting solutions. As I discussed in Chapter 2, the vagueness of a constitution often produces indeterminacies when there are no conventional criteria of interpretation applicable. Justice Stewart's view about the historical origin of the Ninth Amendment is debatable as a criterion for interpreting the text. Yet no other criterion seemed available. This was clearly a case in which the constitutional practice was unclear.

Next, we can agree with Justice Harlan that the right to privacy is a fundamental right. As we saw in Chapter 4, the principle of personal autonomy informs the rights that are part of the ideal constitution. This principle is derived primarily from the prohibition against interfering with actions of individuals that do not harm other people, since such interference would violate the ideal of personal autonomy. A presupposition of our practice of moral discourse is that it is valuable for people to guide their conduct and attitudes by standards they freely accept. To prohibit the use of contraceptives is plainly an instance of perfectionism, since the rule would impose on people certain supposed virtues and would not be designed (as a legitimate paternalistic law) to satisfy subjective preferences.[23]

Admittedly, we cannot impose our own judgment about moral truth. Justices Black and Stewart emphasized this, and a similar view is implicit in the positions of Justices Warren and Goldberg. To presume that we are in a better position than those affected to participate in balancing conflicting interests and in reaching an impartial perspective from which moral rights are determined is, as I have said, a manifestation of epistemic elitism. Simply because the Justices of the Supreme Court are men and women of considerable wisdom and culture, they are not in a better position than those directly responsible to the people whose interests are at stake to define the scope and hierarchy of their rights.

The concern with epistemic elitism is not applicable, however, when the rights in question establish positive or negative conditions needed for the democratic process to have epistemic value. If those conditions are not satisfied, there is no reason for a judge, or anybody else, to defer to the result of a putative democratic process. And indeed, these conditions are not satisfied when laws are enacted on the basis of ideals of personal excellence; their validity has nothing to do with the impartial assessment of interests in conflict. The democratic process has epistemic value because it involves a dynamic that verges toward impartiality but has no epistemic quality when dealing with issues in which validity does not depend on impartiality.

The Connecticut statute is a perfect case of a law infringing a condition or limitation of the democratic system. No person has any reason to defer to the legislature of Connecticut when that institution deals with defining an appropriate sexual life, in the same way as when it purports to solve a scientific, philosophic, or religious issue. The decision of the Supreme Court in this case is right not because of the reasons given by its members but because the Court's evaluation of what is right or wrong should not be limited by the outcome of the collective process of discussion and decision. The Court must enable the citizens to act according to the results of their own reflection, since they have no reasons to defer to what the majority decides, and because the Court has the duty to strengthen the epistemic value of the democratic process which requires that it operate within its proper limits.

Roe v. Wade

In *Roe v. Wade*, the Supreme Court invalidated a Texas statute that prohibited abortion except when medical opinion showed that the abortion was necessary to save the life of the mother. The Court established a trimester system, allowing increased governmental regulation of abortions as a pregnancy proceeded.

Justice Harry Blackmun wrote the opinion of the Court. He found that abortion involved a right of personal privacy located either in the Fourteenth Amendment's concept of liberty or in the Ninth Amendment and concluded that the right to privacy was broad enough to encompass a woman's decision whether or not to terminate her pregnancy. The right of privacy itself was grounded on the constitutional practice established in cases such as *Griswold*. Blackmun recognized that the right of privacy with regard to abortion would be constrained if the fetus was understood to be a person, but he concluded that when the Constitution uses the word *persons*, it refers to those already born. He acknowledged that while one might try to defend the law against abortion on the ground of discouraging illicit sexual conduct, Texas did not resort to such an argument. He found some legitimacy in argument based on avoiding unsafe abortions but thought it overly broad. Blackmun also discussed arguments based on the need to protect prenatal life but rejected them ultimately as too contested to be the basis of a decision to limit the privacy rights of the mother.

Blackmun did find, to some extent, that potential life was a legitimate competing interest to the mother's rights and that the state could protect it. He concluded that in the first three months of pregnancy no compelling interests outweighed the privacy interest of the mother, advised by her physician concerning the safety of an abortion. After that period, however, the state could regulate abortion procedures by taking into account the protection of the mother's health. In the last trimester, the state could regulate or even prohibit abortion in the interests of the potential of human life, limited by the state's need to protect the life and health of the mother.

The concurring opinions of Justices Potter Stewart and William Douglas emphasized that the right of the woman to have an abortion was within the liberty granted by the Fourteenth Amendment. They acknowledged that the states retained the power to regulate liberty under their police power; but all exercises of the regulatory power had to be subject to careful scrutiny to determine whether they were used to advance legitimate interests.

Justice Byron White dissented. He argued that the recognition of the right to have an abortion created a new constitutional right and removed power from the people and the states. According to him, the majority's decision meant that "the people and the legislatures of 50 states are constitutionally disentitled to weigh the relative importance of the continued existence and development of the fetus, on the one hand, against the impact on the mother, on the other hand."[24]

Justice William Rehnquist also concluded that the right to an abortion was completely alien to the Constitution's framers and in no way could be inferred from the text. He noted that most states—reflecting the views of the majority of their citizens—had enacted laws against abortion. This, he believed, demonstrated that the right to an abortion is not a right embedded in the fundamental values and traditions of society and that the Texas statute was not so unreasonable as to violate substantive due process.

The constitutional practice was certainly indeterminate on the question of the right to an abortion. Either solution at the time of *Roe* would have been compatible with the preservation of the historical constitution. While it is true that the right to privacy was established by cases like *Griswold*, the question here was precisely whether the autonomy of the mother is the only value to be taken into consideration or whether it should compete with some other value associated with the life of the fetus.

Notwithstanding this point about the historical constitution and abortion, a conflict arose between the ideal set of rights and the result of a legitimate democratic process. Justices White and Rehnquist appealed to the right of the people and the legislatures of the states to decide these issues in a democratic way, while the majority appealed to the right of liberty, autonomy, or privacy of the mother as part of the ideal constitution of rights.

In order to evaluate this conflict, it is necessary to ask ourselves whether a precondition of the democratic process is being ignored. Just because something is a right is not sufficient to remove that question from the democratic process and put it in the hands of nondemocratic officials. Justice Blackmun mentioned the possibility that the prohibition of abortion should be based on discouraging illicit sexual relations or on medical reasons. He disregarded the former reason because it was not relied upon by the state, and he partially accepted the latter. If management of sexual relations had been the rationale of the statute, it would have to be invalidated, in my view, for being openly perfectionist.[25] The problem of the medical rationale is that it does not seem to be genuine, since abortions accomplished under proper care and conditions can be carried out with minimal risk to the mother. Furthermore, any risk can be undertaken by the woman with the proper degree of information. Besides, it is common knowledge that when abortion is illegal, women—particularly poor ones—undergo abortions regardless of much more dangerous conditions. Therefore, paternalist explanations seem to conceal either perfectionist ones, which are illicit, or justifications in terms of the rights of the fetus.

Contrary to Justice Blackmun's assumptions, it does not seem possible to avoid a position about the value of the fetus when dealing with the abortion issue. Justice Blackmun implicitly adopted a view about the fetus. His view necessarily concluded that the life of the fetus does not have a value to be protected with the same vigor as the value of the life of a born person, unless the fetus has reached the moment of viability. The question is not whether we can avoid taking a position about the value of the fetus, since we cannot. The question is whether the position must be taken through the collective process of discussion and decision or outside of it.[26] The issue is not *whether* to decide the value of the fetus but *who* must reach it with binding power over others.

My position is this: The question of whether the fetus's life has the same value as that of a full person is an a priori question that must necessarily be solved as a precondition of the democratic process. The resolution of this issue determines who should act as a subject of the moral discourse constituting the democratic process. If the fetus has value, the courts should grant the same protection to the fetus as to any other person. It would not be enough to reply that the mother's right to privacy or autonomy overrides the rights of the fetus.[27]

A statute that prohibits abortion would certainly be unconstitutional if it relied on a perfectionist rationale. But if the statute restrained the autonomy of the mother on the basis of assigning value to the fetus, I might reach a different conclusion. While I would likely find the statute seriously objectionable, I cannot see how judges are in a better position than the democratic process to assess the comparative values of the autonomy of the parents and that of the life of the fetus from an impartial perspective.

In sum, the decision in *Roe v. Wade* should stand largely on account of the perfectionist rationale of the Texas statute that was concealed behind paternalistic arguments. I acknowledge, however, that it would be very difficult to invalidate the Texas statute if it simply demonstrated a callous scorn on the part of the democratic legislature for the autonomy of women. It is not outside the scope of the democratic process to compromise the autonomy of women to highlight the value of the fetus. Our indignation toward such a statute is comparable to the indignation toward policies that ignore fundamental social rights in order to preserve property rights of the few. This indignation cannot justify thwarting the democratic process by some external intervention motivated by an epistemic elitist zeal.

Brown v. Board of Education

The decision in *Brown v. Board of Education* will only occupy us briefly since it is less theoretically intriguing than the other two decisions of tremendous political and moral importance. Chief Justice Earl Warren wrote for the Court and rejected the doctrine of "separate but equal" as applied to segregated public schools. The result in *Brown* is hard to square with the historical constitution, since, following *Plessy v. Ferguson*, United States constitutional practice may well have permitted educational segregation.[28] Yet I would say that even if segregation were part of constitutional practice, this is clearly a case where the constitutional practice is so contrary to the ideal constitution that one may justifiably depart from it even at the risk of undermining it.

Warren asserted that education was one of the most important functions of state and local government, and that segregated education harmed African Americans by generating in them a feeling of inferiority that retarded their intellect and development. This argument is sound, but it is insufficient to justify the decision. It is not enough to say that a group of the population is harmed by the way a fundamental state service is provided in order to invalidate the democratic assessment as to how to provide that service. But the argument can be completed by noting that the democratic process itself is seriously affected by a policy of educational segregation. Segregation impairs democracy.

The impact of educational segregation on the democratic process stems from the fact that self-esteem and adequate intellectual development are preconditions for sound civic involvement. More important, segregation in the educational sphere precludes close contacts between different individuals and groups and the development of fraternal feelings necessary for the democratic system to obtain the tendency toward impartiality that is the source of its epistemic value. As I have stressed throughout, the moral superiority of democracy over dictatorial systems of collective decisions is its greater tendency toward impartiality, due to the better possibility of knowing and assessing the interests of all the people affected. This ability is very seriously undermined if people are segregated from each other, particularly in their formative years, even in the unlikely event that the facilities are so equal that there is no harm to self-esteem and intellectual development.

In sum, the real greatness of *Brown* therefore resides in the capacity of the Court to understand a priori conditions for the working of the democratic process. Only when these conditions are satisfied can the process be adequate to require judges and others to defer to its result.

Judicial Review and Institutional Design

After dissecting the institution of judicial review to reveal its logical structure, I have tried to reconstruct this institution in a way that respects that logical structure. The result of that reconstruction is a theory of judicial review which, I trust, is less alarming to legal convention than some of my initial conclusions must have led some to fear. Though I generally argue against the justifiability of judicial review for laws originating through a democratic process, there are three ample exceptions to that denial. These exceptions involve the determination of whether the law respects the preconditions of the democratic process; disqualification of laws grounded on perfectionist reasons; and the examination of whether the law in question undermines the preservation of the morally acceptable legal practice.

In constructing this theory, I have assumed an institutional design according to which judges have only an indirect connection with the democratic process. But institutional designs may vary, requiring different options for the judiciary. For instance, a constitutional tribunal, in the European style, with members who are periodically renewed and chosen by different bodies that are representative of popular sovereignty, maintains greater democratic legitimacy than a supreme court (as in the United States and Argentina) to carry out judicial review. It is also possible to consider procedures that would ensure that members of the higher courts which exercise judicial review could periodically receive support from the democratic process. Such mechanisms should not create a dependency of the judiciary on those who exercise political power but would simply provide the judiciary with a wider basis of democratic support.

Similarly, a wide variety of strategies are available to the judiciary when confronted with a claim implicating the unconstitutionality of a law. On many occasions, the optimal form of judicial intervention is not of an all-out invalidation of an unconstitutional statute or administrative order. Judges need not always push aside the results of the democratic process to promote measures they think are more conducive to the protection or promotion of rights. Rather, judges can, and should, adopt measures that will promote the process of public deliberation over the issue or a more careful consideration on the part of political bodies.

For instance, some statutes lie in the zone between a priori conditions for the correct working of the democratic process and the determinations that must be made through that very process. In such a situation, institutional arrangements (such as those in the Canadian Constitution of 1982) might be fashioned by giving judges a "suspensive veto" over a law, which would give the legislature power to override the judicial judgment, but only after it undertook a new discussion and decision on the matter. We should also consider the possibility of a ruling of "unconstitutionality by omission," which would occur when the legislature failed to implement a constitutional prescription.[29] In such a case, the highest court may be authorized to require the legislature (or a commission of it) to explain the reasons for that omission and reveal whether there are any plans to overcome the deficiency.

Through such mechanisms, judges would have an active role in contributing to the improvement of the quality of the process of democratic discussion and decision, stimulating public debate and promoting more reflective decisions. This reconstruction of judicial review would also promote awareness in judges of the complex considerations they must assess in the discharge of their function.

At its core, this conception of judicial review reflects the complex relationship between deliberative democracy and the other two dimensions of constitutionalism, that is, the recognition of individual rights and the preservation of a constitutional practice. A recognition of the epistemic value of deliberative democracy entails a belief in the primacy of the process of collective discussion and majoritarian decision over any other procedure for determining morally acceptable solutions to social conflicts, even those involving rights. But a nuanced form of judicial review can ensure that the epistemic results emerging from the democratic process will be combined with claims ensuing from the ideal constitution of rights and the historical constitution.

Conclusion

· · · · · · · · ·

The Tensions of a
Complex Constitution

The structure of constitutionalism is beset with internal tensions. These tensions have been revealed by the arguments in this book.

We started by assuming that constitutionalism requires a democratic process, respect for individual rights, and the preservation of an established legal practice as first articulated by the historical constitution. At the same time, we confronted the apparent superfluousness of the historical constitution for justificatory legal reasoning, since justificatory reasoning ultimately relies on autonomous reasons, such as those of the ideal constitution. These autonomous reasons justify actions or decisions regardless of the solutions prescribed by the historical constitution. In order to overcome this apparent paradox, we identified the historical constitution with a social convention. This convention originates in a certain historical context, may be materialized in a certain text, and is constituted by patterns of actions and critical attitudes toward those patterns.

The historical constitution, understood as a social practice or convention, includes the rules of recognition for the other rules of the legal system. But this fact supports its significance only if a purely external approach to it is adopted instead of an internal vision which considers the justification of actions and decision. The relevance of the historical constitution for that justification cannot be provided by the communitarian value of tradition, or by the value of integrity, since all these considerations are objectionable as adopting a holistic approach or relying too heavily on contingent social arrangements.

The constitution as a social convention achieves relevance from the internal point of view of justificatory reasoning if we realize that decisions of political agents are not isolated individual actions, but that their efficacy derives from a system of intertwined actions, attitudes, and expectations. A judge's decision is no more than a contribution to a social practice constantly in flux and is operative insofar as it becomes a part of the network of conduct and attitudes comprising that practice. This practice or convention solves coordination problems on the basis of certain salient factors, such as a constitutional text which is generally observed. Thus, the reasoning performed in the practice of justifying an action or decision involves a two-stage structure. The first stage requires us to evaluate the practice on the basis of autonomous principles, such as those conforming to the ideal constitution of rights. If this first stage allows us to justify the practice, it is necessary to go on to a second stage, in which we deploy the practice itself to make the necessary decision.

By reviewing the problems of interpretation, we realize that constitutional and legal practices are not sufficient to determine unequivocal results. There are several steps in the task of interpreting and applying the historical constitution where one must resort, even at the second stage, to considerations of social morality that comprise the substantive ideal constitution. These considerations assist us in overcoming indeterminacies. The practice of which the historical constitution is a part has a "tiled" configuration, since it is first necessary to find support in previous decisions and actions when justifying other actions and decisions. In making a decision within the framework of the constitutional practice, it is then necessary to attempt to satisfy the principles of the ideal constitution. In turn, this effort assists in preserving and perfecting the overall practice.

By examining the assumptions underlying the social practice of moral discussion, we reach the principles of autonomy, inviolability, and dignity of the person. These principles of social morality exclude the triad of totalitarian conceptions constituted by perfectionism, holism, and normative determinism. The claims of equality are satisfied when we realize that the principle of inviolability of the person is infringed upon not only by positive acts but also by omissions that cause harms. This process of extraction generates an ideal constitution of rights that is robust and based on goods necessary for the formation and exercise, in that order, of personal autonomy.

It was also important to articulate, although in an unavoidably summary way, the specific rights recognized as part of an ideal substantive constitution. These rights include the right to life; freedom of expression; freedom of conscience, liberal education, privacy and intimacy, personal property and work, commerce and industry; and the positive contributions of the state to guarantee equal autonomy, equal treatment, and freedom from illegitimate discrimination. The procedural guarantees for the above rights are also important—not only because it is intrinsically important to discuss the bases for these rights, but also because they condition the relationship of different elements of constitutionalism. For instance, the right to privacy combines with the epistemic justification of democracy to limit the operation of the historical constitution.

The ideal constitution of power is based on a justification of democracy that relies on the transformation of people's interests through the process of participatory discussion and majoritarian decision. That process gives an epistemic quality to democracy insofar as it overcomes dispersion of sovereignty, the poverty of public debate, political apathy, and imperfect mediation. This approach to democracy has very concrete implications for institutional design. It prefers a more parliamentary form of government over a presidential one, decentralization of power to avoid the break-down of consensus, promotion of political participation by the citizens, and the democratization of the channels of public communication. The ideal constitution of power—to the extent that it is materialized in the historical one—leads to what should be the ideal constitution of rights. Therefore, at first sight, there seems to be no conflict between the substantive and the procedural ideal constitutions, since the ideal constitution of power is, when realized, the most reliable way of gaining access to the ideal constitution of rights. The most important goal is, thus, to achieve the ideal constitution of power: deliberative democracy.

This account of the participatory component of constitutionalism does not appear to leave much room for judicial review. This is all the more true when it is shown that judicial review is not a logical consequence of the recognition of either the supremacy of the constitution or individual rights. However, in an epistemic theory of democracy, judicial review is legitimized as a means of insuring that the conditions are present for giving collective participation an epistemic value. These conditions include the procedural requirement for the collective process of discussion and decision to generate a dynamic toward impartiality. The first exception to the general denial of judicial review under the epistemic theory consists in insuring that these procedural conditions are met. The second exception consists in disqualifying democratic enactments based on perfectionist reasons. Since people have the right not to be interfered with on the basis of personal ideals, the democratic process lacks epistemic superiority when it is engaged in such questions. Finally, democratic decisions are not relevant and efficacious unless they are taken in the context of the historical constitution and the social convention of which it is a part. This third exception to the denial of judicial review is aimed at preserving the constitutional practice, which in turn gives the democratic process significance and efficacy.

Ultimately, the structure of justificatory reasoning leads us to the ideal constitution of rights. But the power of that ideal constitution to validate a historical one is conditioned by the fact that the ideal can be materialized only through an existing constitutional convention. In order to know the substantive ideal constitution, we must know the ideal procedural constitution and to put this latter constitution into operation, we must rely on the historical or actual constitution of power. By implementing this particular constitution of power, we produce the actual constitution of rights. This last constitution presumptively coincides with the ideal constitution of rights as long as the actual constitution of power accords with the ideal constitution of power. In turn, the actual or historical constitution must be interpreted by resorting at various stages to the ideal constitution.

The complexity of the notion of constitutionalism is immediately perceived. Three elements emerge from the analysis of this book and are ordered according to the sequence of considerations in justificatory legal reasoning. The first element to be considered in that reasoning is the a priori component of the ideal constitution of rights. Second, the ideal constitution of power must be considered, and we must evaluate whether the historical constitution of power conforms to the requirements of the ideal constitution of power, including its presupposition of an a priori ideal constitution of rights. The operation of the historical constitution indicates presumptively the content of the a posteriori ideal constitution of power, including its presupposition of an a priori ideal constitution of rights. The operation of the historical constitution indicates presumptively the content of the a posteriori ideal of constitutional rights. The ideal constitutions must serve as parameters for justifying and interpreting the historical constitution so as to enable us to employ it for justifying individual actions and decisions. The justification of the historical constitution on the basis of the ideal ones is conditioned by the need to rely on a historical constitution in order to satisfy the requirements of the ideal constitutions. This creates a full circle in our analysis, since it means that the historical constitution will have an impact on the ideal ones.

The three elements of constitutionalism are in permanent and reciprocal tension. The tensions between rights and participatory democracy, on the one hand, and the preservation of the rule of law, on the other, are easy to perceive. All those who participate in a legal practice—judges, legislators, and even citizens—must achieve a permanent equilibrium between perfecting the practice according to the ideals of liberal democracy and preserving its continuity. Continuity must be preserved insofar as the legal practice is, in general, morally acceptable in securing the efficacy of the decisions, including the efficacy of those decisions seeking to bring that practice closer to moral ideals. Occasionally, it becomes sufficiently urgent to alter constitutional practice to maximize its moral legitimacy—either in relation to the recognition of substantive rights or in relation to the improvement of the democratic method—that one must risk the continuity of the practice. On other occasions, it is so important to prevent a break in the continuity of the practice that we must permit solutions that are less satisfactory from the moral point of view, although in the long run they are justified on the basis of other moral consideration.

Initially, it may seem that a conflict does not exist between individual rights and the democratic method under this theory. Democratic discussion and decision making is the most reliable method of determining rights—more reliable than any other method, including the judicial process. But this initial impression is an illusion; conflicts still emerge. For instance, the democratic method requires the satisfaction of certain preconditions to have epistemic value, such as freedom of expression and equal liberty of political participation. These preconditions constitute rights that we have called a priori, since they are determined by Kant's transcendental method and constitute presuppositions of an a posteriori moral knowledge. Recognition of these rights is required for democracy to have epistemic value. What is considered a precondition may be broadened enormously. In fact, all so-called social rights (which I have defended as natural extensions of individual rights) might be seen as a priori rights, since their nonsatisfaction harms the proper working of the democratic process and its epistemic quality.

As we attempt to satisfy preconditions of the democratic process, we expand its epistemic value but at the same time reduce its scope. We face the danger of having an optimal method for deciding very few things, when we take away most questions from the scope of the democratic process as preconditions for its effective operation. If a judge, as a supervisor of the proper working of the democratic process, decides that a citizen must have adequate medical attention, lest her equal and free participation in the democratic process be prejudiced, the judge undoubtedly contributes to the better operation of the democratic process. However, the judge simultaneously takes away from democracy the power to decide how medical resources should be distributed.

In light of this dilemma, it is necessary to achieve a highly delicate balance. First, we must determine an adequate scope for the democratic decision-making method, hoping that the process can self-correct. Second, we must contemplate external intervention to promote democracy's epistemic value when its vices are so entrenched and serious that they will be perpetuated without external intervention.

Ultimately, after the threshold is surpassed and democracy is able to make its much-needed self-corrections, each of the three elements of constitutionalism—rights, democracy, law—may also find support from the others. The democratic process acts as the most reliable method of recognizing fundamental individual rights. In turn, respect for those rights promotes the epistemic value of the democratic procedure of discussion and decision. The continuity of the constitutional practice grants efficacy to the decisions taken through the democratic method, clarifying the rights recognized through that method. Additionally, the voice of public deliberation— the essential component of democracy—and respect for individual rights generate a deep consensus that promotes the continuity of the constitutional practice.

Unfortunately, there is no exact science available to resolve the tensions among rights, democracy, and law. The challenge for all those committed to the ideal of constitutionalism is to balance these three elements when they conflict. By seeking this balance, we seek to reach the threshold where vicious, debilitating, and mutual antagonisms convert themselves into virtuous, fortifying, and perhaps liberating support.

Notes

Chapter 1: The Complexity of Constitutional Democracy

1. See Jon Elster, introduction to *Constitutionalism and Democracy: Studies in Rationality and Social Change* (Cambridge: Cambridge University Press, 1988), ed. Jon Elster and Rune Slagstad, 2–3.

2. Bruce Ackerman, *We the People* (Cambridge: Harvard University Press, 1991).

3. See Edgardo Catterberg, *Los argentinos frente a la política: Cultura política y opinión pública en la transición a la democracia* (Buenos Aires: Editorial Planeta Argentina, 1989).

4. Giovanni Sartori, *Democratic Theory* (Detroit: Wayne State University Press, 1962), 4–5.

5. Ronald Dworkin, *Law's Empire* (Cambridge: Harvard University Press, 1986), 66.

Chapter 2: The Observance of the Historical Constitution

1. Simon Blackburn describes those conventions as follows: "a conventional regularity in group G that one utters S with indicators of assertive force only if one intends to display belief that P." Blackburn, *Spreading the Word: Groundings in the Philosophy of Language* (Oxford: Oxford University Press, 1984), 124.

2. The difficulties associated with discerning the intention of the emissor of a legal or constitutional text are many. The first problem involves selecting the facts that constitute manifestations of the intention. The rationale expressed, the parliamentary discourse, and the action of the legislator or the constitutional convention may point in different directions as to which normative proposition the legislator or constitution maker wanted to formulate.

Second, we confront the problem of constructing intentions when the enactment of the law is due to the intervention of a plurality of agents, or collective organs. In the case of legislative statutes this is specially complex when, as in the American or Argentine federal systems, two collective organs intervene, the Senate and the House of Representatives.

Third, we face the issue of the extent to which it is admissible to reconstruct the intention of the constitution maker by taking into account counterfactual circumstances. For example, I take a glass with the intention of drinking it under the belief that it is lemonade; if I knew that it contained cyanide, I would not have the intention of drinking it. Frequently, the intentions of the authors of a very old constitutional text endorsed some of its norms by relying on factual beliefs that the progress of science has proved to be false or taking into account a set of phenomena that have varied with time. For example, the Argentine Constitution talks about "freedom of the press," because printing was the only means of mass communication in that epoch. If the founders had foreseen radio, cinema, television, video, etc., would they have extended the same protection to them, including a prohibition on federal regulation?

Finally, we must deal with the issue of the level of abstraction with which the intention of the legislator must be described. We can assert that the intention of limiting the taking of private property for public use, as stated in the Fifth Amendment of the U. S. Constitution, was to impede the redistribution of property among individuals. That intention would be frustrated if something were taken from someone in order to transfer it to someone who needed it more. But surely, someone could legitimately argue that the intention of the constitution maker when limiting takings for public use was to assure that takings would not harm but benefit society. In that instance, we could conclude that redistributing property would be in accord with the intention of the framers if that redistribution benefited society. There are no value-neutral criteria to determine the appropriate level of abstraction with which the intention of the constitution makers should be described.

3. See Alf Ross, *On Law and Justice* (Berkeley and Los Angeles: University of California Press, 1974), 121.

4. See *McCulloch v. Maryland*, 17 U.S. 316 (1819).

5. See Carlos Santiago Nino, *Los límites de la responsabilidad penal* (Buenos Aires: Editorial Astrea, 1980), 270–304.

6. For example, a model of "rationality" of the legislator or of the founders is often used, according to which the individual is assumed to be coherent, economical, precise, and operative, foresees all the possible circumstances, etc. In reality this obviously fictitious model presupposes a series of normative principles. The same duplicity appears in the conceptual analysis and in the proposal of legal definitions. Something similar occurs with the method of "legal induction." As Alchourrón and Bulygin say, this method would be perfectly legitimate as a logical, normatively neutral operation if it limited itself to replacing a group of norms with a more economic, but logical, principle. The jurists themselves often present this method in this way. But if they limited themselves in that way, the resulting principle would not be useful for overcoming the indeterminacies of the original norms because the equivalence would only exist if they had the same blanks, contradictions, and imprecisions as those norms. If the resulting principles are useful for finding the solution to cases that the replaced norms could not solve, it is because such principles surely have a greater extension than those norms, implying a modification of them. See Carlos Alchourrón and

Eugenio Bulygin, *Introducción a la metodología de las ciencias jurídicas y sociales* (Buenos Aires: Editorial Astrea, 1971), chap. 7.

7. *Modus ponens:* short for "modus ponendo ponens," the principle of inference allowing us to pass from p, and $p \to q$, to q. *Modus tollens:* short for "modus tollendo tollens," the rule of inference entitling us to pass from *not-q*, and $p \to q$, to *not-p.*

8. The right to life as used here should not be confused with the rhetoric of the abortion debate. I use the term in the same spirit as the text of the Fifth and Fourteenth Amendments to the U.S. Constitution.

9. One might argue that the omission of the right to privacy or to life is not a logical gap but an axiological one. According to how the norms of closure of the system are interpreted, the absence of that right could imply some other normative solution even when that solution seems an aberration (for example, the competence of the Congress for enacting laws that dispose of the life of the people).

10. See Hans Kelsen, *Pure Theory of Law,* trans. Max Knight (Berkeley and Los Angeles: University of California Press, 1978), 205–208.

11. See Alchourrón and Bulygin, *Introducción,* chap. 7.

12. If the word is used in the sense of "not prohibited," it is true that all systems include this principle, because it is a mere tautology. But interpreted this way it does not serve closure functions because it does not assign any normative solution to the nonprohibited conducts. If, instead, "permitted" is interpreted as "positively authorized," it is true that the principle eliminates the gaps of the legal system, but it is not true that it is necessary because the system may or may not include such principle.

13. Carlos Santiago Nino, "A Philosophic Reconstruction of Judicial Review," 14 *Cardozo Law Review* 799, 816 (1993).

14. For further discussion of the problem of self-reference, see Carlos Santiago Nino, *La validez del derecho* (Buenos Aires: Editorial Astrea, 1985), 69–68.

15. This is especially pertinent in regard to the perverse doctrine of the validity of "de facto" legislation. Such rules cannot grant themselves validity, and if they are to be conceded validity, it must be on the basis of independent normative considerations. This implies legitimizing them from a moral perspective and charging the regimes that enacted the rules with moral responsibility for their behavior.

16. See Carlos Santiago Nino, *El constructivismo ético* (Madrid: Centro de Estudios Constitucionales, 1989), chap. 2

17. Robert Alexy, *A Theory of Legal Argumentation: The Theory of Rational Discourse as Theory of Legal Justification,* trans. Ruth Adler and Neil MacCormick (Oxford: Oxford University Press, 1989), 16. (*Sonderfall* means "special case.")

Consider a habeas corpus petition by John Smith, arrested by a police officer. The practical argumentation of the judge deciding his claim concludes with the normative proposition that (1) *John Smith has to be released immediately.* How is this normative proposition justified? Let us suppose that the judge does so using two propositions: (2) article 18 of the Constitution declares that *nobody can be arrested without a written order from a competent authority* and (3) *a police officer is not a competent authority.* What type of proposition is (2)? If it were a description of the social convention that conforms to the constitution in a descriptive sense, proposition (1) could not be inferred from (2) and (3), since, as Hume demonstrated, a normative proposition cannot be inferred from descriptive propositions alone. Proposition 2 must be a normative proposition in order for (1) to result from (2) and (3).

In contrast, the judge may really be thinking is something like: (2') "Nobody can be arrested without a written order from a competent authority." He might be thinking along these lines in reference not to the social practice of accepting a rule but to the rule itself. If this were so, then an additional question would ensue: how do we know that (2') is a legal rule? Putting aside any distinction based on the content, we can only argue that (2') is a legal rule by taking into account its origin and basis, for example, whether it is accepted by the judge because it was formulated by an authoritative source. This means that (2') is only a legal rule when it is based on a proposition such as (4): *Authority C has prescribed that "nobody can be arrested without a written order from a competent authority," and this is observed as a generalized practice.* But again, (2') cannot be derived from (4) alone, since the latter is a purely descriptive proposition. To derive (2') from (4), we need yet another higher premise such as (5): *Rules prescribed by C should be followed, since authority C is legitimate or competent to formulate prescriptions.* Again one must ask what kind of rule (5) is. It will only be recognized as legal on the basis of its enactment by some authority, which in turn requires a new normative proposition on the duty to obey such authority.

Since this process cannot be continued ad infinitum, it must be that some rule regarding the duty to obey a given authority is accepted on its own value, not because it has been formulated by another authority. That rule cannot be a legal rule, because it is not accepted on the basis of its origin. A rule that is accepted on its own merit, not because it has originated from an authoritative source, has the element of autonomy that Kant required of moral rules. It is a moral rule if—as can definitely be said of (5)—it refers to an issue in which the interests of various individuals are involved. This means that, paradoxically, in determining if a rule is a *legal* rule, one must be certain that the rule derives from a *moral* rule granting legitimacy to a certain authority, and from a description of a prescription of that authority. If we accept that a rule which derives from a moral rule is in itself a moral rule, a legal rule—as it appears in the justificatory reasoning used by judges—is also a kind of moral rule.

18. For a discussion of the concept of operative reason, see Joseph Raz, "On Reasons for Action," in *Practical Reason and Norms* (London: Hutchinson, 1975).

19. The justificatory proposition (2') not only derives from the moral proposition (5) but also from proposition (4), descriptive of the constitution understood as a social practice. Without (4), the consequences of (5) would be very different.

20. See n. 17 above for and explanation of the moral principle represented as premise (5).

21. In the terms of n. 17 above, a principle like (5) cannot be true, and therefore the description (4) of the constitutional practice will fail to permit the derivation of justificatory propositions like (2').

22. Applying this argument to our example, (5) should derive from a more basic moral principle, which says that (6) *since nobody can be arrested without a written order from a competent authority, a constitution is only legitimate if it contains such a prescription.* Given this moral statement (6), necessary for both (5) and (2'), (4) is superfluous. (2') could be based on (6) directly, without reliance on (4) and (5).

23. See Neil MacCormick, "Constitutionalism and Democracy," in Richard Bellamy, ed., *Theories and Concepts of Politics: An Introduction* (Manchester: Manchester University Press, 1993), 145.

24. See David Lewis, *Convention: A Philosophical Study* (Cambridge: Harvard University Press, 1969), 5.

25. See Carlos Santiago Nino, *El constructivismo ético* (Madrid: Centro de Estudios Constitutionales, 1989).

26. See Ronald Dworkin, *Taking Rights Seriously* (Cambridge: Harvard University Press, 1977), chap. 3.

27. Carlos Santiago Nino, "Las limitaciones de la teoría de Hart sobre las normas jurídicas," in *Anuario de filosofía jurídica y social* 5 (1985).

28. This idea, applicable to law, can be extended to positive morality. In *The Ethics of Human Rights*, I maintain that a society's current sense of morality presupposes references to an ideal morality, given that the actions and attitudes that constitute it would not occur if the agent had to justify them subjectively on the basis of the social practice itself, that is, those same actions and attitudes. First of all, such actions and attitudes constitute facts that are as compatible with one action or decision as with its opposite. It is thus inconceivable that an agent would pretend to justify a decision, even to himself, solely on the basis of those facts, without presupposing—tacitly or even unconsciously—a normative principle to make them relevant. Second, propositions whose acceptance provokes actions and attitudes cannot be based on those same actions and attitudes without being self-referential and therefore empty. Persons who employ a practice or convention, including one that constitutes the positive morality of a society, must therefore justify its use on the basis of propositions based on principles whose validity does not depend on their being adopted as part of the practice or convention. In other words, ideal morality has logical priority over positive morality, as is normal in all manifestations of the human praxis. Third, a distinction must be made between propositions to which one refers from the internal point of view, and actions and attitudes reflecting one's adherence from the external point of view. Without the intention of the agents referring to ideal principles—which, for law as for positive morality, must be ideal moral principles, because it is they that, by definition, refer to the conflicting interests of diverse people—practices and conventions that constitute, from an external point of view, the phenomena of law and morality would not arise, nor remain. Carlos Santiago Nino, *The Ethics of Human Rights* (Oxford: Oxford University Press, 1991), chap. 5.

29. What I have tried to show regarding the construction of a cathedral may be applied in connection to rather more fictitious examples than the construction of an artifact—a car, for example—done by different people who each can only provide a few parts independent of the rest, or, as in a now fashionable example developed by Dworkin, the case of a narrative developed successively by separate authors. See Dworkin, *Law's Empire*, 228–238.

30. See Lon Fuller, *The Morality of Law*, rev. ed. (New Haven: Yale University Press, 1978).

31. Karl Popper, *The Open Society and Its Enemies*, vol. 2 (Princeton: Princeton University Press, 1966), chap. 17.

32. Stephen Holmes, "Precommitment and the Paradox of Democracy," in Jon Elster and Rune Slagstad, eds., *Constitutionalism and Democracy: Studies in Rationality and Social Change* (Cambridge: Cambridge University Press, 1988), 227.

33. The preservation of the historical constitution as a convention or social practice does not imply freezing that convention or practice. Social practices can evolve without falling apart. Dworkin convincingly describes how an objective that grants meaning to a practice can change, and how the conduct and attitudes constituting the practice also change. That evolution is compatible with the preservation of the practice. But it does not imply, contrary to Dworkin's view, that new decisions must be made according to principles which provided

coherent justifications for other actions or decisions constituting the practice. A principle may well be proposed that is incompatible with many of the actions or decisions adopted up to that point, since the justificatory basis of the practice may not have been clearly understood. But it is true that without some respect for past types of conduct and decisions that constitute the practice, the practice may be fatally undermined. The tension between allowing the practice to evolve toward the expansion of democracy and rights, and simultaneously preserving it, cannot be solved by an exact formula. It requires prudence and a dose of good luck to be measured by the degree of acceptance of the new orientation. Confused and ambiguous reactions to the changes, skepticism about the possibility of limiting unpredictable behavior connected to the practice, and a weakening of the practice's legitimacy are all signs that an audacious attempt to reorient the practice has failed.

34. The two-staged structure of practical reasoning for applying the constitution can be schematically differentiated from its two main competitors: conventional collectivism and reasoning projected from isolated actions to collective actions. In conventional collectivism, a certain social practice is the basis for inferring valid justificatory principles. For the other alternative, the only relevance a social practice has in justifying actions is as part of the factual circumstances that, according to basic evaluative principles, determine a particular normative consequence for the individual action. In contrast, a conception based upon staged legal reasoning uses basic normative principles, those found in the ideal constitution, to determine which social practices are legitimate. Once this is determined, those practices are used to justify actions and decisions. In this way, my theory gives moral relevance to the historical constitution as a convention—without resorting to conventionalism or communitarianism—and adopts an intermediate position between the extremes of deriving justificatory principles from certain facts alone and denying any significance to facts which are constitutive of basic social conventions. Only those principles that are derived in an autonomous way and are part of the ideal constitution can determine which social facts are morally relevant. Once identified, however, those facts are sufficient for inferring justificatory reasons.

35. This type of staged practical reasoning is in fact presupposed by Rawls when he maintains that his principles of justice are applied not to particular actions or decisions but to the basic structure of a society, that is, the fundamental institutions that regulate relations between individuals, and between them and the power of the state. John Rawls, *A Theory of Justice* (Cambridge: Harvard University Press, 1971), chap. 2. More explicitly, this type of reasoning is defended by Marcus Singer, in his article "Institutional Ethics," when he maintains that there is an inferential breach between moral propositions that refer to institutions and moral propositions referring to the actions constituted by the institution. According to Singer, given a proposition about the justice or injustice of an institution, one cannot infer, without the help of additional premises, any proposition regarding whether an action of the institution should or should not be undertaken. Singer, "Institutional Ethics," in *Ethics*, ed. A. Phillips Griffiths (Cambridge: Cambridge University Press, 1993), 223–245.

36. The actions of citizens, like those of legislators and judges, can be seen as a form of collective action. As John Searle has said, collective action is not reducible to individual actions. Searle, *Minds, Brains, and Science* (Cambridge: Harvard University Press, 1984), 72. Yet that in no way implies, as Dworkin supposes, the existence of a collective subject. Ronald Dworkin, *A Matter of Principle* (Cambridge: Harvard University Press, 1985), 321–326. Collective action pre-

supposes a collective intention, implying the necessity of common objectives, since without them there can be no collective intention, which in fact underlies Dworkin's thesis regarding the value of integrity as the coherent acceptance of shared principles. But collective objectives can be very general; an example might be the just resolution of social conflicts on the basis of legitimate standards. Using this approach, it is possible to identify the collective action embodied by the legal practice of a society: it is distinguished by its intention to refer to the same collective practice. This kind of self-reflectiveness is characteristic of all practices that are more than merely convergent actions. Reference to such practices, however, does not necessarily define the objective of the collective action. That objective may be constituted by autonomous principles, and the reference to the social practice constituting the historical constitution may be a part of the necessary means for satisfying them.

Chapter 3: The Ideal Constitution of Rights

1. Carlos Santiago Nino, *The Ethics of Human Rights* (Oxford: Oxford University Press, 1991).

2. Wesley Newcomb Hohfeld, *Fundamental Legal Conceptions as Applied in Judicial Reasoning and Other Legal Essays*, ed. Walter Wheeler Cook (New Haven: Yale University Press, 1923), 36–60, and Hans Kelsen, *Pure Theory of Law*, trans. Max Knight (Berkeley and Los Angeles: University of California Press, 1978), 145.

3. Some philosophers conceived of those norms as irreducible, others as acts of abrogation of those permissions, others as norms which establish prohibitions and promises of not interfering.

4. Nino, *Ethics of Human Rights*, chap. 3.

5. Moral rights are established by the fact that, according to certain principles which are assumed valid, it is improper to deny to any individual constituting part of a relevant class access to a situation which is beneficial for each class member. The existence of a moral right does not necessarily presuppose that there is a correlative moral duty, unless some conditions are satisfied regarding the possibility of providing the good in question on the part of other individuals, and with the distribution among them of the burdens involved in that provision. Nino, *Ethics of Human Rights*, chap. 1.

6. This inconsistency arises from the incompatibility between the action of formulating a normative proposition and the action endorsed by it or by some necessary presupposition of it.

7. Note, however, that those results may have an epistemic relevance, as will be discussed later.

8. This feature of autonomy was underscored by Kant as distinctive of the acceptance of moral principles.

9. See Joseph Raz, *The Morality of Freedom* (Oxford: Oxford University Press, 1986).

10. See, for instance, ibid., chap. 4 and John Rawls, *A Theory of Justice* (Cambridge: Harvard University Press, 1971), chap. 1.

11. See Thomas Nagel, *The Possibility of Altruism* (Oxford: Oxford University Press, 1970).

12. Nino, *Ethics of Human Rights*, chap. 5.

13. Elie Kedourie, *Nationalism* (New York: Praeger, 1961), 32–50.

14. See this point in Carlos Santiago Nino, *Introducción al analisis del derecho* (Barcelona: Ariel, 1984), chap. 4.

15. See Thomas Nagel, *Mortal Questions* (Cambridge: University Press,

1979), 83–84; Thomas Scanlon, "Contractualism and Utilitarianism," in Amartya Sen and Bernard Williams, eds., *Utilitarianism and Beyond* (Cambridge: Cambridge University Press, 1982).

16. See Nino, *Ethics of Human Rights*, chap. 5.

17. See Carlos Santiago Nino, "A Consensual Theory of Punishment," 12 *Philosophy and Public Affairs* 289 (1983).

18. See Nino, *Ethics of Human Rights*, chap. 5.

19. Nino, "Consensual Theory."

20. Nino, *Ethics of Human Rights*, chap. 5.

21. Ibid., chap. 1.

22. See Chap. 1 above.

23. 494 U.S. 259 (1990).

24. The case involved a Mexican extradited to the United States for drug trafficking. His house in Mexico was searched by U.S. agents, with the knowledge of the Mexican police but without a judicial warrant.

25. For a discussion of these authors, and citations to their relevant works, see Nino, *Ethics of Human Rights*, chap. 4. See also Nino, "The Communitarian Challenge to Liberal Rights," 8 *Law and Philosophy* 37 (1989).

26. See Charles Taylor, "Atomism," in *Philosophy and the Human Sciences: Philosophical Papers*, vol. 2 (Cambridge: Cambridge University Press, 1985), 187.

27. See Joseph Raz, *Ethics in the Public Domain* (Oxford: Oxford University Press, 1994), essays 2, 3, 11.

28. See Alasdair McIntyre, *Is Patriotism a Virtue?* (Lawrence: University Press of Kansas, 1984), 6–8. McIntyre arrives at analogous conclusions using slightly different premises. According to his theory, the rules that ascribe rights are justified on the basis of certain goods. These goods are internal to various social practices. Hence, a moral evaluation of individual rights is subject to the conventions and traditions of each society.

29. See Nino, *Ethics of Human Rights*, chap. 4.

30. McIntyre, *Is Patriotism a Virtue?*

31. Nino, *Ethics of Human Rights*, chap. 6.

32. For instance, Larry Temkin shows how this idea of equality involves different parameters of comparison with incompatible consequences, such as those which take into account the situation of disadvantage and comparing it to some of the situations of an average person, or the situation of the person who is best positioned in absolute terms, or the situation of anybody who is relatively better positioned. Temkin, *Inequality* (Oxford: Oxford University Press, 1993), 91–102.

33. As Jeffrey Reiman describes it, "In capitalism, Marx held that workers work without pay because they give their bosses more labor-time than the amount of labor-time they get back in the form of their wage. A worker works, say, a forty-hour week and receives back a wage which will purchase some amount of goods that it takes (whoever produces them) less than forty hours of labor to produce. The worker gives a surplus of labor over the amount he receives in return, and this surplus labor is held to be unpaid." Reiman, "Exploitation, Force, and the Moral Assessment of Capitalism: Thoughts on Roemer and Cohen," 16 *Philosophy and Public Affairs* 6 (1987).

34. However, this concept of exploitation presupposes the Marxian theory of value in terms of labor, an approach almost universally rejected by social theorists. See, for instance, John E. Roemer, "Property Relations vs. Surplus Value in Marxian Exploitation," 11 *Philosophy and Public Affairs* 281 (1982). This has led to attempts to define the idea of exploitation in non-Marxian terms—for

example, the proposal of Hillel Steiner, which uses a liberal concept of exploitation. See Steiner, "A Liberal Theory of Exploitation," 94 *Ethics* 225 (1984).

35. The requirement of strict equality in the democratic process has broad implications since it presupposes an idea of equal citizenship that extends over factors which have to do with personal identity, integrity, and individual self-esteem.

36. Of course, this would be the same if we adopted some varieties of realist meta-ethics, such as intuitionism or naturalism. Only if we endorsed noncognitivist views of meta-ethics, such as emotivism or prescriptivism, would those individual assertions of moral truth lack all authority. Many have therefore thought that adopting ethical skepticism is the only way of securing democracy and tolerance.

Chapter 4: Alternative Conceptions of Democracy

1. The former approach, more often than the latter, ascribes to these conceptions both an explanatory and a justificatory import. See Joseph Schumpeter, *Capitalism, Socialism, and Democracy* (New York: Harper & Row, 1976), 250. Robert Dahl gives explanatory prominence to the conception of democracy as a "polyarchy" over the populist and Madisonian models of democracy. See Dahl, *A Preface to Democratic Theory* (Chicago: University of Chicago Press, 1956), 64–89. In contrast, C. B. Macpherson argues for a model of participatory democracy. See Macpherson, *The Life and Times of Liberal Democracy* (Oxford: Oxford University Press, 1977), 93–115. Jürgen Habermas defends a democratic system that uses as a model a process of ideal communication, in *Communication and the Evolution of Society*, trans. Thomas McCarthy (Boston: Beacon Press, 1979), 186–187. Cass Sunstein favors a republican vision of democracy, or at least a conception which mixes republican with "pluralist" conceptions. See Sunstein, "Interest Groups in American Public Law," 38 *Stanford Law Review* (1985): 29–87. Finally, Bruce Ackerman puts forth an outlook which he calls "dualist," opposing it to two others which he deems "monist" and "fundamentalist." Ackerman, *We the People* (Cambridge: Harvard University Press, 1991).

2. Giovanni Sartori, *The Theory of Democracy Revisited* (Chatham, N.J.: Chatham House, 1987), 241–247.

3. See Chap. 3 above.

4. Thomas Scanlon, "Rights, Goals and Fairness," in S. Hampshire, ed., *Public and Private Morality* (Cambridge: Cambridge University Press, 1978).

5. Peter Singer, *The Expanding Circle: Ethics and Sociobiology* (New York: Farrar, Straus, and Giroux, 1981), 62–63.

6. Ronald Dworkin, *Law's Empire* (Cambridge: Harvard University Press, 1986), 186.

7. Owen M. Fiss, "The Death of the Law?" 72 *Cornell Law Review* 1 (1986).

8. John Rawls, *A Theory of Justice* (Cambridge: Harvard University Press, 1971), 23–24, 187.

9. Carlos Santiago Nino, *El Constructivismo ético* (Madrid: Centro de Estudios Constitucionales, 1989), 22–27.

10. Carlos Santiago Nino, *The Ethics of Human Rights* (Oxford: Oxford University Press, 1991), chap. 7. In utilitarianism, this leads to what I have elsewhere deemed "the quatrilemma of consequentialism." See Nino, "El Cutrilema del consecuencialismo," 4 *Doxa* (1987). Either utilitarianism relies on the very principle of utility for making those normative judgments, and hence is circular; or

it relies on other valuative principles, which contradicts the pretension of using the principle of utility as the final valuative principle; or it relies on a purely factual concept of causation, which produces results that are extremely counterintuitive; or it rests on social or positive morality for making those normative judgments implicit in causal attribution, thus losing critical distance with that positive morality.

11. See Anthony Downs, *An Economic Theory of Democracy* (New York: Harper & Row, 1957). Downs's intention is more descriptive than normative. One of his conclusions is that under certain conditions the government has no alternative but to enforce the policy supported by the majority of voters, and that the minority has no alternative but to propose the same policy, though better implemented. He also shows, however, that a coalition of minorities with intense preferences may sometimes defeat the majority.

12. Richard A. Posner, *Economic Analysis of Law*, 2d ed. (Boston: Little, Brown, 1977), 405–406, 411.

13. Ibid., 406–407.

14. James M. Buchanan and Gordon Tullock, *The Calculus of Consent: Logical Foundations of Constitutional Democracy* (Ann Arbor: University of Michigan Press, 1962).

15. In fact, the criterion of efficiency as productivity directly responds to the principle of utility, though, as Jules Coleman says, there could be some differences between the two. The Paretian criterion of efficiency is usually considered as the "second best" with regard to the direct application of the principle of maximization of utility, since it avoids the problems of interpersonal comparisons that the latter requires. Coleman, *Markets, Morals, and the Law* (Cambridge: Cambridge University Press, 1988), 97–100.

16. Allen Buchanan, *Ethics, Efficiency, and the Market* (Totowa, N.J.: Rowman and Allamhead, 1985), 9.

17. Ibid.

18. Carlos Santiago Nino, *Un país al margen de la ley* (Buenos Aires: Emecé Editores, 1992), chap. 4.

19. Max Weber, "Politics as a Vocation," in *From Max Weber: Essays in Sociology*, trans. H. H. Gerth and C. Wright Mills (New York: Oxford University Press, 1958).

20. Schumpeter, *Capitalism, Socialism, and Democracy*, 232–296.

21. Giovanni Sartori's vision of democracy can be classified under this heading despite the fact that he wages a forceful and subtle attack against the theoretical usefulness of this category of "elitism." He continually warns us about the need to distinguish descriptive from normative theories and the ensuing risks from both excessive idealism and extreme realism in analyzing democracy. Accordingly, he emphasizes the descriptive nature of most elitist visions of democracy. But his own normative theory is explicitly elitist, insofar as it requires elites to be selected on the basis of merit. Sartori defines his ideal vision of democracy as selective polyarchy on the basis of merit. Sartori, *Democracy Revisited*, 157–163.

22. Hannah Arendt, *On Revolution* (New York: Viking, 1963), 276.

23. Macpherson, *Liberal Democracy*, 88–89.

24. Michel Crozier, Samuel P. Huntington, and Joji Watanuki, *The Crisis of Democracy: Report on the Governability of Democracies to the Trilateral Commission* (New York: New York University Press, 1975).

25. Dahl, *Preface to Democratic Theory*, 34–62.

26. The polyarchic model is of Madisonian inspiration, the features of which may be gathered from the following passage of Dahl's (ibid., 131–133): "I am not suggesting that elections and interelection activity are of trivial importance in determining policy. On the contrary, they are crucial processes for insuring that political leaders will be somewhat responsive to the preferences of some ordinary citizens. But neither elections nor interelection activity provide much insurance that decisions will accord with the preferences of a majority of adults or voters. Hence we cannot correctly describe the actual operations of democratic societies in terms of the contrasts between majorities and minorities. We can only distinguish groups of various types and sizes, all seeking in various ways to advance their goals, usually at the expense, at least in part, of others. . . . We expect elections to reveal the 'will' or the preferences of a majority on a set of issues. This is one thing elections rarely do, except in an almost trivial fashion. Despite this limitation the election process is one of two fundamental methods of social control which, operating together, make government leaders so responsive to non-leaders that the distinction between democracy and dictatorship still makes sense. The other method of social control is continuous political competition among individuals, parties, or both. Elections and political competition do not make for government by majorities in any very significant way, but they vastly increase the size, number and variety of the minorities whose preferences must be taken into account by leaders in making policy choices. I am inclined to think that it is in this characteristic of elections—not minority rule but minorities rule—that we must look for some of the essential differences between dictatorships and democracies. . . . The distinction comes much closer to being one between government by a minority and government by minorities. As compared with the political processes of a dictatorship, the characteristic of polyarchy greatly extend the number, size, and diversity of the minorities whose preferences will influence the outcome of governmental decisions."

27. Robert A. Dahl, *Democracy, Liberty, and Equality* (Oxford: Oxford University Press, 1986).

28. Ibid., 242.

29. Robert A. Dahl, *Democracy and Its Critics* (New Haven: Yale University Press, 1989), 280–298.

30. Lowi describes the steps by which pluralistic theory is transformed into an ideology: "(1) Since groups are the rule in markets and elsewhere, imperfect competition is the rule of social relations. (2) The method of imperfect competition is not really competition at all but a variant of it called bargaining—where the number of participants is small, where the relationship is face-to-face, and/or where the bargainers have 'market power,' which means that they have some control over the terms of their agreements and can administer rather than merely respond to their environment. (3) Without class solidarity, bargaining becomes the single alternative to violence and coercion in industrial society. (4) By definition, if the system is stable and peaceful it proves the self-regulative character of pluralism. It is, therefore, the way the system works and the way it ought to work." Theodore J. Lowi, *The End of Liberalism: The Second Republic of the United States*, 2d ed. (New York: Norton, 1979), 35.

31. Carlos Santiago Nino, "Transition to Democracy, Corporatism and Constitutional Reform in Latin America," 44 *University of Miami Law Review* 129 (1989).

32. As with elitism, some pluralists warn against opening excessive channels of participation for the population in order to avoid overload of social demands

which may put the political equilibrium in crisis. They see generalized apathy as a functional prerequisite for equilibrium. Crozier, Huntington, and Watanuki, *Crisis of Democracy*.

33. For the defense of this conception of the moral person, see Nino, *Ethics of Human Rights*.

34. Lowi, *End of Liberalism*, 36, 58–59.

35. Nino, *Un país al margen de la ley*.

36. Lowi, *End of Liberalism*, 58.

37. Rawls, *Theory of Justice*, 18.

38. Ibid., 221–228.

39. See, for instance, Ronald Dworkin, *Taking Rights Seriously* (Cambridge: Harvard University Press, 1977).

40. Martín Farrell, *La democracia liberal* (Buenos Aires: Abeledo-Perrot, 1988).

41. Carlos Santiago Nino, *Introducción a la filosofía de la acción humana* (Buenos Aires: Eudeba, 1987).

42. Nino, *Ethics of Human Rights*, chap.6.

43. John Locke, *The Second Treatise of Government*, ed. Thomas P. Peardon (Indianapolis: Bobbs-Merrill, 1975), para. 119.

44. Peter Singer, *Democracy and Disobedience* (Oxford: Oxford University Press, 1973).

45. See Chap. 6 below.

46. Jean-Jacques Rousseau, "The Social Contract," in Sir Ernest Barker, ed., *Social Contract: Essays by Locke, Hume, and Rousseau* (New York: Oxford University Press, 1962), 180–182 (emphasis in original).

47. Ibid., 185.

48. At one point, Rousseau describes that process of transformation by referring to "individuals engaged in deliberation," but he is alluding to individual reflection or monologic discourse. He immediately adds that the general will can be reached "if no means existed by which the citizens could communicate one with another."

49. This construction gave rise to what Benn and Peters call the "Jacobin theory of democracy." This theory, defended by Robespierre and by a host of his intellectual and political heirs, holds that there is a "will of the people" which transcends electoral results and is directed toward the common good. S. I. Benn and R. S. Peters, *Social Principles and the Democratic State* (London: Allen and Unwin, 1959), 344.

50. Barker, introduction to *Social Contract*.

51. John Stuart Mill, "Considerations on Representative Government," in *Three Essays: On Liberty; Representative Government; The Subjection of Women* (London: Oxford University Press, 1975), 168–170.

52. Ibid., 186.

53. Ibid., 186–187.

54. Ibid., 190.

55. Ibid., 196–198.

56. Of course, the latter was very much influenced by the former. See Cass R. Sunstein, "Beyond the Republican Revival," 97 *Yale Law Journal* 1539 (1988).

57. Sunstein, "Interest Groups," 36.

58. In the context of his moderate defense of the republican constitutionalist vision, Frank Michelman states: "As its Aristotelian source, 'public happiness' doctrine attributes to human beings a telos, a defining end or purposive essence, preinscribed by nature. But the idea that citizenship (or any other specific social

role or form of life) is the essence of the human subject runs against the modern liberal temper. It seems that to urge on such grounds the renewal of civic life is to reject liberalism's historic deliverance of individuality from pre-Enlightenment oppressions of mind and spirit." Michelman, "Traces of Self-Government," 100 *Harvard Law Review* 4, 22 (1986).

59. Macpherson, *Liberal Democracy*, chap. 3.

60. Bruce Ackerman, "Why Dialogue?" 86 *Journal of Philosophy* 5 (1989).

61. Rawls, *Theory of Justice*, 580–587.

62. Sunstein, "Beyond the Republican Revival," 1558–1564.

63. Sunstein, "Interest Groups," 47.

64. Ackerman, *We the People*, 3–33.

65. See Bruce Ackerman and Carlos Rosenkrantz, "Tres concepciones de la democracia constitucional," 29 *Cuadernos y Debates* 13 (1991).

Chapter 5: The Foundations of the Deliberative Conception of Democracy

1. Carlos Santiago Nino, *The Ethics of Human Rights* (Oxford: Oxford University Press, 1991), chap. 7.

2. With regard to the justification based on self-interest, see David P. Gauthier, *Morals by Agreement* (Oxford: Oxford University Press, 1986). For the justification grounded on consent, see David A. J. Richards, *A Theory of Reasons for Action* (Oxford: Oxford University Press, 1971) and James M. Buchanan and Gordon Tullock, *The Calculus of Consent: Logical Foundations of Constitutional Democracy* (Ann Arbor: University of Michigan Press, 1962). For an account based on intuition, see Morton White, *What Is and What Ought to Be Done: An Essay on Ethics and Epistemology* (New York: Oxford University Press, 1981).

3. John Rawls, *A Theory of Justice* (Cambridge: Harvard University Press, 1971), 130–136.

4. Although other works of Rawls's lie outside the limits of this comparison, it is worth mentioning that in his transitional work, "Kantian Constructivism in Moral Theory," 77 *Journal of Philosophy* 515 (1980), Rawls is explicit in saying that the procedures by which the first principles are chosen ought to be adequately grounded on practical reasoning.

5. Rawls, *Theory of Justice*, 356.

6. Jürgen Habermas, "Discourse Ethics: Notes on a Program of Philosophical Justification," in *Moral Consciousness and Communicative Action*, trans. Christian Lenhardt and Shierry Weber Nicholsen (Cambridge: MIT Press, 1990), 43–115.

7. P. F. Strawson, *Skepticism and Naturalism: Some Varieties* (New York: Columbia University Press, 1985).

8. Habermas acknowledges the difficulties for grounding this principle of universalization without falling prey, as Karl-Otto Apel warns, to Munchhausen's trilemma: either an infinite regress, or a vicious circle, or a dogmatic cut in the justification. Habermas maintains that this trilemma may be avoided if we dismiss a deductivist conception of justification and, following Apel, seek a transcendental-pragmatic rationale based on the presuppositions of practical discourse. For this we must appeal to the concept of practical inconsistency that applies when a speech-act which refers to a certain proposition relies on assumptions which oppose that proposition. This argument is operative insofar as the discourse in question is so general that, as R. S. Peters says, it cannot be replaced by functional equivalents. Karl-Otto Apel, "The A Priori of the Commu-

nicative Community and Foundations of Ethics," in *Towards a Transformation of Philosophy* (London: Routledge and Kegan Paul, 1980), 225; Habermas, "Discourse Ethics," 79–82.

9. As pointed out by Alexy, a series of more specific rules of argumentation implies this general principle. Robert Alexy, *A Theory of Legal Argumentation: The Theory of Rational Discourse as Theory of Legal Justification,* trans. Ruth Adler and Neil MacCormick (Oxford: Oxford University Press, 1980), 187–208; Habermas, "Discourse Ethics," 75–76.

10. In defense of this position, Habermas agrees with Ernst Tugendhat, who maintains that if it is true that the postulate of universalization is not a semantic but a pragmatical criterion and is not to be used in monologic reasoning but rather in a real intersubjective discourse in which all those concerned must determine whether a norm is equally good for them, then it is not a postulate for the formation of judgment but only for that of the will. Tugendhat conceives discourse as a means of assuring that all the people concerned have, through the rules of communication, the same opportunity to participate in a solution of equitable compromise, a solution that everybody would autonomously accept. Habermas, "Discourse Ethics," 68.

11. Ibid., 72.

12. Ibid, 103.

13. Ibid., 103, 94.

14. Stephen K. White, *The Recent Work of Jürgen Habermas: Reason, Justice and Modernity* (Cambridge: Cambridge University Press, 1988), 50.

15. Recently, Rawls appears to be paying more attention to something he calls, enigmatically, "free public reason." He refers to the shared social practice of public justification as evidence of the existence of an objective order of reasons. With regard to his overall epistemological position, Rawls seems to accept E1 even though—in the section on democracy—he flirts with E2, the thesis which I called "epistemological constructivism." He ultimately rejects this in referring to the determination of basic liberties. John Rawls, "The Idea of Public Reason," in *Political Liberalism* (New York: Columbia University Press, 1993).

16. See Habermas, "Discourse Ethics," 84–94.

17. If the principles were not universal, public, final, etc., a consensus about some of them would hardly serve as a basis for the convergence of actions and attitudes needed for cooperation.

18. Michael Walzer, "Philosophy and Democracy," 9 *Political Theory* 379 (1981).

19. See Chap. 7 below.

20. There are also conceptual problems concerning what has been deemed "the problem of private language." See Ludwig Wittgenstein, *Philosophical Investigations* (New York: Macmillan, 1973), §§243–309, and Ernst Tugendhat, *Self-Consciousness and Self-Determination,* trans. Paul Stern (Cambridge: MIT Press, 1986), 77–98.

21. See Jon Elster, "Arguments for Constitutional Choice," in Jon Elster and Rune Slagstad, eds., *Constitutionalism and Democracy: Studies in Rationality and Social Change* (Cambridge: Cambridge University Press, 1988), 303.

22. These dynamics are the subject of the famous footnote 4 in Justice Stone's decision in *United States v. Carolene Products Co.,* 304 U.S. 144, 152–153 (1938).

23. See "Essai sur l'Application de l'Analyse à la Probabilité des Decisions Rendues a la Pluralité des Voix (1785)," in *Condorcet: Selected Writings,* ed. Keith Baker (Indianapolis: Bobbs-Merrill, 1976), 33. The theorem was proved

by Bernard Grofman, Guillermo Owen, and Scott Feld in "Thirteen Theorems in Search of the Truth," 15 *Theory and Decision* 261 (1983).

24. Lewis A. Kornhauser and Lawrence G. Sager, "Unpacking the Court," 96 *Yale Law Journal* 82, 82–117 (1986).

25. They also argue that the assumptions of these theorems can be relaxed without altering the result.

26. Grofman, Owen, and Feld, "Thirteen Theorems."

27. For treatment of this problem of conflicts of rights, see Nino, *Ethics of Human Rights*, Chap. 7.

28. Ibid.

29. Carlos Santiago Nino, *Fundamentos de derecho constitucional* (Buenos Aires: Editorial Astrea, 1992) (discussing the doctrine of de facto laws).

30. Kornhauser and Sager, "Unpacking the Court," 107–109.

31. Alexander Hamilton, *The Federalist*, no. 84, in *The Federalist Papers* (Cambridge: Harvard University Press, 1972), 531–541.

32. They may be associated with Kantian a priori judgments that are known by a transcendental method of probing into the preconditions for empirical knowledge. These rights are known for being preconditions for the knowledge of the rest of intersubjective morality, including other rights.

33. See Chap. 2 above.

34. This position resembles Ronald Dworkin's advocacy of articulate consistency in the process of legislation and adjudication. The crucial difference with Dworkin, however, is that here I am resorting not to the dubious value of intersubjective integrity but to the need to maximize the epistemic value of democracy, taking into account the change of interests underlying successive or adjacent democratic decisions.

Chapter 6: Establishing Deliberative Democracy

1. Carlos Santiago Nino, "Autonomía y necesidades básicas," 7 *Doxa* 21–34 (1990).

2. South Dakota adopted the initiative and referendum in 1898, Utah in 1900, Oregon in 1902, and Massachusetts in 1981. The recall was adopted in 1908 by Oregon and in 1911 by California for all elected officials. Thomas E. Cronin, *Direct Democracy: The Politics of Initiative, Referendum, and Recall* (Cambridge: Harvard University Press, 1989), 51, 126–127.

3. Cronin, *Direct Democracy*.

4. While the intensity of interests is relevant to the utilitarian and economic views of democracy, this is not the case with regard to the epistemic conception.

5. Cronin, *Direct Democracy*, 10–11, 57–58.

6. Ibid., 212.

7. Ibid., 211.

8. Ibid., 211–212, 214–222.

9. Ibid., 225–226.

10. Robert A. Dahl, *Democracy and Its Critics* (New Haven: Yale University Press, 1989), 340.

11. James S. Fishkin, *Democracy and Deliberation: New Directions for Democratic Reform* (New Haven: Yale University Press, 1991), 81–104.

12. For a consideration of the requirements of workplace democracy, see Robert A. Dahl, *A Preface to Economic Democracy* (Berkeley and Los Angeles: University of California Press, 1985).

13. Michel J. Crozier, Samuel P. Huntington, and Joji Watanuki, *The Crisis of Democracy: Report on the Governability of Democracies to the Trilateral Commission* (New York: New York University Press, 1975).

14. Carlos Santiago Nino, "La participación como remedio a la llamada 'crisis de la democracia,'" in *Alfonsín: Discursos sobre el discurso* (Buenos Aires: Eudeba, 1986), 123–137.

15. See, for instance, the well-known analysis of Raymond E. Wolfinger and Steven J. Rosenstone, *Who Votes?* (New Haven: Yale University Press, 1980).

16. Robert M. Entman, *Democracy without Citizens: Media and the Decay of American Politics* (New York: Oxford University Press, 1989), 26–27.

17. Carlos Santiago Nino, "El voto obligatorio," in *Segundo Dictamen Sobre la Reforma Constitucional del Consejo para la Consolidación de la Democracia* (Buenos Aires: Consejo para la Consolidación de la Democracia, 1987).

18. See Fred W. Riggs, "La supervivencia del presidencialismo en EEUU: prácticas para-constitucionales," in *Presidencialismo vs. Parlamentarismo: Materiales para el Estudio de la Reforma Constitucional* (Buenos Aires: Eudeba, 1988), 45–94, 73.

19. Karl Polanyi, *The Great Transformation* (New York: Farrar and Rinehart, 1944), 223–226.

20. See Jennifer Nedelsky, *Private Property and the Limits of American Constitutionalism: The Madisonian Framework and Its Legacy* (Chicago: University of Chicago Press, 1990), 195.

21. Carlos Santiago Nino, *Radical Evil on Trial* (New Haven: Yale University Press, 1996).

22. Adam Przeworski, *Democracy and the Market: Political and Economic Reforms in Eastern Europe and Latin America* (Cambridge: Cambridge University Press, 1991), 30, 32, 33.

23. This dynamic can be analyzed by resorting to the structures of interaction developed by game theory. Edna Ullman-Margalit describes situations where one of two or more parties pretends to maintain a status quo of inequality in his or her own interests. See Ullman-Margalit, *The Emergence of Norms* (Oxford: Oxford University Press, 1977).

24. See Chap. 7 below for a discussion of the role of the judicial branch.

25. Giovanni Sartori, "Video-Power," 24 *Government and Opposition* 39 (1989).

26. Entman, *Democracy without Citizens*, 128.

27. For distortions produced by the commercial controls of mass media, see Owen M. Fiss, "Free Speech and Social Structure," 71 *Iowa Law Review* 1405 (1986).

28. Ibid., 1412–1413.

29. Entman, *Democracy without Citizens*, 22.

30. I was enlightened on this point by the thorough paper that Ken Levit wrote for my course at the Yale Law School in the spring of 1992. See Levit, "Campaign Finance Reform and the Return of *Buckley v. Valeo*," 103 *Yale Law Journal* 469 (1993).

31. Cass R. Sunstein, "Interest Groups in American Public Law," 38 *Stanford Law Review* 29, 44–45 (1985).

32. Carlos Santiago Nino, "Transition to Democracy, Corporatism and Constitutional Reform in Latin America," 44 *University of Miami Law Review* 129 (1989).

33. See this characterization of American federalism in Bernard Schwartz, *El federalismo norteamericano actual* (Madrid: Civitas, 1984).

34. This is not an uncommon phenomenon in Argentina. The German Bundesrat is particularly interesting in this regard; it not only has differential representation according to population, as in the Canadian Senate, but also asserts specialized competencies and is formed by the delegates of local governments.

35. C. B. Macpherson, *The Life and Times of Liberal Democracy* (Oxford: Oxford University Press, 1977), 108–109.

36. Jean Blondel, "Mass Parties and Industrialized Societies," in Blondel, ed., *Comparative Government: A Reader* (London: MacMillan, 1969), 117–126.

37. See a description of these and other systems in Andrew Reeve and Alan Ware, *Electoral Systems: A Comparative and Theoretical Introduction* (London: Routledge, 1992).

38. See Juan Linz, "Democracia presidencial o parlamentaria ¿Hay alguna diferencia?" in *Presidencialismo vs. Parlamentarismo*, 26–31.

39. In Argentina, the president is elected at the same time as half of the House of Deputies. However, very few people actually separate their ballots for the two offices. Therefore, the polarization typical of presidential elections is reflected in the election of deputies, and as a result the finely tuned ideological options theoretically offered by proportional representation are undermined.

40. Linz, "Democracia presidencial," 33.

41. See Stephen Holmes, "Precommitment and the Paradox of Democracy," in Jon Elster and Rune Slagstad, ed., *Constitutionalism and Democracy: Studies in Rationality and Social Change* (Cambridge: Cambridge University Press, 1988), 195–240.

42. Ibid., 231.

43. The U.S. Constitution requires amendments to be passed by supermajorities in the House and Senate along with ratification in three-fourths of the states or in a constitutional convention. Reform of the Argentine Constitution requires a two-thirds vote of the total membership of Congress to pass a "declaration of need," which must specify whether the reform is partial or total and which part of the constitution is to be reformed. There is then a call for a popular election of a constitutional convention, which will draft the reform according to the guidelines set out in the declaration of need.

Chapter 7: Judicial Review in a Deliberative Democracy

1. *Marbury v. Madison*, 1 U.S. 137 (1803).

2. Alexander M. Bickel, *The Least Dangerous Branch: The Supreme Court at the Bar of Politics*, 2d ed. (New Haven: Yale University Press, 1986).

3. Montesquieu, *The Spirit of Laws*, ed. David Wallace Carrithers (Berkeley and Los Angeles: University of California Press, 1977).

4. Michael Walzer, "Philosophy and Democracy," 9 *Political Theory* 379, 387–390 (1981).

5. Hans Kelsen, *Pure Theory of Law*, trans. Max Knight (Berkeley and Los Angeles: University of California Press, 1978), 4–10, 30–58.

6. Hans Kelsen, *General Theory of Law and State*, trans. Anders Wedberg (New York: Russell and Russell, 1961), 38.

7. The criterion of validity that Kelsen offers for nonprimitive norms of the system determines that a norm is valid when it satisfies the conditions established by another valid norm of the legal system.

8. *Bowers v. Hardwick*, 478 U.S. 186 (1986).

9. The ambiguities and problems of these characterizations of the con-

cept of validity are discussed in my book *La validez del derecho* (Buenos Aires: Editorial Astrea, 1985). See Joseph Raz, *Practical Reason and Norms* (London: Hutchinson, 1975), 222.

10. See Eugenio Bulygin, "Sentencia judicial y creación de derecho," in *La Ley* 124, 1307.

11. See Nino, *La validez del derecho*, chap. 2.

12. This has been proposed by Constantineau in his famous doctrine of de facto laws. Albert Constantineau, *A Treatise on the De Facto Doctrine in Its Relation to Public Officers and Public Corporations Based upon the English, American, and Canadian Cases, Including Comments upon Extraordinary Legal Remedies in Reference to the Trial of Title to Office and Corporate Existence* (Toronto: Canada Law Book Company, 1910).

13. Ronald Dworkin, *Taking Rights Seriously* (Cambridge: Harvard University Press, 1977), chap. 4.

14. See Chap. 4 above.

15. John Hart Ely, *Democracy and Distrust: A Theory of Judicial Review* (Cambridge: Harvard University Press, 1980); Carlos Santiago Nino, *The Ethics of Human Rights* (Oxford: Oxford University Press, 1991), chap. 6.

16. There is a certain analogy between this determination of a priori rights and the transcendental method through which Kant determined the truth of synthetic a priori propositions, which is provided not by empirical observation but by detecting the conditions of those empirical observations.

17. See Chap. 3 above.

18. Nino, *Ethics of Human Rights*, chap. 3

19. This position depends heavily on a nonretributivist view of punishment. See Carlos Santiago Nino, *Radical Evil on Trial* (New Haven: Yale University Press, 1996), chap. 3.

20. 381 U.S. 479 (1965).

21. 410 U.S. 113 (1973).

22. 347 U.S. 483 (1954).

23. Moreover, most perfectionist policies are counterproductive and irrational, since ideals of virtue typically require spontaneous adhesion in order to be satisfied and cannot effectively be imposed by others.

24. 410 U.S., at 148–150.

25. As discussed earlier, paternalism may be justified in certain situations. For instance, paternalism may legitimately be used to overcome problems of ignorance, coercion, weakness of the will, or coordination problems that impede people from satisfying their subjective preferences.

26. I believe we can ascribe intrinsic value only to those entities which have the capacity of valuing—specifically, autonomous persons. See Chap. 3 above. It is obvious that the fetus has no such intrinsic value, but neither does the recently born child or, for that matter, a comatose person. However, these entities may experience some reflex value. There are three possible relationships between something that has intrinsic value and another entity in order for the latter to receive reflex value from the former. The first is the relationship of identity, the second is the relationship of turning itself into the entity with intrinsic value, and the third is the relationship of being valued by an entity with intrinsic value. The first relationship is not present between the fetus in its first stages and the autonomous person: it only arises in an attenuated way in the last stages of pregnancy. The second relationship does not transmit the same degree of value. The same could be said about the third alternative, which is dependent upon the existence of somebody who values the fetus as part of his or her life plan (which is not the

case when the parents ask for the abortion). Therefore, the fetus seems to have a tenuous value in its early stages, although that value grows with its development.

27. Similarly, one cannot infer the mother's obligation to take care of the fetus from this assertion of the value of the fetus. Nothing much follows from my conclusion that the fetus does not have value, only that a statute that permitted abortion would not be unconstitutional, unless perhaps it permitted abortion in the later stages, where there would be more value.

28. 163 U.S. 537 (1896).

29. See German Bidart Campos, "La justicia constitucional y la inconstitucionalidad por omisión," 78 *El Derecho* 785 (1978).

Editor's Note

Carlos Santiago Nino was born in Buenos Aires in 1943. He received his first law degree from the University of Buenos Aires and his doctorate in jurisprudence from Oxford. He became involved in politics in the early 1980s in an effort to restore democracy in Argentina and later served as an adviser to President Raúl Alfonsín on human rights and constitutional reform. He held a chair in philosophy of law at the University of Buenos Aires and, starting in 1986, was a regular visiting professor at the Yale Law School.

Professor Nino died suddenly on August 29, 1993 while on a trip to La Paz to work on the reform of the Bolivian constitution. Immediately before his death, Owen Fiss of the Yale Law School had visited Professor Nino in Buenos Aires and received the manuscripts of two books, *The Constitution of Deliberative Democracy* and *Radical Evil on Trial*, both written in English. The two men discussed the manuscripts and a number of revisions that Professor Nino was contemplating.

Upon Professor Nino's death, Professor Fiss assumed the responsibility of readying the two manuscripts for publication by Yale University Press. On *The Constitution of Deliberative Democracy*, he was principally assisted by Kenneth Levit, a student close to Professor

Nino at Yale. Richard R. Buery, Jr., Sunny Chu, Leah Cover, Gadi Dechter, Noah Feldman, Zecharias Hailu, and Elisabeth Layton also helped in bringing this project to completion. A copy of the manuscript for *The Constitution of Deliberative Democracy* as it existed upon Professor Nino's death is at the library of the Yale Law School.

Index